The
PHOTO CD *Book*

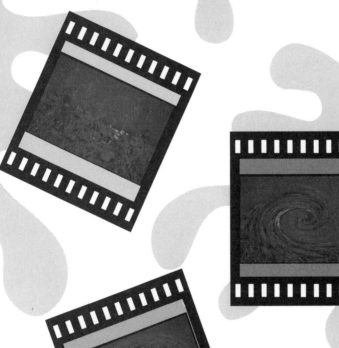

Heinz von Buelow
Dirk Paulissen

Abacus

 **COREL** **Cover photos courtesy of the Corel Corporation**

A Data Becker Book

Printed in the U.S.A.

ISBN 1-55755-195-2

10 9 8 7 6 5 4

Managing Editor:	Scott Slaughter
Editors:	Louise Benzer
Technical Editors:	Gene Traas, Rob Lun
Language Specialists:	Brooks Haderlie, Elke Walsworth
Book Design:	Scott Slaughter
Cover Art:	Abby Grinnell
Proofreading:	Robbin Markley

Contents

Contents

Contents

Contents

Contents

Welcome to the World of Digital Image Processing

The **Photo CD Book** is your first source for learning and understanding the digital technology invented by Eastman Kodak to "replace" conventional photography. It's written for CD-ROM/multimedia fans, photography buffs, graphic artists, desktop publishers, and the "technologically curious". **The Photo CD Book** is an important source for learning and understanding the "whats" and "how-tos" of this new digital image technology.

This book is a "hands-on" way to learn and use this technology. You'll see how to turn your personal computer into a digital photo studio and art gallery. *The Photo CD Book* also includes the following:

- ➢ Background and uses for photo CD

- ➢ Elements of photography and image processing

- ➢ Information on how to set up a Photo CD (PCD) system (including hardware and software configurations)

- ➢ How to create Photo CDs

From the basics of image processing and the tricks of photo retouching and enhancement, to visual presentations and the special effects of morphing, you'll get complete coverage of where this technology is taking us.

The **Photo CD Book** will teach you how the different hardware is used to record, manipulate and output Photo CD images. You'll also see how the most popular software packages can transform ordinary images into sensational images. One entire section is devoted to describing how you can use and enhance Photo CD images with Micrografx PhotoMagic, Microsoft Publisher, Corel's CorelDRAW!, Aldus FreeHand and PhotoStyler, Adobe PhotoShop, and other popular software.

The companion CD-ROM includes samplers such as Microtek's Photo Star graphic utility, a slideshow viewer program that lets users see photos in thumbnail or full size, real PCD photo examples that were used in the book and a stellar collection of the most popular shareware graphics utilities including PaintShop Pro and Graphics WorkShop. Also included are selected photographs from Abacus and Corel's photo CD sampler collection.

Introduction To The Photo CD

CHAPTER 1

1. Introduction To The Photo CD

The photo CD is a revolutionary invention that allows you to save photos electronically, with the best possible quality. Therefore, it represents an ingenious link between conventional photography and the electronic world.

With the photo CD, it's possible to generate almost digital photos with existing photo technology at a cost that is affordable for both personal and professional use.

The original method of producing an electronic image using the camera was complicated, time-consuming, and expensive. A still video camera, such as the Canon Ion, is an excellent alternative. It allows you to use only a tape, but usually it cannot generate images in photo-quality, which produces the best and highest resolution. You can save an individual picture in about 2 million pixels on a disk, compared to the photo CD, which can store 18 million pixels.

What Is The Photo CD?

By using the photo CD, you can change new and existing photos into high-quality digital images. The photo CD also makes it easy to use this new technology. It not only revolutionizes photography, but it also opens new opportunities in computer technology and entertainment electronics.

A photo CD can hold up to 100 pictures in photo quality at a cost of about 65 cents per picture. However, the prices still vary significantly and will continue to decrease. However, a professional scan of equal quality can cost $50 or more. Therefore, this process is very expensive when compared with the photo CD.

Obviously, with these advantages, the photo CD is sure to be a success. Before discussing its other advantages, we'll provide an overview of the photo CD's development.

The Kodak catalog CD is part of the Kodak family of photo cd discs

Photo CD development

1990

In September 1990 Eastman Kodak introduced the photo CD system as the first affordable digital system for taking and storing photographs. This system provides a new way to archive photos, because up to 100 pictures can be stored on one CD. Also, the pictures can be shown on a normal television. So, you don't have to use a screen and a slide projector. For the first time it's also possible to incorporate photo-quality 35 mm black and white or color photos or slides into computer applications inexpensively.

A month later, Kodak announced a series of new developments for computer applications of the photo CD. Software and hardware companies can use the photo CD developer tool to integrate digital data of the photo CD into new and existing applications. Users that have application programs that weren't modified for this system can use a special application software that lets them access photo CD data. Because of the Kodak color management system, system-wide digital color signal manipulation, independent from the output system, is possible. This system guarantees a constant and excellent color quality even with different types of software, computers, and peripherals. The leading manufacturers of computer hardware and software, such as Adobe, Apple Computers, IBM Corporation, and Sun Spark Systems, support the photo CD system.

In the same year, the first photo CD players were introduced at the "Photokina" camera show in Cologne, Germany. Then, in November 1990, Popular Science magazine named the photo CD system "Best of what's new."

1991

Kodak released a handbook for developers in June 1991. This handbook provides information about the technical aspects of the photo CD system for companies that want to develop new products based on the photo CD system.

In August 1991, Kodak received three important European awards for the photo CD system:

> ➤ The International Inkama Gold Medal for the development of the photo CD system as a link between traditional photography and electronic technology

> ➤ "Best Design Technology" from the Technical Image Press Association

> ➤ "Top ten products" status of the Photo Expo 91

The first time Kodak displayed the photo CD system at an international electronics fair was in Berlin. As a result, the photo CD system received very positive reviews.

In September 1991, Fuji Film accepted a licensing agreement, which lets them use photo CD technology. By the Fall of 1992, Fuji successfully transferred photos to the photo CD with its photo finishers.

Then Philips Interactive Media Systems announced that it would begin marketing the photo CD player in September 1991. The Philips CDI player is completely compatible with the photo CD.

A group of photo magazine editors from 13 countries selected the photo CD system as the "European innovation of the year 1991/92."

By October 1991, Intel supported the photo YCC color system also used for the Kodak photo CD system. This makes it faster and easier to transform high-resolution photos for use on Intel action media II boards in desktop publishing applications.

In December 1991, MCI telecommunications announced that they would start using Kodak recordable data CDs in 1992 for complex billing for its biggest customers. This was the first commercial application of Kodak CD technology and helped promote the use of the photo CD system.

1992

Next, Kodak announced the photo CD system will provide additional interactive possibilities when it's introduced on the market in the summer of 1992.

By slightly downgrading the high photo resolution, the photo CD can store up to 800 color photos in TV resolution. A combination of photos in TV-quality with tone, text, and graphics is possible up to a total memory capacity of 600 Meg. By using the menu, the contents of the photo CD can be accessed with a television or PC monitor.

Agfa Gaevert announced that it will use the photo CD system as input medium for the Agfa digital print system. Because of this, digital photo data can be read by the photo CD and then color pictures can be printed.

In February 1992 Kodak published details of the photo CD imagining work station during the PMA Show. Then, in March, the Kodak photo CD developer software was produced. The first Kodak photo CD imagining work station was delivered to large photo labs in Germany in May 1992.

In the summer of 1992, the photo CD system and the photo CD player were introduced in North America, Western Europe, Japan, and other key markets. Then it was presented, with much publicity, to the general public during Photokina '92.

1993

In January, Kodak ships the Kodak Photo CD Access developer toolkit for the Sun/UNIX platform. This helped application developers build flexible user interfaces to images stored on Photo CD discs. The toolkit consists of a library of the basic C-language functions required to read images from a Photo CD disc into memory in formats compatible with the Sun/UNIX environment.

In February, Kodak starts taking orders for the Kodak Professional Photo CD Imaging Station 4200.

In March, Toshiba America Information Systems announces it signed a license to brand its CD-ROM drives with the Photo CD logo.

Also in March, the Photo CD Portfolio disc format is improved with the addition of a new feature set and authoring software. The new features allows users to create discs combining:

- ➤ Photographic images
- ➤ Audio
- ➤ Graphics
- ➤ Text
- ➤ Programmed access

Photo CD uses

When you use the photo CD system, your photographs are still processed by a film processing lab. However, your photos will be in two forms: Celluloid (film) and Digital (CD).

How long this process takes depends on the price. Some processing labs will finish your CD within 24 hours, but this will probably cost about $3 or more per photo. However, this price includes individual enhancement of each photo.

The large Kodak labs can do this work more inexpensively. In this case, the price will be about 63 cents per photo, but the process takes up to 3 weeks. Therefore, you should consider both prices and turnaround times before selecting a processing lab.

When you receive your photo CD, you can view the photos by using the photo CD player, which can display the pictures on your television as well as play music CDs.

With the Kodak photo CD player 860, you can create your own show to go with each photo CD. This player also lets you determine, either manually or automatically, the sequence in which the photos are displayed. It's also possible to zoom in on the separate images and arrange them on the screen. You can also save the new setting for each photo.

Professional photographers don't need special equipment to use the photo CD system. Instead, they can use their existing camera equipment. They can determine the final results before having pictures saved on a photo CD. Therefore, he/she can sell a photo CD with selected pictures and keep the originals.

By using the photo CD, photo agencies can now provide completed pictures to their clients. These digital photos can be adapted with appropriate desktop publishing programs and simply transferred into flyers, newspapers, books, etc.

Since the images have been digitized, the photo can go directly to the print setup. Therefore, using photo CD technology not only saves money, but also protects valuable original photos from being lost or damaged.

The photo CD is also an excellent way to store pictures. Film goes through a natural aging process that can affect the quality of a photograph. The organic fabric, which is extremely sensitive to its surroundings, will begin to show slight discoloration after about four years of storage.

Obviously, this could eventually destroy a photo. However, digital images cannot change. So, they don't lose any of their quality.

The photo CD is an efficient way to store photos because it can hold several photos, which can be accessed easily.

Unlike traditional film development, creating a photo CD is a very clean and fast process. It takes approximately a quarter of an hour to produce a photo CD. Also, photo CDs don't have to be processed in a dark room. In comparison, films can be permanently destroyed if they are exposed to light during processing.

This process is even faster if the film is still in a strip. The scanner can take in the entire film strip automatically by using a motor. For individual pictures, each slide (or frame) must be manually placed onto a special film platform.

Despite these technical advances, you'll probably still want printouts of many of your photos so you can frame them and pass them on to friends and family. This is still an option because the photo CD is only another way of storing pictures electronically.

It's possible to get printouts of pictures from the photo CD. However, this is much more expensive than a traditional print. However, if the original photos are lost or destroyed, this is the only way to get a printout of a photo on paper.

Compact discs

In the photo CD system, photos are stored on compact discs (CD). The CD has been used as an optical storage medium for about 20 years. However, only the music CD has been a major success. For the last 10 years, it has been a vital part of the music industry.

There are three kinds of CDs:

1. Read-only CD, called ROM (Read Only Memory). This CD is pressed in a special process and is extremely expensive to manufacture.

2. One time written CD, called the WORM (Write Once, Read Many). Data are inscribed with a laser on a blank disc. The photo CD is based on this technology.

3. The optical disc that can be written on and deleted several times. This type of disc doesn't have a special name. It is still in the development stage and a standard hasn't been established yet. Because of this, manufacturers are reluctant to develop this disc.

Open system

The photo CD system is an open system, which means that it contains interfaces to all available operating systems, such as OS/2, MS-DOS, UNIX, and Apple Macintosh. It also has a data format, which is compatible with the Philips CD-I system.

CD formats

In addition to the standard photo CD, Kodak provides four other CD formats.

The Kodak family of photo CD discs

Professional photo CD

This professional photo format, called the "Kodak Pro Photo Master Disc", allows the professional photographer to store pictures in middle or large formats on the CD to attain much higher image quality.

Depending on their film format, 25 to 100 pictures can be stored on the Pro Photo CD. This means that it can only hold about 25 8 x 10 inch pictures, while it can contain 100 35 mm slides.

There are also safety features, that are important in professional use. There is a special identification, which represents the copyright of the photographer.

Kodak Pro Photo CD

Also, it's possible to attach a watermark, which cannot be altered, to the image. Finally, a photographer can use a code to prevent unauthorized use of high resolution pictures.

These CDs can store images from standard rolls of film, typically 35 mm. However, images from the large film formats favored by professionals, including 120, 70 mm, 4 x 5 inch as well as 35 mm can also be used.

Photo CD Portfolio

The Kodak photo CD Portfolio is a new format that enables you to create your own multimedia presentations by combining photo CD pictures with text, graphics, and stereo sound.

For example, you can easily create a family tree presentation by using family photos, narration, and songs.

The photo CD portfolio can also be used for advertising presentations or employee

Kodak photo CD Portfolio

training. This CD can store up to 800 images at video resolution for display on TV sets or computer monitors.

These images are lower resolution than standard Kodak Photo CD Master Discs.

The number of pictures will be reduced by the amount of sound you use. For example, if you use a half hour of sound, only 400 images can be stored. Using the photo CD Portfolio is an excellent way for businesses to demonstrate products or services to potential customers.

Kodak photo CD catalog

With this format, it's possible to digitize a vast amount of pictures, but only in television-quality. This disc was designed for direct mail order companies, photo agencies, and art galleries that want to store several pictures on one disc for wide distribution.

This disc is then mailed to customers or clients. This is easier than mailing a traditional catalog, which can weigh several pounds.

However, since the images are saved on the disc in low resolution, they are intended only for information purposes.

Kodak photo CD catalog

The customer or client can select and order the desired pictures or products shown on the CD catalog. The images can be combined with text and graphics and divided into separate chapters similar to a traditional catalog. A photo CD catalog disc can store about 4,400 pictures in low resolution.

People that have photo CD players can access the catalog by using the menu that's included and can then view the desired chapters by remote control. Computer users can select the pictures with a special index program. Each CD contains one of these programs. This makes it easy to find a specific product or picture.

Medical photo CD

The last format is the medical CD. This CD stores x-ray images, CAT scans, and other medical documentation.

Creating your own CDs

If you want to place manipulated images on a CD, Kodak and Philips provide a CD writer. This equipment allows you to make your own CD-ROMs. However, you cannot create your own photo CD. This is only possible with a complete Kodak imaging station.

The Kodak Photo CD Imaging Workstation 2400

However, this presents more of a legal problem than a software/hardware problem. For a photo CD to be recognized and subsequently read by a particular piece of equipment, it's imprinted with a specific code. Kodak owns all the rights to this code, which can be used only on Kodak photo CDs.

Another problem is the compression of the photos in the special photo CD format. To do this in a reasonable amount of time, you need, in addition to the CD writer, an equally powerful computer.

When you consider the volume of data for each individual picture, it's best to store them on a CD-ROM. Another advantage is the unlimited readability of a CD-ROM. Since the CD writer with the software costs approximately $6,900 and the individual blank discs cost another $40, it's used mainly by professionals.

Using photo CD technology

To ensure that software and hardware manufacturers can integrate photo CD technology into their products, Kodak works closely with these manufacturers. Kodak provides a developer toolkit, called the "Photo CD Access Developer Toolkit", for software manufacturers. This software lets you decompress the digital images of the photo CD as well as store them in existing graphics formats.

The photo CD software provides an overview of the pictures contained on the disc by displaying miniature versions of them. Double-clicking loads the image in the desired resolution and saves them again in the proper format.

To ensure these functions, Kodak has developed a comprehensive list of computer commands, which are actually small programs, that are located in the toolkit. Therefore, you need the toolkit in order to use the photo CD format.

Currently, several programs can access the photo CD. As photo CD technology is updated, software manufacturers will offer these new features in updates for registered customers.

Displaying photo CD images

Besides using the photo CD for storing pictures, you'll also want to display these pictures. There are several ways to do this.

Photo CD player

Special photo CD players let you replay the digital pictures. Currently, Kodak and Philips offer photo CD players. However, soon other manufacturers will produce photo CD players.

An important advantage of a photo CD player compared to a regular CD player is its ability to display pictures and play music in stereo quality for about the same price.

The Kodak Photo CD player Model PCD 5870

It's very easy to display the pictures. Simply use the remote control to access all the functions. Depending on the equipment's capabilities, you can create pre-programmed slide shows, while letting the Autoplay function display one picture after the other automatically. The individual pictures can also be enlarged, rotated, moved up, down, and sideways, and much more. All of these settings can be saved and replayed automatically the next time the picture is displayed. It's even possible to save an image in several settings. By doing this, a picture can appear in an overview and then, in a larger size, during a presentation.

Even a portable machine, which is about the size of a portable music CD player, is available. This portable photo CD player enables you to display electronic pictures wherever there is a television.

Portable photo CD player

CD-I player

The Philips CD-I (CD interactive) player lets you modify the CD-I discs by using a joystick. These machines will soon be able to play movies on discs. CD-I players are more expensive than photo CD players, but provide significantly more functions. These players contain the photo CD format.

Philips CD-I player

Displaying photo CDs on computers

To use photo CDs on a computer, you must have an XA-capable, internal or external CD-ROM. Although the CD-ROM should be able to support multiple sessions mode, this isn't absolutely necessary.

The photo CD files have their own format, which differs from the usual formats of familiar graphics processing programs. You also need the proper software for displaying the PCD files (i.e., the picture files) with the photo CD on the computer.

Kodak and Toshiba offer special programs at reasonable prices. However, many popular graphics programs have add-ons for loading PCD files directly.

We'll describe the various graphics processing and desktop publishing programs and the software using the photo CD in Chapter 3.

The Photographic Process

Before you can place your own photo CD in your CD-ROM, your film or slides must be developed at a film processing lab. Then you can select which pictures you want to include on your photo CD. In this section, we'll provide some tips on taking successful photographs.

Camera equipment

You can take photos with any camera. However, your best quality photos will be taken with an adjustable type camera with interchangeable lens capabilities. Higher quality lenses when used correctly will render the highest quality photo image. The most popular camera on the market today is the 35mm camera.

There are basically two kinds of 35mm cameras: Point and shoot and adjustable SLR.

Point and shoot camera

The first is the point and shoot camera which has a simple non-adjustable lens with a built-in flash and takes 35mm film. They are totally automated so there's no need to set any camera settings. You simply point and shoot. For occasional photography around the home or on vacation, these simple cameras produce a good quality photo for the occasional picture taker.

Adjustable SLR

The second type of 35mm camera is the adjustable SLR (single lens reflex). This type of camera also takes 35mm film. However, it offers the flexibility of interchangeable lenses and is fully automated with a manual (creative) override. It has a more sophisticated light metering system that allows the photographer greater accuracy and creativity in taking photographs.

SLR cameras come in different price ranges and configurations suiting the photographer for his/her own personal needs.

Other 35mm cameras

There are other 35mm cameras available on the market which have a blend of features from both the simple point and shoot camera and the SLR camera. It's only important to remember that no matter what type of camera you're using, all cameras work under the same principle. All cameras we're accustomed to have a lens, a shutter and need both film and light to capture a photo image.

Lenses

Because SLR's are so commonly used today and because they are the most desired choice among serious photographers, we'll discuss the use of the SLR in more detail. And, how to obtain the best possible photos using this type of equipment.

Zoom lenses

Using any of the lenses you currently own for your SLR will render a high quality photo. However, most popular lenses used today for the SLR are the short zoom lenses (approximately 28-80 mm). These lenses are capable of taking both wide angle and short telephoto views of your subject.

The second is the medium range zoom lens (approximately 70-210mm). These lenses are used for some portraiture photos and still offer enough magnification for pulling a distant subject in much closer without the need of a tripod to hold your camera and lens steady.

These lenses, due to their design, are usually poor choices for shooting in low lighting situations without a flash. However, today's choices of high quality fast films can remedy the situation with only minimal quality loss.

Zoom lenses also are more convenient when taking photographs because they eliminate the tedious task of changing lenses for every photographic situation. By using the zoom lens you can compose you're photo right in the view finder, zooming in or out to include or eliminate certain elements that may add or detract from your final photo.

Standard telephoto and wide angle lens

A more economical choice in lenses is the standard telephoto and/or wide angle lens. The choice of these lenses would depend on which type of photography you do (i.e., 105mm lens for portraiture photograph or a 28mm lens for general landscape photography).

These types of lenses typically have two important advantages over their zoom counterparts:

1. They allow you to shoot in lower lighting situations because of design without the need for faster film or the aid of a tripod.

2. In many cases, these lenses render a sharper image on film with more contrast.

The standard 50mm lens you purchase with your SLR is a good all around lens for capturing pictures around the home and on vacations. Although it is neither a wide angle or a telephoto lens, the standard lens produces a sharp, crisp image on film of people and things around you. For general photography the 50mm lens will produce an image in life size, or as we see the subject, just before we trip the shutter.

Film

Slide film (transparencies) offers the most economical way of editing your photos for those you plan on putting on a photo CD. They're very easy to handle because they come back from the photofinisher individually mounted in cardboard holders.

If you plan on shooting photos on print film so you can pass along pictures to your friends and family, you can have duplicate photos made economically from your negatives. At the same time, they're acceptable to be transferred to a photo CD.

When choosing a film for shooting pictures, select a film that is best suited for your shooting situation:

➢ Slower films in the range of 25-200 ISO (film speed) for general flash and daylight photography.

➢ Fast films in the range of 400-1000 ISO for low light and sports photography.

The general rule is:

Lower film speeds produce richer colors and sharper pictures

Film consists of light sensitive particles. The faster the film, the larger the particles that make up the film. These particles, called grain, make up the light sensitive fiber of transparancies and negatives of our photo. Black and White prints can also be transferred to Photo CD as well.

Subjects

Any images are suitable for transfer to a photo CD. However, since the photo CD is still an expensive option, use only your best photographs. Also, when taking pictures, try to create quality photos.

Helpful tips

Now that we've briefly discussed the different types of camera equipment and film, we'll provide answers to some of the most commonly asked questions about photography.

Automatic features

Most automatic SLR cameras will produce average results under most lighting conditions. The creative photographer who is looking to create a different mood in their photographs may opt in many cases to do one of the following:

> ➢ Switch to the manual feature of the SLR

> ➢ Alter the automatic settings of the camera to obtain a different result than what the automatic camera has in mind

A photographer can make an average picture more dramatic with the following techniques:

> ➢ Controlling the amount of light reaching the film using creative lens filers

> ➢ Carefully selecting the proper shutter speed

> ➢ Adjusting the aperture (f/stops) of the lens

Viewfinder

All SLR cameras allow the photographer to view his/her subject directly through the lens by means of a sophisticated mirroring system and prism inside the camera body. What the photographer views when looking through the viewfinder will be precisely what will appear in the photograph. Proper film exposure will determine if your picture is too light, too dark or pleasing to you.

Although the human brain records things three dimensionally, traditional photos can only be captured by cameras two dimensionally. This means that depth, for example, can be represented in a photograph only by certain elements that make up the composition of the photo, such as foreground, background and the size of an object in relationship to the size of other objects in the picture.

Composition

Consider your viewfinder as a painter's canvas. Divide the viewfinder horizontally into 3 equal portions: Lower, middle and upper. Each portion should contain some important element of the landscape on which you're planning to take a picture:

> ➢ In the lower portion, or the foreground, place your horizon line where lower meets middle, such as placing a tree or branch in the immediate foreground.

> ➢ In the middle portion, place the most important element of your photo. For example, place people, homes or farmland in the foreground of the middle section instead of directly in the center.

> ➢ In the upper portion of the photo, place the sky or mountains.

Refrain from placing your subject in a landscape directly in the middle of your viewfinder. The best landscapes depict several elements which make up your photo using the rules regarding composition we listed above.

Special note on viewfinders

Also, be aware of the potential differences in composition between a viewfinder camera such as the point and shoot cameras and an SLR camera. With the SLR, you see exactly what the lens sees when you look into the viewfinder.

Point and shoot cameras have a viewfinder that is slightly offset from the lens, thus creating the problem known as parallax view.

Parallax view occurs when what you're viewing is not exactly the composition the camera is viewing. A very slight position adjustment, either left or right from your view (depending on which side the viewfinder is located relative to the lens) is needed prior to taking a picture. This will give you a truer representation of your composition.

When shooting an individual, compose your photo with the axis of the camera in the vertical rather than the horizontal position. Move in close and fill the viewfinder with the upper third of their body and focus on the eyes for maximum sharpness.

Whatever kind of picture you are shooting, make sure you gently squeeze the shutter button, keeping your arms as close to your body as possible before snapping the picture. This will prevent blurred pictures. Other factors which can give the appearance of blurred pictures are:

> ➢ Finger print smudges or dirt on the front element of your lens.

> ➢ Incorrect focusing.

> ➢ Weather conditions (haze, fog, etc.).

> ➢ Using the wrong film for the kind of lighting conditions under which you're shooting pictures.

> ➢ Improper camera settings in automatic or manual mode.

Spatial appearance

Placing an object, such as a branch, leaves, or a bench, in nature shots is an old, but effective technique. The picture gains spatial depth by emphasizing the foreground, which can be unfocused.

A picture with spatial appearance

Flare

A flare is one or several bright yellow or white blotches appearing in your photographs, washing out a part or all of your photo. Flare occurs because scattered light rays strike your lens the moment you take a photo.

These scattered light rays are not part of the light rays that you've brought into focus on your film plane (where the film is located) which will make up your photo just prior to snapping your picture.

Flares can occur when photographing in extreme contrast lighting situations. An of this is backlit subjects where a person is looking directly into the camera and the sun is directly behind the subjects head, giving a bright halo affect around the hair.

NOTE

If you're using a camera with a separate viewfinder, don't shade the lens. This may block your view of the subject from the viewfinder.

Flasres can also occuer when shooting a sunset where you are taking a picture directly into the brightest areas of the sunset.

A portrait with high flare

Flare can sometimes accentuate a photo and other times it can deter from it. Using an inexpensive lens shade can prevent a great deal of flare appearing in your photos, by preventing direct sunlight from striking the lens at right angles. Flare is more likely to occur when the sun is closest to the horizon and you are shooting pictures towards the same direction.

Underexposure

Pictures which appear dark are considered underexposed. This can occur because your camera was incorrectly set or you were taking a flash picture with your point and shoot camera beyond the 10 or 12 foot maximum range of the flash. Even adjustable SLR's require periodic adjustment to prevent underexposure.

When using a flash with an SLR you need to allow more light to strike the film when shooting dark subjects against a light background. This is because the light from the flash will be absorbed by the dark subject rather than reflecting back to the film. The light being reflected off the light background will dominate the brightness of the entire photo and make the dark subject darker than it really appears. Therefore, some manual adjustment to the lens aperture is needed to allow more light to reach the film from the dark subject. This produces a truer lighting ratio between light and dark, creating a more pleasing photo.

Overexposure

Pictures which appear too washed out are considered overexposed. This can occur because your camera was incorrectly set or you were taking a flash picture with your point and shoot camera within 4' of your subject, thus exposing your subject with too much light.

Even adjustable SLR's require periodic adjustment to prevent overexposure. For example, suppose you're shooting a beach scene on a sunny day. A white beach towel and a subject are in the foreground. In this case, camera light meters tend to read the overall bright tonal range of the scene, overlooking the white beach towel and subject in the forground which is important for this photograph.

If you let the camera select the exposure, it would probaby expose correctly for the sand. However, because the white beach towel is brighter and reflects more light to the film plane, the most important portion of the photo (the beach towel and the subject) will be overexposed. In this case, you must make an adjustment to the aperature, or the shutter speed, or both. This adjustment will allow less light to reach the film plane which will give a correct exposure for the beach towel and the subject.

Sharpness

The following factors affect the sharpness of photos:

> ➢ Lens

> ➢ Focus

> ➢ Depth of field

> ➢ Movement (you or the subject)

> ➢ Weather conditions (haze, fog, etc.)

> ➢ Type of film

> ➢ Size of print made from the negative

In photography, sharpness is extremely important because the technical quality of a photo is based on it. A sharp photo isn't necessarily a good photo, but it meets at least the technical requirements for a good photo. Sometimes a blurry photo is considered good.

An example of an intentionally blurred photo is a track star jumping over hurdles. This would give the impression of speed and motion versus a crisp shot of the runner frozen in mid air over the hurdle. In this instance, the photo is blurred intentionally using the photographer's creativity and manipulating an adjustable camera.

The choices you make about film speed and resolution affect the sharpness of the photos you take. Film speed and resolution are closely related. The lower the film speed, the less grainy the film and the finer the detail.

However, the slower the film speed, the more light is needed for exposure. Using slower film speeds in low lighting situations increases the danger of a blurred photo due to movement.

When sharp photo reproduction is required and large blow-ups are needed, a slow film with high resolution is recommended. In sport photography, where fast shutter speeds are needed for capturing the rapid movements of an athelete, a high speed film is preferable.

Over the last several years, films have improved dramatically and even high speed films yield exceptional results in color saturation and resolution. Even 8 x 10 inch enlargements made from fast 35mm films produce sharp prints without noticable graininess.

Depth of Field

Depth of Field is the area in a photo which appears to the naked eye in sharp focus, in front of and in back of the primary subject which you've focused on.

There are three elements which affect depth of field:

> ➤   The lens you're using.

> ➤   The distance from you and the subject on which you're focusing.

> ➤   The aperature (f/stop) at which your lense is set.

Change any one or all these elements before taking your photo and you will change the depth of field. A photo which is sharp from front to back can be very impressive. However, a photograph with very limited depth of field can be equally appealing.

Generally, wide angle lenses offer the greatest depth of field because of their optical design. A telephoto, however, has more limited depth of field. As the size of the telephoto increases in focal length, the depth of field becomes smaller. Wide angle lenses are more forgiving to the photographer if you do not focus accurately.

Focusing a telephoto lens is crucial because depth of field can only be a matter of inches in front of and in back of your primary subject in the picture. We recommend supporting your camera and telephoto lens with a monopod or tripod to prevent movement that could blur your photos.

This is especially true when using telephoto lenses beyond 300mm focal length. Remember, not only is your subject being magnified by your telephoto lens, but so is any movement by your equipment during exposure.

A picture with great depth of field

Remember, sharpness isn't necessarily good either. By experimenting with the depth of field, you can separate the subject from the background. Also, slight blurring produces the illusion of movement.

A picture with shallow depth of field

Generally, the minimum shutter speed used in general outdoor photos without a tripod should be the reciprocal of the focal length (1/focal length). If the exact shutter speed is unavailable, use the next fastest speed. The focal length used also determines the highest allowable shutter speed - in fractions of a second. This is the slowest shutter speed allowed, which will still yield acceptable results.

For a wide angle lens with a focal length of 28mm, the shutter speed should be 1/30th of a second or faster. A 200mm telephoto lens requires a minimum shutter speed of 1/250th of a second.

This is a general rule. Therefore, following these shutter speeds won't guarantee that your photo will always be sharp or that not using these shutter speeds always produces a blurry photo.

Halo

To create a halo effect, the light source must be directly behind the subject but not visible in the picture.

For indoor shots, do this by positioning the lamp so it's level with the subject's head.

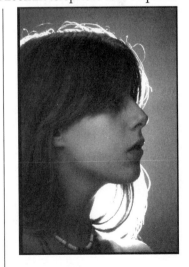

Portrait with halo

For outdoor shots, take the photo late in the afternoon when the sun is so low that it disappears behind the subject's head. You can intensify this effect by using a telephoto lens.

Diffusion effects

Instead of special diffusion filters, you can use inexpensive gauze or nylon stocking in front of your lens. A nylon stocking with round holes makes an excellent diffuser.

A section choice for a diffuser is to position a piece of glass in front of your lens and lightly smear it with Vasoline.

Pictures of television images

To take photographs of images on a television, use a slow shutter speed (1/8th to 1/30th of a second). The slow shutter speed is necessary because the TV image is formed by scan lines, rather than as one immediate image.

Photograph taken with a diffuser

If the shutter speed is too fast, the photos will not capture part of the screen. Therefore, you'll probably get blurring effects from moving pictures.

To avoid this, try waiting for moments when there isn't too much movement during a segment on the television. Also, make certain the room is completely dark. Lamps and light from windows can cast reflections on the screen.

Use a short telephoto lens to eliminate distortions caused by the curved screen. Most standard or wide angle lenses emphasize these distortions. Also, use a tripod so you can continue watching the television until you're ready to take the picture.

Pictures of computer monitors

It's difficult to take photos of computer monitors. The curved screen causes distortion and colors are generated differently than on a printout. Therefore, shifts in color composition are unavoidable.

The quality of monitors has improved significantly because of flatter screens, improved resolution, and better colors. However, photographs of monitors still contain distortions and show the scan lines of the monitor.

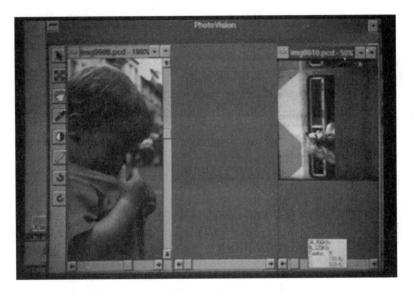

Picture of a computer monitor

Make certain the room is completely dark when taking photos of a monitor. The light from windows and lamps cast reflections on the screen. Also, clean the screen thoroughly. Use a short telephoto lens to eliminate distortions caused by the curved screen. Normal or wide angle lenses emphasize these distortions. Also, use a tripod so you can continue watching the monitor until you're ready to take the picture.

Remember the image on the monitor is formed by lines and this formation takes time. If the shutter speed is too fast, the photos will appear striped. Set your shutter speed to 1/15 second or slower, such as 1/4 second.

If you're taking photos of computer graphics, you're dealing with still pictures. Therefore the shutter speed isn't important, as long as the camera is on a tripod. The following lists the problems that occur when taking photos of computer graphics directly from the monitor:

> ➢ A choice of limited colors or resolution. There are still quite a few systems with 640 x 200 pixels with four colors.

NOTE

You can eliminate moiré effects by keeping the camera slightly out of focus. After determining a precise setting, take the camera slightly out of focus, so the actual focal point lies slightly in front of the screen.

The image will lose the moiré effect without visibly sacrificing sharpness. Also, the slight de-focusing will make the color areas appear more solid and calm because it suppresses the line structure of the monitor.

> ➢ Distortion caused by the curved screen.

> ➢ Even with a high quality monitor, the lines are obvious if the focus is not slightly off.

Aerial photos

If you want to take aerial photos, first you must find an airport where you can make arrangements with a pilot. Most likely, you'll need to go to one of the smaller airports in your area. Make certain to tell the pilot that you want to take aerial photos. This is important because you must be able to open the window (you don't want to shoot through a dirty window). Also, be sure the wing doesn't appear in the picture.

Take along only a small amount of equipment because space is limited on most private planes. Be sure you have a wide angle telephoto, or zoom lens. Use the following lenses:

> ➢ 28mm or 35mm lens for landscapes

> ➢ 105mm to 135mm lens for individual objects

The shutter speeds should be as high as possible because of the vibrations of the plane. A high shutter speed is also important because the relative speed of a plane at low altitudes (under 500 ft) is quite high. In hazy weather, use a red filter for black and white photos. This will increase the contrast in your photos.

Because there is a tremendous amount of ultraviolet light in the atmosphere, your photos may render more blue than usual when processed. Therefore, we recommend using an ultraviolet (UV) filter over your lens. This filter will give you truer colors when your photos are processed. You may even want to experiment with a polarizing filter. It will enhance your photos by bringing out richer color in your aerial landscape.

An aerial photograph

If you're really lucky and have a facility available, taking aerial pictures from a hot air balloon is much easier and produces excellent results.

Time lapse photos

Events that occur over a certain period of time, such as a flower blooming, can be captured on film by using a time lapse technique. Depending on how long the event takes, the camera takes a picture every second, minute, or hour.

A tripod and a motorized camera are required when taking time lapse photos. Some cameras can be preset so they take the pictures automatically. Sometimes it's even possible to preset the time between the exposures, which can be a few seconds or up to several hours.

Winter photos

If you want to take pictures of snow scenes, you should remember a few things. In winter scenes, you're likely to have a large bright area in front of you. Because of the whiteness of the snow, the light meter in the camera attempts to read the light reflecting off the snow and disregards the trees or people in the scene which require more light. So, the trees or people in the scene are not exposed correctly.

To correct this, take a meter reading of the back of your hand. Make sure the front of your hand is at the same angle to the sun (if it's out) as your subjects in the snow scene. Also make certain the back of your hand, in relatio to your subject, is in the same light. Set your camera to the exposure you've just read from the back of your hand to properly expose for trees and subjects in your snow scene. The meter reading of your hand will usually be 1 to 2 f/stops less (more light) than your meter reading directly into the scene.

Make the correction in your exposure on your camera by changing your shutter speed, or f/stop, by 1 or 2 stops. Since the film should get more light than appears necessary to the light meter, you must fool it into believing that a slower film, needing more light, is in the camera.

A winter photo

Also, remember the film in the camera becomes very brittle and cold at low temperatures. The low humidity can also cause static charges. This can lead to flashes, which appear as light exposures to the film. Battery-driven cameras can stop working at low temperatures.

Avoid these problems by keeping the camera under your jacket or under your arm inside your jacket. Also, carry some replacement batteries in your pocket.

LCDs (Liquid Crystal Displays) may not work at low temperatures. So, if you take a lot of outdoor photos in the winter, you may want to use a mechanical camera, which doesn't depend on an energy source.

Rain

Although you can take pictures in the rain, you should protect your camera from water as much as possible by using an umbrella. Usually you'll need another person to hold the umbrella while you take the photo. If some rain gets on your camera, wipe it with a clean, lint-free cloth.

Rain can create interesting effects in photos

Another recommendation is to shoot through a plastic bag placed over your camera. Make certain the plastic is flush against the lens at the time of shooting. You could also cut a hole in the bag so the lens has an unobstructed view.

Finally, you can always look for a shelter (for example, a doorway) to protect yourself from the rain while taking a picture.

Fill-in light

Fill-in light can be used in low light conditions. Using additional light will increase contrasts, brighten highlights and enhance shadows. There are several ways to do this:

Flash unit

Many point and shoot cameras automatically activate the flash when there's not enough light to properly expose the film. With manual cameras, you need to set your camera and flash to expose your photo properly.

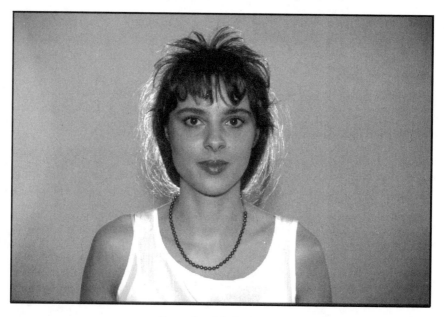

Portrait with flash unit

Reflecting light

Light surfaces, such as cardboard and projector screens, can be used to reflect existing or artificial light onto the parts of the subject which you want to brighten.

To create a reflector, simply cover a cardboard box with aluminum foil. You could also use white Styrofoam boards or use your flash to bounce off reflecting surfaces.

> **NOTE**
>
> In black/white photography, you can diminish skin blemishes by using an orange filter. Use a blue filter to define lips and skin tones.

You can control the intensity and effectiveness through the following methods:

> ➢ The structure and color of the material.

> ➢ Move these reflecting surfaces closer or further away from your subject to get your desired affect.

> ➢ Place your subject next to light colored walls and reflect light off these walls.

Candle light

To take photos in candle light, you can use either fast or slow film (we also recommend using a tripod). Normally, the more candles you use, the less exposure to your film is needed. Candle light will give you a very soft lighting effect as well as giving your photos a yellow hue cast.

With adjustable cameras, you should bracket your exposures (using different f/stops or shutter speeds which are slower and some faster than what your camera exposure meter is reading). Bracketing will give you different exposures during candle light shooting that can dramatically change the mood of the photo, allowing you to choose one or several different photos which you can enjoy.

Also, there are several special effect filters available, such as star filers, mirage filers, etc., that you can put on the front of your lens. These filters can change the entire appearance of your photo.

Portraits

When shooting a portrait, you attempt to capture the personality or expression of the subject. This is difficult to do. A portrait doesn't necessarily have to be beautiful but could convey a personal mood about the subject.

For inside shots, try using existing light besides flash. For outside photos in sunshine, try backlighting or shady areas under a tree where the light is more even and softer.

> **NOTE**
> You'll need an additional light source like flood lamps which can be purchased at a photo dealer. These flood lamps are color balanced for the film you're using.

It's important to use a short telephoto lens for portrait photography because short focal length lenses (like a 28mm lens) tend to exaggerate the proportions of the face and a large focal length lenses tend to flatten out the proportions too much. The ideal focal length for an adjustable 35mm camera when shooting portraits is 85-105mm lenses.

A diffusion filter can be used to create a soft flattering photo and minimize skin blemishes.

Portrait of a mother with child

Nature photography

In nature photography, you can experiment with aperture, perspective, focal depth, and location. You can also use filters to create dramatic effects.

You can use all camera formats, including even the simplest cameras, in nature photography. For example, you can achieve the effect of a wide angle or a telephoto lens with a normal lens simply by elevating the camera. Standing on high ground without a clear foreground produces the same effect as a telephoto lens, while a low position with a foreground produces the same effect as a wide angle lens. This is why eye level isn't always the best choice for taking a picture. Little changes, like changing the height of the camera, can often have surprising benefits.

Film processing

Once you've taken your photos, the next step is to develop them. You'll probably take them to a local photo processor, maybe the local drug store or supermarket. This shop then sends the photos, either sorted or in random order, to a larger photo lab, which creates the photo CD. If you want your photos sorted in a specific order, you'll probably have to pay extra.

Select only your best slides by using a slide projector or light table and a loupe (magnifier) to see the sharpness of your slides or negatives. The photos you select can be digitized on a photo CD.

If you want your slides to appear in a certain order on the CD but don't want to pay extra, you can place the slides in the slide protectors used for filing and storage. These protectors, each of which can hold three slides, hang on a perforated paper band. You can sort your slides and insert them in these protectors in the desired order.

Now you're ready to take your film to a processing lab. Try calling some labs to determine which ones have the best prices and turnaround times. A 36 exposure roll of 35mm film processed and copied to a photo CD will cost around $35. Two or three weeks is normal for obtaining a photo CD.

Once you have your photo CD, it's possible to have it copied by taking it to the processing lab. Unfortunately, copying a CD costs the same as producing the original item.

Creating a photo CD

In this section, we'll explain how your film is transformed into a photo CD. First, framed slides are inserted separately into a platform of the slide scanner and, with a five second rapid scan, transferred into the attached computer. The scanner reads 2,048 lines with 3,072 dots each, which are identified with a resolution of 12 bits per primary color (red, green, blue). This is a tremendous amount of data to be processed within 5 seconds. You can calculate this yourself:

```
2048 lines * 3072 dots * 12 bits * 3 colors = 226,492,416 bits
= 28,311,552 bytes = 27,648K = 27 Meg
```

The computer that's used for this process is called a "Sun Sparc station", which was specifically designed for this task. The lab technician can correct the color of the pictures, change their sharpness, or select only sections of a picture by using this computer. However, remember there is usually a fee for all these services.

A typical photo CD Mastering Station

Once all corrections have been made, the individual photos are transferred to the writer. A Philips CD writer burns the digital image data into a blank photo CD. Up to 100 pictures can be inscribed on a photo CD.

Although the photo CD can be inscribed only once, this can be done in several sessions. To make this possible, the data management on the CD must be structured accordingly. You'll need a table of contents for a photo CD written in sessions so you can easily find a specific photo.

For your computer to read a photo CD, which was written in several sessions, you need a CD-ROM which is able to access interlaced management structures. This is called a "multiple session CD-ROM."

If you have only a single session drive, you can load only the pictures burnt into the CD during the first session. We'll discuss the structure of a photo CD in more detail later.

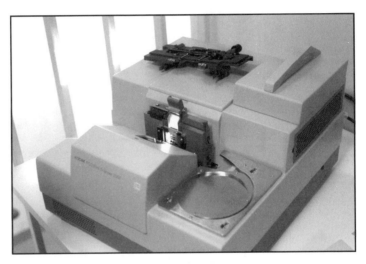

The Kodak PCD 2000 scanner

After the writing procedure is complete, a special thermal transfer printer, called the Kodak PCD Index Printer 200, will output a table of contents in the form of miniature pictures. These pictures are enclosed in the cover of the CD. The printout contains the identity number of the photo CD. This will help you find the individual photos again.

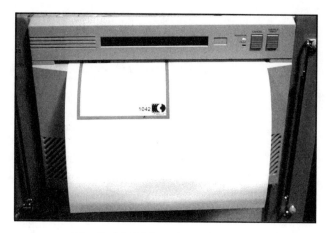

The Kodak PCD Index Printer 200

Duplicates of the photo CD are created with a simple copying process from a CD-ROM to the photo CD writer. It's possible to duplicate the entire CD and transfer individual pictures to another photo CD.

Using the photo CD

There are many ways to use a completed photo CD. If you're using the Kodak photo CD for your personal use, you can display the CD on your television for your friends and family. To do this, you'll need a Kodak photo CD player, Philips photo CD player, or (since October, 1993) a 3DO player. You can use these machines to present slide shows on the TV. Since these photo CD players are also excellent audio CD players, you'll have two devices in one.

For the best results, you should display your pictures on a high-quality large screen TV. Televisions with 100 Hz display frequency are especially suitable. Since the images on the photo CD are still images, there might be a noticeable flickering, especially on large screens of some televisions.

To use the photo CD on your computer, you need a CD-ROM drive. Before purchasing a CD-ROM be sure that it's the latest model. The drive should be able to read Mode 2 Form 1 Data in multiple sessions. The other components in your system (i.e., CD ROM device driver, host adpater card, etc.) must also support this mode of reading.

You can easily add a CD-ROM to your computer. However, the computer system must have at least a 386 coprocessor and 4 Meg of memory. You need as much memory for an Apple Macintosh and the lowest possible model is the Apple Macintosh LC.

The prices of CD-ROMs vary. However, these price differences are usually justified. If you'll be using the CD-ROM only for personal use, you can use a less expensive drive because speed probably isn't that important. However, if you'll be using the drive for professional presentations, you'll want more power and speed. Therefore, you'll probably need to buy a more expensive CD-ROM.

Kodak color prints

Printing photos directly from the photo CD will be possible within the next few months. Many companies and film processing labs have thermal printers, which Kodak has also integrated into their scan stations for printing proofs. Soon it will be possible to get direct printouts (up to 11 x 11 inches) from a photo CD. However, this process will be quite expensive.

Creating A Home Theater

Kodak and Philips provide photo CD players that have similar functions. These players are mainly intended for household use.

The Philips photo CD player

These players make it easy to show your pictures to your friends and family. Unlike typical slide presentations, you don't need a projector, screen, a darkened room, and a long pause between slides. Also, since videotaping is so popular and people are used to watching videos of special events, the electronic slide show is a natural progression.

With the photo CD, you can easily present an "electronic slide show." Simply switch on the TV, insert a CD into the player, and start the show. Later, you can replace the photo CD with an audio CD and play your favorite music.

Not only is this process simple, but it also protects your photos from the elements that can destroy them. You can store an amazing amount of photos on one CD.

Kodak photo CD players

Remember, you must have a photo CD player before you can view your pictures on your television. Kodak offers four machines with different capabilities. Besides photo CDs, each can also play audio CDs.

All photo CD players include an infra-red remote control and all necessary connector cables. All devices are programmable for audio as well as for video. This means that you can program the presentation and the sequence of the pictures.

The simplest machine is the Kodak photo CD player PCD 270. This player allows the viewer to delete some pictures from the playback sequence. The manufacturer's suggested retail price is $379.

The Kodak photo CD player PCD 870 offers more advanced viewing options. This player is easy to use and allows you to save your programs because of its relatively large memory. The manufacturer's suggested retail price is $449.

The Kodak photo CD players PCD 5850 and PCD 5870 offer the same features as the PCD 870 and also have a CD changer, which can accommodate up to five CDs simultaneously. This allows access to 500 pictures or more than five hours of music. The manufacturer's suggested retail price is $549.

The following is an overview of the functions of the Kodak photo CD players:

Photo functions	PCD270	PCD870	PCD5850/587
Automatic play	•	•	•
FPS (saving of selected subjects)	•	•	•
Interval (selectable picture interval)		•	•
Pan up/down	•	•	•
Pan left/right		•	•
Insert (pictures in other areas)		•	•
Rotating the image clockwise	•	•	•
Rotating the image counter clockwise		•	•
Normal view (filling the whole screen)	•	•	•
Full View (decreased image display)		•	•
Frame On/Off (section frame for selecting the zoom area)		•	•
2 X Tele (doubles the section)		•	•
Reverse Display (playing in reverse order)	•	•	•
Scan (of the full images)		•	•
On screen display			•
Multiple disk changer			•

Music functions	PCD270	PCD870	PCD5850/587
Shuffle (random order of titles)	•	•	•
Search forward/reverse	•	•	•
Program (programmed order of titles)	•	•	•
FTS (saving chosen titles)		•	•
A to B		•	•
Time Edit (CD stops after defined playing time)		•	•
Scan (short playing of all titles)	•	•	•
Earphone jack		•	•
Multiple disk changer			•

Photo and music functions	PCD270	PCD870	PCD5850/587
Play	•	•	•
Pause	•	•	•
Stop	•	•	•
Next (image/piece of music)	•	•	•
Previous (image/piece of music)	•	•	•
Repeat	•	•	•
Skip	•	•	•
Keep (save settings on exit)	•	•	•
Program memory	2K	8K	8K

Kodak also has a portable photo CD player, called the Kodak photo CD portable Player PCD 970. This player is ideal if you want to show your pictures to friends and family who do not have a photo CD player. The manufacturer's suggested retail price is $449.

Connecting the CD player

Before you can access the pictures and sound provided by your photo CD player, you must not only integrate the equipment into your audio and video system, but also connect the necessary cables.

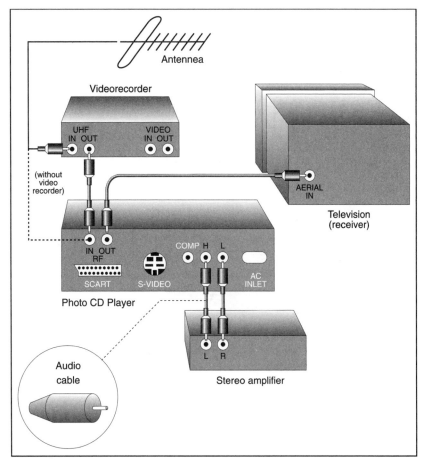

Connecting a photo CD player through the antenna input

For the audio output, there are two RCA phone connectors for the right and the left channel. Connect these to the CD input of your amplifier. If your stereo system doesn't have separate input for a CD player, use the auxiliary connection.

There are several ways to display the pictures on your TV. If your TV doesn't have a video input, you can transfer the image through the antenna input. This connects the photo CD player, like a video cassette recorder, between the antenna and the TV. Plug the external antenna cable into the photo CD player and the cable that came with the CD player between the output of the CD player and the antenna input of the TV. With this setup, the player sends the signal of the image across a TV channel, which can be selected using a Channel selector switch, usually found on the rear of the photo CD player. Obviously, you must switch your TV to the correct channel to receive the picture.

However, this method doesn't provide the best display quality. The signal of the image must be modulated to a carrier wave, which is processed by the receiver of the TV. Then it again filters out the signal of the image and transfers it to the video section of the TV.

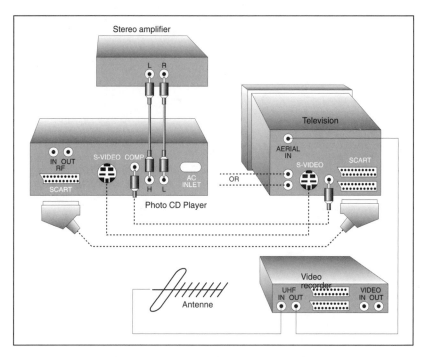

Different connections for a photo CD player

You'll obtain a better display if you can feed the image data directly into the TV through a video input. There are several ways to do this. You can transfer the signal of the image with a video cable with RCA plugs or with an S video cable. If your TV has an RGB port or an S video port, you should connect your photo CD player to it. This transfer guarantees the best display.

If the only video port on the TV is already being used by your VCR, you can connect the photo CD player to its input. This connection has another advantage. You can record a slide show on video tape and add sound to it.

With a high-quality video recorder and a good tape, you can record an almost perfect copy of the pictures on your photo CD. Then you can play the video on any video recorder. This is helpful because currently more people own video cassette recorders than photo CD players.

Therefore, if you create your own videos using a camcorder and also take 35mm photos, the photo CD system can be extremely useful. You can add still photos to videos.

As we mentioned, you can attach a photo CD to any television. However, the quality of the display depends on the quality of the TV. This means that ideally your TV should have an RGB or S video port to be able to display the information it receives from the CD player. These connections lead to unaltered transport of the information to the screen.

Unlike videos, which consist of moving pictures running at 50 frames per second, the photo CD only issues individual pictures and displays them as still images on the screen. However, because of the television technology, the individual pictures appear on the screen in the display frequency. This leads to the same problems that occur with computer monitors.

The human eye sees flickering if the display frequency is below 70 Hz. This flickering isn't very noticeable in moving pictures, because each individual image contains different information.

This isn't the case with still pictures. A slight flickering is especially noticeable on big screen TVs at the normal display frequency of 50 Hz. Only the newer, high quality TVs, with a display frequency of 100 Hz, can eliminate this problem.

Uses for the photo CD player

Besides home use , the photo CD player can also be used professionally in various ways. The Autoplay function makes the photo CD player a perfect tool for presentations. Also, since they are easy to use, photo CD players can be used by anyone.

The following lists some of the ways a photo CD player can be used:

Travel agencies

Travel agencies can display photos of various travel destinations on televisions displayed in their windows or within their offices. Photos of hotels, beaches, and points of interests can also be displayed.

Stores

The photo CD system can be used to display sale items or specialty products.

Health services

Information about various health services and procedures can be shown.

Sales representatives

Using a portable photo CD player, sales representatives can show their products to clients.

Universities and colleges

Universities and colleges can use photo CDs to manage their large collections of pictures. Students can easily access the pictures, without damaging the originals.

Schools

Photo CDs can be used in schools for subjects such as geography and biology.

> **NOTE**
>
> Since using a photo CD player is as easy as using an audio CD player, we won't explain the basic functions. Creating a personalized slide show from the pictures on your Photo CD is easy.
>
> Your photo CD includes an index print. This is a printout consisting of thumbnail images of the pictures on your photo CD.

Photo agencies

Photo agencies can index and save a photographer's numerous photos on separate CDs so they are easy to find. Also, numerous pictures can be placed on a CD and sent to clients.

This also prevents others from processing the pictures illegally. The client simply selects the desired photos and then receives the originals or a photo CD with high-resolution pictures.

Personnel departments

Businesses can use photo CDs to keep a pictorial database of their employees. These photos can be useful for identification purposes.

As you can see, photo CD players can be used in various ways. They are useful and can be used wherever photos are used.

Creating a slide show

Once you've connected the photo CD player to your equipment, you can start your first slide show. In our explanations, we'll use the Kodak Photo CD player PCD 5870.

For most cameras, the images on your photo CD are stored in the order in which you took the pictures. However, pre-wind cameras unwinds the film from the cartridge when the film is loaded and winds it back onto the cartridge as the pictures are taken. This places the pictures on the film in reverse order. The Kodak Photo CD player includes a [Reverse] button to correct this.

Use the Favorite Picture Selection (FPS) list to create an interesting slide show by programming your own sequence and display mode.

Function keys on the remote control let you rotate, enlarge, pan, zoom in on sections of pictures, or display an entire picture.

Several steps are involved in creating a complete show. First, determine the specific display mode for each picture and then its sequence. The best way to do this is by cycling through the pictures on your CD twice. You might want to make some notes for later reference.

Press the [FPS] button on the front of your photo CD if the display does not already indicate the FPS is active. First, move from picture to picture and decide whether each should appear in the preset position.

If you want to include the picture, indicate how it should appear in the show and save the setting by pressing the [Keep] button on your remote control (some other photo CD's call this button "Store").

If you do not want to include a picture in the preset position, press the [Skip] button and the picture will be excluded from the sequence.

The second time, use the [Insert] button to include pictures that you want to view but which are at different locations on the CD. Again, you can alter the display mode individually. It's even possible to insert a picture several times into your slide show in various display modes, such as complete and partial views.

If you want the displayed picture to remain at its present location, select the desired display changes and save the setting by pressing the [Keep] button. The [Next] button moves to the next picture.

If you don't want the picture displayed at this location, press [Skip] on your remote control. The photo CD player automatically displays the next picture.

Repeat this process to remove all the pictures you don't want to use and select the display modes for the other pictures.

Then, insert all the desired pictures at different locations. Select the picture behind the desired location. Press the [Insert] button and choose the picture to be inserted. You can do this by entering its number or by displaying it on the screen with [Previous] and [Next]. Select the display mode and finally press [Keep].

It's possible to edit your programming. Simply display the picture you want to edit, erase it from the sequence with [Skip] or display it in a different form and save it again with [Keep].

By pressing the [Autoplay] and the [Repeat] buttons, your slide show will operate automatically and without interruptions.

The information for your slide show is stored in your photo CD player. Playing your photo CD on another player will not display your presentation on that player. The programming applies only to the PCD on which you created it. When you change the CD, the player identifies it and activates its own program from memory.

You can also turn off FPS without losing the slide show you created. Switch off the FPS option. All the pictures will appear in normal display and sequence. Pressing the [FPS] button again reactivates the program.

Ready-made CDs

Besides using your own photos on a CD, you can use ready-made CDs, which contain various types of photos. For example, many CDs containing various sights of interest from around the world are currently available.

Photo CDs from Philips

The following CDs are available from Philips:

➢ Dream land America

➢ Film legends (with sound)

➢ Fashion trends 92/93

➢ Esthetic nudes

➢ Old timers (with sound)

➢ The Windsors

➢ Marilyn Monroe

➢ Dream hotels

Philips photo CDs

Professional photo CDs from Corel

The Corel professional photo CD-ROM is available from Corel, the maker of CorelDRAW!. Each CD contains 100 photo CD pictures that aren't copyrighted. However, remember the Corel DRAW! disks are not player compatible; they can be read using a CD-ROM drive with the appropriate software.

The professional-quality photos on this CD cover various topics, such as nature photos, cars, and planes. Different types of photos are always being added.

Each CD also contains several useful utilities:

Corel Screensaver

This lets you use your own photos as a screen saver.

Corel CD Audio

This is a fully-operational CD player.

Corel Mosaic Visual File Manager

This is a display and file management program.

Corel photo CD-Lab

This is a slide show program with automatic or manual functions. This program also lets you add music to your presentations.

Windows Wallpaper Flipper

This program allows you to change backgrounds automatically.

The contents of the CD are compatible with Windows and Apple Macintosh. Comprehensive user manuals are also included.

Installing A CD-ROM Drive

As you already know, before you can use photo CD pictures on your computer, you must attach a CD-ROM drive that can read photo CDs. This drive can be connected internally or externally to the computer.

In any case, you'll need an interface suitable for the CD-ROM for data exchange with your computer and through which it's controlled. If you already have a SCSI (Small Computer Standard Interface) controller in your computer, simply plug in the new drive and activate the necessary drivers according to the user's manual. Otherwise, you'll need an additional controller or a sound card with a CD-ROM-compatible interface.

Besides the CD-ROM, you'll also need sufficient memory in the form of RAM as well as on your hard drive. If you only want to display the photos on your monitor, 4 Meg of RAM and 20 Meg on the hard drive are sufficient. However, if you want to process your picture on the photo CD in a higher resolution, you'll need a minimum of 8 Meg of RAM. It's best to have 20 Meg or more of RAM. This also applies to the space on the hard drive. You need at least 100 Meg for optimum processing.

Before purchasing a CD-ROM drive, be sure it has the following minimal requirements:

> ➢ A free plug for the controller or an existing SCSI controller, or a sound card with a plug for a CD-ROM. (The drive must have a sound card-compatible interface.) If you want to add a sound card and a CD-ROM, you should purchase a kit that contains all the components. You'll need a free 16-bit socket for the sound card.

> ➢ For an internal CD-ROM, you need a free drive slot that opens to the front.

> ➢ For an internal CD-ROM, you need a free electrical socket to supply the electricity. If a socket isn't available, use a Y-cable, which lets you attach two devices with cables.

> ➢ For an external CD-ROM, you need a separate electrical socket.

> ➢ For an internal CD-ROM, which you want to connect to an existing SCSI adapter, you need a data cable with a free plug for the drive. Usually, a SCSI data cable comes with three plugs (one for connection to the adapter and two for attachment to the SCSI devices). If you've already attached two SCSI devices, you'll need a cable for three machines. You can either make this cable yourself or have it made for you.

> ➢ If you want to do more than simply display the pictures, you need sufficient RAM. When expanding RAM memory, think of the future. For example, if your computer has a 4 Meg capacity, don't expand it to 8 Meg using 1 Meg SIMMS if you plan on expanding further later.

> ➢ If you want to expand your computer with 8 Meg in the form of 1 Meg SIMMS, you can usually just do this by exchanging the SIMMS for 4 Meg SIMMS. The old 1 Meg SIMMS are usually less expensive than their original purchase price.

Before you install and attach the new CD-ROM, you should be aware of your computer configuration. This is especially important if you already have several attachments on your computer.

To access the data on the CD-ROM and for controlling it with the computer, you need certain data and control ports, which may already be occupied by other devices.

➤ I-/O Port
  This is the address where the computer communicates with the interface.

➤ IRQ (Interrupt ReQuest)
  This is the connection the drive uses for requesting time on the CPU.

➤ DMA (Direct Memory Access) channel
  Moves data in and out of memory without burdening the CPU.

➤ Basic address of the card specific BIOS (Basic Input Output System)
  This is the address for the programs requiring an intelligent interface like a SCSI controller for managing independent data transfer.

To avoid crossovers, write down how the addresses listed above are used by other cards and, before the installation, check whether there are any conflicts with the basic settings of the new controller card.

Internal CD-ROMs

Carefully insert the CD-ROM into a free drive duct and screw it in. Slip the interface card, which is usually provided, into a free slot of the motherboard. Attach the drive to the interface card with the included cables and connect the drive to an electrical outlet.

After you've examined all the connections, switch on your computer. Now you can start the installation software. Normally the original values of the setup program are automatically used. It's helpful if you have the settings of your other built-in computer cards available.

After you reset the computer, the CD-ROM is ready. If you encounter problems, refer to Chapter 2 for more information on installing a CD-ROM drive.

External CD-ROMs

External CD-ROMs are easier to connect because you must insert only a few plugs.

If you connect the drive through your own controller, insert the controller card into a free slot. Usually you can leave all the settings on the card in the preset locations. If you already have many additional cards in your computer, you might encounter crossover. If this occurs, refer to Chapter 2 for information on what to do.

After attaching the drive, you must install the drivers with the included installation program.

Software requirements

Most photo CD-compatible programs run under Windows. Therefore, Windows 3.1 should already be installed on your computer.

Since the photos are placed on the CD in a complex format, you need special software to display them. Several photo CD kits, which contain all the necessary equipment (CD-ROM and software), are available. For example, Sony's photo CD kit contains Kodak's Access.

The enclosed software varies depending on the manufacturer (see the illustration on the following page). However, all the programs let you load the pictures and save them in a common graphics format.

After activating the appropriate program, miniature versions of the pictures appear. To display a full-size version of a picture, double-click it. Another window opens and the picture is displayed in the desired size.

Since Windows' Paintbrush is an image processing program, you can make simple changes to the picture without buying a special program.

Need More Information?

On Chapter 3, we'll provide an overview of the programs you can use to process the pictures on a photo CD.

Toshiba photo CD kit

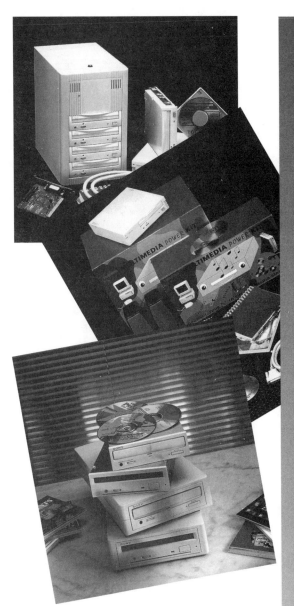

Computers And The Photo CD

Computers And The Photo CD

Chapter 2

Computers And The Photo CD

In this chapter, we'll discuss photo CD technology in more detail. First, we'll discuss the various CD formats and then focus on the photo CD format. You'll also find information on the hardware that's needed to display the pictures of the photo CD on a computer monitor.

CD Formats

If you've ever seen an audio CD, you already know the basic design of any compact disc. With ordinary records, a needle picks up the information mechanically.

However, with a CD, a laser reads the information without touching the CD. Also, while a record contains analog data, a CD contains digital data, which consists of zeros and ones.

The surface of a CD consists of a paper-thin reflective layer of aluminum. The data exists on the CD in the form of "pits" and "land." The "pits" are the hollows in the surface ("land").

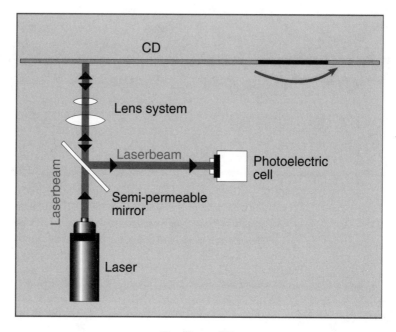

Reading a CD

After a CD is inserted into the drive, the laser focuses on the land in order to achieve the maximum reflection. If the laser hits a hollow, it loses its focus and the photo receptor determines a much decreased intensity, corresponding to a switch from 0 to 1.

Each shift from pit to land and from land to pit translates to the value 1; everything else has the value 0. Therefore, the lengths of the pits or the land represent a sequence of zeros until the next change, as shown in the following figure.

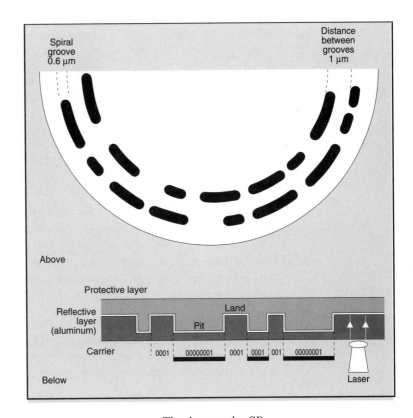

The data on the CD

Since the hollows are a physical indentation, the electronic and magnetic rays cannot harm the data. However, a deep scratch on a CD can create misinterpretations during the reading of the hollows.

Small scratches don't influence the readout, because the active reflective layer lies beneath a relatively thick, clear protective surface. Shallow scratches in this protective coating are outside of the focal area of the laser and don't influence the read out (result).

The data on a CD are deposited in data blocks according to a special inscription and coding procedure. To avoid a constant change from 0 to 1 and back, the data is formatted in 14-bit format instead of 8-bit. Because of this coding change, this procedure is called EFM (Eight to Fourteen Modulation) coding.

65

The arrangement of the data on a CD is similar to the arrangement on a phonograph record. All data blocks and sectors lie behind one another on a spiral groove about 0.6 μm wide. The distance between the grooves measures 1.6 μm. Since a diameter of 12 cm accommodates about 20,000 tracks on a normal CD, the memory capacity is 125,000 bits per square millimeter.

Starting at the innermost track, the sectors are counted in minutes, seconds, and sector numbers. A second contains 75 sectors; the entire CD lasts about an hour. The following calculation determines the capacity:

```
(75 sectors * 2352 bytes) / 1024 = 172.3K/second
(172.3K * 3600 sec) / 1024 = 605.7 Meg/CD
```

Constant Linear Velocity (CLV)

For this procedure, which is called "constant linear velocity", each sector is the same length. Therefore, the outer track, with the greater radius, holds more data sectors than the innermost track (smaller radius).

Since the laser beam (with a strength of 1.5 to 1.7 μm) moves between the inner and outer track when reading the data, different rotation speeds must ensure a constant transfer of data per time unit to the read head. Consequently, the rotation speed slows from the inner (500 RPM) to the outer track (215 RPM).

With a CAV (Constant Angular Velocity), which is used for hard drives, the medium turns at a constant speed and all concentric tracks contain the same amount of data. This creates a faster data transfer rate but wastes a lot of space. This occurs because the outer track, which is several times longer than the inner, contains exactly the same amount of data.

CD standards

The structures we just discussed are the only similarities found among the various CDs. As you learned, digital data exists in data blocks, called sectors, on the CD. A certain format is needed in order for this data be read correctly.

Otherwise, for example, a simple string of zeros and ones would probably cause a read error. Also, you must be able to locate certain areas on the CD.

Therefore, control structures are needed to identify individual sectors and provide additional data, such as a checksum of the sector for improved protection of stored data. Unfortunately, this improved protection takes up memory space. If a bit is read incorrectly on an audio CD, this error is almost inaudible. However, this isn't the case if a wrong bit is read on a data CD.

The method of coding and managing the data on a CD is defined in a collection of "colorful books."

Red Book (Digital audio, CD DA)

This determines the properties of audio CDs:

A sector contains 2,352 bytes of usable data. Besides that, 784 bytes are used for detecting errors and 98 bytes for operational purposes.

Yellow Book (CD-ROM)

This standard describes two modes, which have different error detection methods and maximum rates of data transfer.

Mode 1

A sector contains only 2,048 bytes of usable data, since 280 bytes are reserved (for additional correction of errors). Also, you'll need 12 synchronous bytes and 4 header bytes, which must also be subtracted from the usable data reserved in the Red Book.

Since, unlike an audio CD, each sector of the data CD must be accessible, each sector is identified with a number. This number resides in the 4 header bytes. The 12 synchronous bytes are needed to separate the rest of the data and to mark the sector identification. This allows relatively fast access to the individual sectors.

Since this standard is based on the Red Book, it also contains 784 bytes for detecting errors and 98 bytes for data control per sector.

All usable data can be restored from the 290 bytes of the additional error correction with the help of a statistical algorithm, even if only a small part of the usable data is recognized correctly. The result is an error potential of 10^{-12}. This means that statistically one read error can occur within 1,000 gigabytes.

However, the small amount of usable data provides a maximum reading speed. As mentioned above, 75 sectors are read per second, which means a data transfer rate of 75 x 2048 = 150K per second.

Mode 2

This mode omits the additional error correction in favor of increased reading speed. Therefore, only the 12 synchronous bytes and the 4 header bytes necessary for complete identification of the individual sectors must be subtracted from the 2,352 bytes of usable data, which are available according to Yellow Book specification. 2,336 bytes of usable data remain.

This produces a maximum data transfer rate of 75 x 2336 = 171K per second. However, the error potential in this mode is still 10^{-8}, but this is sufficient for image or sound files.

Green Book (CD-I)

This format is based on mode 2 of the Yellow Book. However, it uses another 8 bytes for a CD-I subheader. This standard also defines the coding procedure for the various data used (graphics, audio, etc.).

Orange Book (CD-WO, CD-MO)

This book contains the specifications for write-once CD-ROMs and magnetic optical drives.

CD-ROM XA standard

When the standards of the CD-ROM were defined in the Yellow Book, it was obvious the formats described there were insufficient for the expanding multimedia industry. So, this standard was expanded. The most important innovation is the ability to mix (almost without errors) music, video, and image data inside a track with programming data. It's even possible to output image and sound signals simultaneously through special definition and output procedures.

The basis for the XA standard (eXtended Architecture) are the mode 2 sectors of the CD-ROM standard. There are two form types in the XA standard, called mode 2 form 1 and mode 2 form 2, which allow the storage of very sensitive program data with less sensitive data in this sector form. An 8-byte subheader precedes the usable data of both types. These bytes remain unused at the end of the usable data in the normal mode 2 sector. This subheader allows a clear data identification within the subsequent usable data.

For the form 1 sectors, 280 bytes are subtracted from the 2,328 bytes of "user data" for increased error detection. Again, 2,048 bytes of usable data remain. Consequently, this form corresponds to the mode 1 sector of the CD-ROM standard.

The form 2 sectors can store fewer sensible data like audio, video, or image data. Data wasn't deducted for increased error detection. Therefore, it contains 2,328 bytes of usable data, which can be read with a maximum data transfer rate of 2328 * 75 = 170K.

XA standard and old drives

Since the arrangement of the XA sectors is almost identical to the old CD-ROM standard, many old drives can read this type of a sector. However, they may not be able to identify the 8 bytes of the subheader. The controller and the driver software control the identification of the data and their correct use.

If it's "firmware", which means the built-in electronics and logics can enable the drive to read the information in the subheader, then the drive can be adapted to have limited XA capacity with a specific driver. This means the drive can read and interpret the information of an XA CD.

However, changing the driver won't give it the ability to read and process encapsulated sectors. To do this, you need a faster memory buffer to quickly store temporary data during the reading of the next sector, so the image and the sound data can be emitted simultaneously (in parallel). For adequate speed, the controller must have direct access to the buffer. A software solution with the driver and the computer memory is too slow.

Current photo CDs don't contain encapsulated sectors. Instead, they contain only equal sectors written in the XA standard mode 2, form 1. To read a photo CD, a drive only has to be able to identify these sectors and a driver has to be able to use this information.

The file system of a CD

After defining the physical format for storing data on a CD, you must define how data are organized on the CD. Therefore, a standard that ensures optimal expansion of the CD was defined. Representatives of the leading companies met and decided on a standard, called the "High Sierra Standard", which was named after their conference hotel. Because of an effort to create an international standard, this standard later became "ISO 9660."

The ISO 9660 standard defines a hierarchical file system, which is used on your computer. The only differences or limitations are related to file names. With MS-DOS, you can use only 8 characters for the name and three characters for an extension. With Amiga and Macintosh computers, you can use file names of any length.

To guarantee compatibility between the two types of computers, the ISO 9660 standard defines two levels:

> ➢ Interchange level 1
> follows the DOS convention

> ➢ Interchange level 2
> allows file names of any length.

Special drivers perform the transfer of the file organization on a CD to the appropriate operating system. The MSCDEX.EXE program handles this for MS-DOS.

Photo CD Technology

Technically, the photo CD resembles a CD-ROM XA disc. The format developed by Kodak is based on a future capability that will be able to mix images and sound, which is a mandatory condition of the XA format. However, currently the photo CDs are written with the same sectors of the XA standard mode 2, form 1.

One feature of the photo CD is that it allows you to add the data to the CD in several steps called sessions. Unfortunately, this ability causes several technical problems.

Each time a CD is inscribed, the appropriate tracks are framed by a "Lead In" and a "Lead Out." These structures reveal to the drive the start and the end of the written sector of a CD. Firmware prevents other areas of the CD from being read. Drives that cannot find several sessions on a CD, with multiple sessions capability, can identify and read only the first session. If you own such a device, collect as many pictures as will fit on a photo CD, before you have it made. Writing a photo CD in a single session has another advantage. Since less memory is used for supervision, you can place up to 120 pictures on the CD in one session.

The physical disc format

With the photo CD, Kodak and Philips have developed a design that can be combined with various applications. The structure of the photo CD combines the qualities of the audio CD, the CD-ROM, and the CD-I with the attributes of inscribable CDs.

The data structure of the photo CD guarantees an efficient display on photo CD players. Additional data structures permit a display on CD-ROM XA drives. The structure of a CD is determined in one of the "colorful" books, which define the individual formats.

The Red Book describes the audio CD, the Yellow Book defines the CD-ROM in various modes, the Green Book deals with the CD-I, and the Orange Book defines the CD WO and CD MO. (CD WO stands for Write Once. This is a CD that's inscribed once, such as a photo CD. CD MO stands for Magnetic Optical, which is a CD that can be inscribed more than once.)

So, the photo CD is defined by the Orange Book, the Yellow Book, and the Green Book. There is also a multiple session capability.

Single session

This is a digitizing procedure. If a CD is inscribed only once, up to 120 pictures can fit on a photo CD.

Multiple session

These are several digitizing procedures. Pictures are randomly transferred to the photo CD. In this case, the maximum storage capacity is 100 pictures, because it must include information and control data for each session. Each session occupies about 20 Meg for informational data, which is located in the Lead In and the Lead Out, for consolidating the individual sessions.

The photo CD system uses a hybrid disc as described in the Orange Book in order to write data on the CD sequentially, while retaining compatibility with simple players. This hybrid disc contains multiple program areas called sessions.

The hybrid disc technology permits the creation of a photo CD as a single or a multiple sessions CD. If the user wants to add pictures to a partially filled photo CD, the subsequently digitized images are added during a later session.

A session is framed by Lead In and Lead Out addresses. These addresses contain information, which differentiate the various sessions for multiple session devices. Single session devices recognize only the first digitizing process.

Special CD WO structures

Each session contains control structures, which regulate the access to various elements of the photo CD. The device needs the index table structure for locating the images on the CD. This structure holds information for disk identification, indicators to the image packs, which are the files that contain the picture data, and other necessary information for displaying images on the device.

When a new session is written on the photo CD, new index table structures and additional control records are inscribed on the disc and placed over the previous information.

The index hierarchy or subsequent sessions has the same structure as previous sessions. The last index sequence describes all input data from all sessions on the disc. Files, such as INFO.PCD, contain the updated information about all sessions on the CD.

Characteristics of the WO (Write Once) CD

A blank Kodak CD isn't pressed like an audio CD or a CD-ROM. Instead, it must be formatted to ensure exact guidance for the inscribing laser, so it can burn the data into the CD. This is one of the reasons why a CD WO blank is more expensive than a blank that includes pressed information.

The formatting consists of a microscopic groove, into which the carrier material is pressed. Electronics guides the inscribing laser along this groove and alters the revolution of the CD according to the distance from its center.

A CD WO consists of four layers. The carrying material is covered by a reflective layer. This layer is coated with an organic dye. Then there is a protective layer.

The writing laser alters the reflective properties of the organic dye. A low energy pick-up laser reads the changing energy levels emitted from the modified dye.

The file system of a photo CD

The image files are stored in a hierarchical file structure on the photo CD. This structure is shown on the following page.

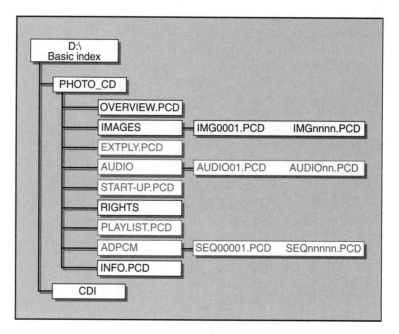

Index table structure of a photo CD

Like every CD-ROM, the photo CD is organized according to the ISO 9660 standard. The "interchange level 1" specifies the requirements of the file name, which are very similar to the DOS requirements for file names (i.e., 8 characters with a three character extension).

The pictures, with all pertinent information about the photo CD, are stored in the IMAGES subdirectory in the PHOTO_CD directory. This directory also contains three important files.

INFO.PCD

This is an information file that contains the serial numbers and information about the photo CD and processing lab.

OVERVIEW.PCD

This file contains the preview images of all pictures stored in the file.

STARTUP.PCD

This file is the first image the Photo-CD player displays. It contains the contains the photo CD logo (in Image PAC format). It is possible to customize this screen.

IMAGES directory

This directory contains all image packs. The individual pictures are numbered from IMAG0001.PCD to IMAGnnnn.PCD. Besides the PHOTO_CD directory, you'll also find the CD-I directory. This contains the necessary data for playing the photo CD on a CD-I player.

The root directory can also contain other subdirectories, which contain various types of data. A good example is the companion CD. In addition to the PHOTO_CD directory, you'll find other directories, which contain programs and data for this book.

How a picture is saved

Now that you're familiar with the structure of the general file system, we'll discuss the picture files, called "image packs", that are stored on the photo CD. These image packs are usually named "IMAG0001.PCD" to "IMAGnnnn.PCD."

NOTE

Don't confuse these files with "normal" picture files in the BMP, PCX, or TIF formats.

A picture is stored in an image pack in five different resolutions. This is done not only for clarity, but also for effective compression of the pictures.

A 1 x 1 1/2 inch picture is scanned with a resolution of 2048 x 3072 pixels and saved on the CD. If this picture is saved in the BMP format, it requires about 18 Meg. In this case, 30 pictures would barely fit on a CD.

The photo CD player picks up data with a speed of 150K per second. At this data transfer rate, it would take two minutes to transfer an image in full resolution to the computer. For the fastest possible image construction and maximum storage of pictures on the CD, the photo CD system cuts up and compresses the individual pictures and saves them encapsulated within a file. This ensures that pictures of different resolutions are quickly loaded and displayed upon demand.

For example, to show pictures on a TV, an average resolution is sufficient. However, you need the highest resolution for a DTP application. The resulting loading time lasts an average of four minutes because the image also must be decompressed. Usually only one or two pictures are loaded and saved in the working memory of the computer.

The PCD file consists of the following formats:

Picture components	Resolution
Base/16	128 lines x 192 pixels
Base/4	256 lines x 384 pixels
Base/4 and Base/16 pictures are saved in uncompressed form on the CD.	
Base	512 lines x 768 pixels
4 Base	1024 lines x 1536 pixels
16 Base	2048 lines x 3072 pixels
4 Base and 16 Base pictures are saved in compressed form on the CD.	

The uncompressed pictures can be displayed very quickly because complicated decompression procedures aren't needed.

64 base format

The 64 base format, used for the Professional CD, is new. This format produces an image in a resolution of 4096 x 6144 pixels. This resolution is intended for professional use. The Kodak Scanner 4045 is used for digitizing the images. It digitizes from a small picture format to a medium format, and the picture data of the small picture print corresponds to the original data. So this format provides absolute photo quality.

Also, a copyright file was added to the file system. This file contains the rights of the creator of the picture. The copyright information is burnt on the CD during the scanning process. This capability is useful for professional photographers.

Unfortunately, because of their high-quality, professional photo CDs are much more expensive than normal CDs.

For compatibility with other formats, additional picture data is saved in separate files. In addition to the IMAGES directory, you'll find the RIGHTS directory, which contains the copyright files for every picture and an IPE, which contains a directory with the same name for each picture, under the name "IMGnnnn" (nnnn represents the number). These directories contain files for the 64 base format.

Besides the information file, you'll find another subdirectory, which contains the C1_0001.ICR and C2_0001.ICR files.

These files contain color information. The Y0001.ICR file contains brightness information in packed form.

Kodak photo YCC standard

Another difference between photo CD pictures and normal pictures is the color system that's used. Instead of the RGB color scheme used in computer applications (8 bits for each basic color: Red, green, and blue), the photo CD pictures are saved according to the YCC color coding system.

This 24-bit wide system splits each color pixel into two components: An 8-bit luminosity providing 256 gradients of brightness and two 8-bit chrominance, which determine the color components. These components are specially designed for the output of natural colors.

For important colors like red, several more hues are available than for colors like dark blue. The YCC system also permits easy adaptability to the desired output medium.

The separation of the brightness data from the color data is also an important aspect of the compression and interlacing of the pictures within an image pack. The brightness data is most important for the resolution of an image because the eye is most sensitive to it.

The color data of a picture barely changes for the different resolutions or it can simply be calculated through interpolation. For that reason, the color section of a picture is saved only once in base resolution within an image pack, while the brightness data is saved for each resolution, and is occasionally compressed. For example, in reading an image in base/16 resolution, the uncompressed brightness data is tied to the color data of the base picture, which is calculated to the lower resolution through interpolation. The resulting data is changed to the desired output format, for example RGB for display on the computer monitor.

Image resolution

The image resolution, measured in pixels in the electronic image, is measured in lines in the photography and printing. For example, compare the pixel of an electronic image with the graininess of a photo. A direct comparison is impossible because of the different recording and measuring procedures. Instead, you should evaluate the final product-printouts of the same size.

The more information a picture contains, the more it can be enlarged. This is easy to do. The enlargement distributes the image data over a larger area. But after a certain size, the human eye can distinguish the distance between the individual pixels. In this case, the image appears unsharp or grainy. The farther the distance to the picture, the smaller the picture appears to the viewer, and the more the sharpness increases.

To return to the comparison described above, if a photo clearly shows graininess at a certain point of enlargement, the electronic image will also show its separate pixels. Therefore, the more information a picture contains, the more the print of a picture can be enlarged without losing any quality.

Suppose that a small format slide consists of about 15 million pixels, and a middle format slide consists of 200 million. However, the photo CD has only 6.2 million pixels for the small format. The Professional photo CD easily eliminates this discrepancy; it comfortably reaches the amount of pixels of a small format slide.

But the larger the starting format of a film, the more it surpasses the image data density of a digitized picture. So, you must consider whether this amount of image data is useful. A printed photo cannot provide the original photo quality. Even the human eye can notice the difference in quality.

Perhaps you're wondering why we're discussing photo quality for a digital image. However, this is an important consideration because a picture is rarely printed in its original form. Usually before it's printed, a picture is changed several times. Each change decreases the quality. Therefore, the better the starting quality, the less noticeable is a decrease of quality after the image is treated. The loss of quality is obvious, if only a segment of the picture is enlarged or if the total printout is extremely large.

If you need quality electronic images for advertisements or slides, the photo CD provides high quality pictures inexpensively.

Until now, only very expensive drum scanners could produce top quality pictures. Their production costs were much higher than those of a photo CD.

This implementation planning is no longer necessary with the photo CD. Because of the various resolutions stored in the PCD file, the necessary resolution is used. This is helpful because the processing times for images with a low resolution is much shorter than for pictures with higher resolutions.

This applies everywhere because, as we mentioned, it makes sense to work with low resolution images because of their higher processing speed and fewer demands on the system resources. Since the photo CD was introduced, the costs of a scan are no longer a determining factor. Now you have all the vital resolutions of each image available at low cost.

A printout of a 3 1/2 x 5 inch picture needs about 1.7 million pixels for good quality reproduction. A 5 x 7 inch picture requires 3.4 million and a 8 x 10 inch picture requires 7.2 million pixels. These values are for a viewing distance of about 12 inches.

For reproductions in magazines, you can use much fewer pixels, since the print technology doesn't have the same capabilities as, for example, a dye sublimation printer.

Regardless of how the printouts of photo CD pictures are used, you can find a suitable application. Remember, using too many pixels in the final product doesn't cause problems but using too few may cause problems.

Production Process

 The actual process of placing films (pictures) on a CD is very complex. This process consists of the following steps:

1. The images are scanned with a special high resolution scanner.

2. The data is transferred to a powerful computer.

3. The image is displayed and modified.

4. The picture data is converted from the RGB format to the YCC format. This isn't a simple conversion. As we mentioned, the YCC color system is designed for photography. Therefore, it provides adaptability to the output device. This requires a comprehensive calculation of the colors in the entire picture.

5. The brightness values of the individual pixels for various resolutions are calculated.

6. The brightness values of the 4 base and 16 base resolutions are compressed.

7. The pictures are written on the CD.

8. The pictures are printed.

Four devices are needed for these procedures:

➢ Scanner

➢ Central computer

➢ CD writer

➢ Printer for the contact prints

The following figure shows the individual components of a photo CD master originator station.

A typical photo CD mastering station

Kodak scanners

Kodak uses the following scanners for digitizing images:

PCD scanner 2000

This scanner is used exclusively for processing small format films. A motorized film transport for uncut films makes this device easy to use. Individual pictures can also be processed with a special "picture platform."

The scanner digitizes negatives and slides (black and white or color) with a maximum resolution of 2,048 lines times 3,072 pixels with 12 bits in each of the three primary colors. It generates an original file of 27 Meg.

The PIW scanners 2200 and 2400 are kits sold by Kodak and contain either a recorder or two CD writers, but the scanner is always a PCD 2000.

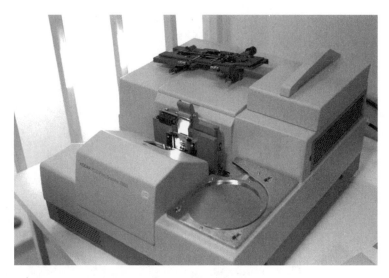

The Kodak PCD scanner 2000

PCD scanner 4045

This scanner can process small format pictures up to a size of 2.25 x 3.3 inches. It can digitize with 4,096 lines times 6,144 pixels, which enables it to scan images for the professional photo CD.

Because of the large picture format, a motorized picture feed cannot be used. So, this must be done manually.

As a kit with either a recorder or two CD writers, this equipment is called PCD scanner 4200 or 4400.

PCD scanner 4045

Central computer

A Sun Sparc Station codes the picture data and converts the color and consistency data for the creation of a high-quality electronic image. This computer isn't much bigger than a pizza box and was designed specifically for use within a Kodak scanning station. The Kodak PCD Data Manager S 200 is a modified Sun Sparc computer

However, don't judge the performance of this device by its size. The scanned image appears on the screen after only five seconds and is ready for processing. You'll notice the immense volume of data only when the data are written onto the blank CD.

Kodak PCD Data Manager S 200

The lab technician examines the individual pictures on the monitor before he/she starts the digitizing process. This is when any corrections are made.

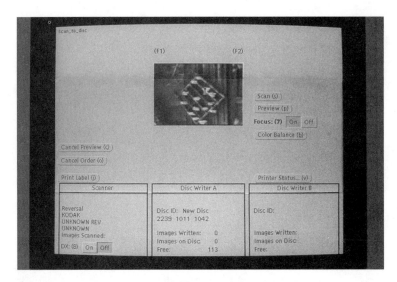

The main screen

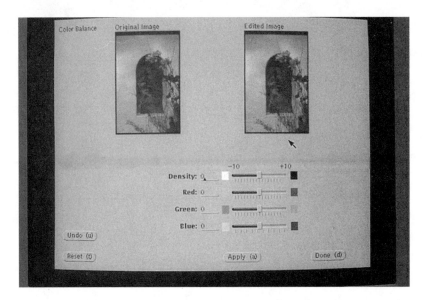

Color correction

The sharpness of the picture as well as its color intensity can be modified.

The data manager is very similar to a computer used for professional image processing.

Kodak PCD Writer 200

A Kodak PCD Writer 200 is attached to the work station. Controlled by the work station, it writes the processed data on the blank photo CD. The laser changes the surface of the CD and burns the image permanently on the CD.

Kodak photo CD reading and writing device

Kodak PCD Index Printer 200

This printer outputs the contact prints of a photo CD. Since these prints are numbered and dated, they are used as an index of each disc. The copies are of photo-quality.

Up to three prints are usually enclosed in the cover of the CD. This makes it easy to locate any of the 120 pictures.

Kodak PCD Index Printer 200

Kodak CD-ROM XA Reader S200

It's possible to copy CDs by connecting a CD-ROM to the Sun Sparc Station. The CD-ROM can copy single files or read an entire CD and save it to another photo CD. The Kodak CD-ROM XA Reader S200 is used for this purpose.

The Kodak CD-ROM XA Reader S200 is a normal XA-capable CD-ROM and can be used as such with any computer.

PC Systems

Whether you're using a PC or a Macintosh system, the new photo CD technology places tremendous demands on hardware. If you're familiar with image processing, you already know that working with pictures on a computer requires powerful hardware.

For many years, Apple was the leader in desktop publishing applications. The Apple Macintosh's image processing capabilities surpassed those of the PC. However, Windows has started to change this. In the meantime, powerful image processing programs have been developed for both Macintosh computers and Windows PCs.

For most users, the decision of which system (Macintosh or PC) to use is based on price. Based on this factor, the PC is the better choice. However, the memory management of DOS is rather antiquated. Because of the 640K limit, a rapid and limitless memory access isn't possible, at least not for DOS PCs. However, this situation is improving, especially with the development of OS/2 and Windows NT.

Many people think that all systems will eventually be completely compatible. This is an important concern of most software developers because their customers want to be able to use their existing files and data with new systems. Otherwise, users will be reluctant to change to these new systems.

Currently, which computer you choose depends on your personal preference. However, remember that as new developments are made, such as Intel's Pentium chip, existing technology becomes more affordable.

Recommended PC configuration

In this section, we'll discuss the minimum requirements needed for a computer that you want to use with a photo CD.

Minimum requirements

As we've mentioned, photo CD technology places tremendous demands on a system's resources. Therefore, we don't recommend using a minimal configuration. A PC 386SX with a 4 Meg memory is sufficient if you want to learn how to use photo CD technology.

Due to the size of the files, you must have at least 25 Meg of memory (real or virtual). If you want to save a photo CD picture on the hard drive, you'll need the space that is required for the picture. This can be a very large amount, depending on the file type and resolution of the image.

You also need a CD-ROM that supports the XA standard.

The larger the systems resources, the faster a photo CD picture is loaded and processed. If a computer doesn't have sufficient resources, it can take up to an hour to load an image in full resolution. To improve the performance of your system, you should use a larger memory and an optimal computer configuration.

Ideal configuration

We recommend using a 486/50 MHz motherboard with a VESA local bus, 32 Meg of working memory, 400 Meg hard drive, cache controller, super VGA card with a resolution of 1,024 x 768 pixels with 32,000 colors, and 2 Meg of video memory in a tower case with enough space for additional expansions. The monitor should be at least 15" diagonal.

At first this configuration may seem too expensive. However, as we mentioned, computer hardware prices are constantly becoming more affordable as new technology is developed. There are many PCs with these capabilities available from various manufacturers. When buying a system, look for expandability.

Built-in components are easier to use and less expensive. Be sure you understand any warranty and service agreements before you purchase your system. In some instances, the warranty becomes void as soon as the case is opened.

In the following sections, we'll provide detailed information about the expansions you can make to your system in order to get the most out of the photo CD.

Motherboard

The best way to improve the capacity of a PC is by installing a more powerful motherboard. Unfortunately, doing this is difficult because the motherboard is the "heart" of the computer. First, most of the existing components must be removed. Also, you need some dexterity to handle the components properly.

If you install the motherboard yourself, you can save some money. However, doing this can be dangerous because you may damage components. Repairing any damages may cost you more money in the long run. Refer to do-it-yourself books, such as *Upgrading & Maintaining Your PC* from Abacus, and videos for helpful information.

If you don't feel comfortable installing the motherboard yourself, your computer dealer can do this for you. Although this may cost an extra $60 or more, you'll have a functioning computer with a satisfactory warranty.

When selecting a new motherboard, generally you should get the fastest motherboard you can afford. Currently you can get motherboards with 486 processors and a clock speed up to 50 MHz.

NOTE

Unfortunately, there's no way to determine whether motherboards are defective. If you install a defective motherboard yourself, usually it's difficult to prove the board was already defective before the installation.

There are also DX2 boards, with which the processor works twice as fast as the system's clock speed. These are 25 MHz boards with 50 MHz DX2 processors and 33 MHz boards with 66 MHz DX2 processors. The 66 MHz DX2 boards are almost as fast as the "real" 50 MHz boards.

Since for the "real" 50 MHz boards, the whole system runs at a 50 MHz speed, the load on the motherboard is significantly higher than with the 66 MHz DX2 boards with a clock speed of 33 MHz. If you work with local bus components, it's better to use a 33 MHz board because a higher clock speed also places heavy demands on the individual system's components.

VL bus

VESA Local (VL) bus technology provides faster access to your peripheral devices. Unlike the normal ISA bus, which provides at most a 16-bit access, VL bus provides direct 32-bit access to the processor. VL boards usually have 2 VESA Local bus interfaces and are about the same price as a comparative ISA board.

For optimum speed, you can insert a VL bus graphics card and a VL bus hard drive controller. Most graphics card manufacturers always offer affordable VL bus cards. Recently Miro introduced a VL bus variation, called Miro Movie Pro, which significantly speeds up your system.

Also, a VESA Local bus controller is available from Ultrastore. This increases the system speed of even fast SCSI 2 hard drives. The IDE controller and the IDE cash controller of VL bus technology are also available. Currently these controllers cost about half as much as a SCSI controller.

A VL bus system provides faster access to the hard drive and an increased graphics organization. This increases processing speed, especially for photo CD technology. When used in high resolution mode, this system eliminates, or at least decreases, the endless waiting periods for the individual processing steps.

Graphics processing will be much faster once the Pentium (586) processor becomes more widely used. Upgrading to a VL bus board will even be useful with this processor. Most VL bus boards already have an upgrade socket so you can easily perform the upgrade to the 586.

In the meantime, there are numerous reasonably-priced motherboards, graphic cards, and IDE controllers of the VL bus standard available. The motherboard costs about $120 more than a comparable ISA board. Although SCSI controllers are still rare, they should be available soon.

If you update your system to the VL bus standard, you'll notice the speed increase immediately. If you also use a VL bus graphics card and a SCSI VL bus controller, images will be processed much more quickly.

PCI bus

The Intel PCI bus is currently being developed. The Intel PCI bus achieves greater speeds than the Local bus. Also, the Intel standard is supposedly much easier to use than any existing bus systems. Adaptec, ATI, AMD, Compac, Dell, IBM, Intel, as well as National Semiconductor and Acer are in the process of working with this standard. Unlike the Local bus, the PCI bus isn't attached directly to the processor and the cache. Instead, it's attached with a separate controller chip. So it doesn't matter to which type of CPU the PCI bus is connected. A memory controller translates the CPU protocol to the bus protocol and back.

The PCI bus board (the motherboard with PCI bus) accommodates at most 4 PCI sockets and an onboard controller. If necessary, several systems can be connected to achieve greater capacity. Besides increased capacity, Intel also claims that original PCI cards will have added capabilities.

Since the insertable cards configure themselves, jumpers for interrupts and DMA access aren't needed. The cards also determine whether they can operate with the system. Also, the peripherals are automatically configured. Computers with this new technology should be available by next year.

Working memory

Expanding working memory (RAM) is the easiest way to upgrade your computer. SIMMs (Single In-line Memory Modules) are affordable and can easily be installed. So, you can double or quadruple your present memory. For optimum performance while processing photo CD pictures, a computer needs 32 Meg of RAM.

Remember the working memory is arranged in banks and each bank can contain only SIMMs of equal value (i.e., 256K, 1 Meg, or 4 Meg SIMMs). The motherboards hold either two or four banks. Motherboards with two banks can be expanded to 32 Meg, and those with four banks can be expanded to 64 Meg.

However, in most computers the banks are usually filled with small SIMMs. For example, in a 2 Meg computer with two banks, both are filled with 256K modules. If you want to expand to 4 Meg, you must insert four 1 Meg SIMMs into the slots of a bank. To do this, you must remove the old SIMMs. If you leave the SIMMs in the second bank, you'll have 5 Meg.

If you want to expand working memory even further, you can also do this by only exchanging SIMMs. The maximum exchange with 1 Meg SIMMs is 8 Meg. For a larger increase, you must eliminate the old SIMMs and use 4 Meg SIMMs.

Hard drives

If you want to add a larger hard drive to your system, first you must consider whether you want to use a SCSI interface or AT bus. Both SCSI and AT bus hard drives are suitable for expanding existing computers. If you're content with two hard drives, the AT bus is sufficient. Special AT controllers are needed if you want to use more than two hard drives.

The SCSI interface provides the most flexibility. One controller can manage up to seven different devices. Another advantage of the SCSI interface is that it's possible to use both controllers (AT and SCSI) in one system.

91

If you want to work with photo CD pictures, a 400 Meg hard drive should be the smallest memory in the system. If you consider price per megabyte, hard drives in the gigabyte range are more affordable.

It's also possible to connect a hard drive to the parallel interface. However, since these hard drives are much slower than internal hard drives, they're less suitable for use as normal mass storage (in connection with photo CD applications). They can be used to exchange large amounts of data.

Cartridge drive

If you want to store numerous pictures, you can also use a cartridge drive. This is an external drive that provides almost unlimited storage capacity. Use this drive to transfer data from a storage medium (disk cartridge) to your hard drive for processing. When you're finished processing the data, you can move it back to the disk cartridge. The storage capacity of the removable storage media is usually 44 or 88 Meg.

Syquest makes some of the most popular cartridge drives. These drives are SCSI devices and can be accessed with SCSI controllers.

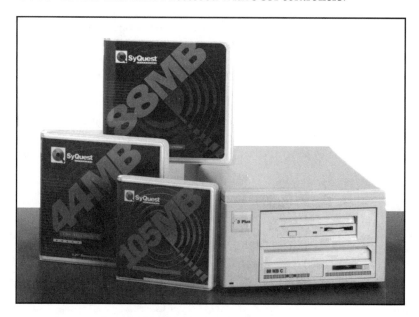

A cartridge drive using Syquest cartridges

Bernoulli box

The Bernoulli box, made by the Iomega Corporation, is a removable disk system that's connected to a computer through a SCSI interface. These drives are easy to use and have a large storage capacity. Their data access time can be compared to that of a normal hard drive. An almost unlimited storage capacity is possible by simply changing disks.

Floptical disk

This drive uses a combination of optical tracking and magnetic recording. Grooves in the disk are used to optically align the read/write head over the tracks.

Iomega recently started selling 21 Meg floppy disk drives. They are accessed with a SCSI controller and are available as internal and external 3.5-inch drives. The floptical drive can save and read 21 Meg of data on special disks. It also supports all 3.5-inch disk formats.

The floptical technology is a combination of optical tracking and magnetic recording. This results in precise tracking, which permits more and denser writing on a floptical than on a common floppy disk.

A floptical disk

A photo CD picture in full resolution will fit almost perfectly on a floptical. So, this disk is an alternative to cartridge drives.

The Iomega floptical drive is connected with a special SCSI adapter. It can also be accessed with an ADAPTEC 1520/1522 SCSI controller or with a 3 PLUS controller.

MO drives

Magnetic optical (MO) rewritable drives are the best way to store large amounts of data. They come in capacities of 128 to 650 Meg. These drives are very expensive. However, if you need more than 1 gigabyte of memory, this is your most affordable option.

The devices that you can buy today have access times equivalent to conventional hard drives. So, you can use MO drives as supplementary hard drives, as backup drives, and as an inexpensive way to exchange large amounts of data. Many processed photo CD pictures can be saved and/or passed on without problems on an MO disk.

All MO drives are compatible with PCs and Macintosh computers. They are connected with a SCSI interface. The disks have a 3.5-inch format and have the same outer measurements as a double density 3.5-inch floppy diskette. The disks can be stored like regular disks and aren't affected by magnetic influences.

The hard drive fills up quickly, considering the size of the files, because processing a picture in full resolution involves about 20 Meg of data. For this reason, the MO technology as storage medium is especially helpful, since there is room for 6 pictures in full resolution on an MO disk.

MO drives are easy to install. The standard connection with a SCSI controller allows immediate access to this inexpensive mass storage device. Although the writing speed isn't very fast, during the reading the IBM MO drive is very powerful.

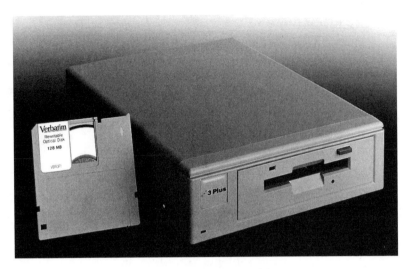

An example of an MO drive

The IBM 0632 Rewritable Optical drive has an amazing storage capacity. A 5.25-inch laser disk can hold up to 1.3 gigabytes. Therefore, this device is suitable for the production of CD-ROMs, since more than 500 Meg can be written and read on each side.

The drive can also be connected to an Apple computer by using a simple switch. The drive we tested had the following features:

> Industrial standard SCSI 2 interface with a data transfer rate of 5 Meg/sec (burst mode).

> Hours of operation at about 180,000 hours.

> Rewritable disk, supported by ISO, ANSI, and ECMA standards.

> 595 Meg, 652 Meg, 1.19 gigabyte, or 1.3 gigabyte per disk.

> Data transfer rate of 1,561K per second.

> 256K read ahead buffer cache.

> The micro code can be updated with SCSI.

CD-ROM drives

As you already know, you must have a CD-ROM drive in order to use photo CDs on your computer. Currently most of the CD-ROM drives that are available are XA and multiple sessions compatible. Older models usually run in a single session mode and can be adapted to be limited XA-capable by using a special driver.

SCSI or AT bus

As with hard drives, you must also determine which interface (SCSI or AT bus) should be used with CD-ROM drives. However, this is easy to do. SCSI drives are generally much faster than AT bus devices, but they are also more expensive. Speed isn't as important for the relatively slow CD-ROM drives. However, the greater flexibility of the SCSI adapter is a definite advantage. You can attach up to seven different devices to a controller.

Caddy or drawer?

There is another difference among available CD-ROM drives. With some drives, the CD is placed in a caddy and then inserted. A caddy is a plastic case that holds a CD. An attached metal shank opens the case inside the drive as with the 3.5-inch disks. Other drives use a drawer like the ones used in audio CD players.

There is some disagreement over the proper way to handle CDs. Some believe the photo CD must be protected from dust and fingerprints. In this case, a caddy provides the best protection. However, this is only effective if you have a caddy for each CD.

Others think using a caddy is awkward. These people think that a drawer is much easier to use, and that a jewel box is the best protection for each CD. Which method you use depends on your personal preference.

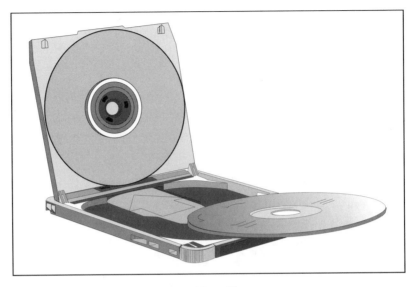

A CD caddy

Internal or external drive

If you have room in your computer, you should use an internal drive. This helps you save space on your desk and protects the drive.

This is also the less expensive option because you don't need an individual power cord or a separate case. However, the installation process is time-consuming.

The following sections provide an overview of the CD-ROM drives that are currently available.

> **NOTE**
> If your drive isn't included in the following pages, refer to your user's guide to determine the drives with which it's compatible.

Toshiba

The XM 3401 double speed drive is XA and multiple session compatible. It's compatible with IBM PCs, Micro Channel, and Apple computers. Also, it's available as an external and internal drive.

This drive's fast access time of 200 milliseconds is quite remarkable. The Toshiba CD-ROM drive can be connected to any PC-compatible SCSI controller. A short SCSI insert card from Future Domain is included with this drive.

Toshiba offers a complete photo CD kit for the PC as well as the Apple. A sample photo CD is also included.

The Toshiba photo CD kit

Installation

The short SCSI insert card from Future Domain is used to install the 5.25-inch internal drive. If there are several SCSI drives in the system, use the necessary jumpers as explained in the user's manual to ensure that you're using an open address. Insert the drive into the 5.25-inch shaft of your computer, which is accessible in the front. Usually you must remove the face plate from the case. Then connect the drive with data cables to the SCSI controller.

If you want to use the Future Domain controller that came with the kit, connect it to the other end of the data cable and insert the controller card into a free slot of the motherboard. To do this, first remove the face plate of this shaft. Then secure the card with the same screw that you just removed.

Close your computer and after rebooting it, insert the installation diskette and start the Setup procedure. Except for some confirmation prompts, the installation procedure is performed automatically.

After restarting the computer, the Toshiba 3401 is ready to use.

If you want to connect to a sound card, you must buy the required audio connection cable separately and use it to link the drive with the sound card during the installation.

Specifications	
Capacity:	
Mode 1	599 Meg
Mode 2	683 Meg
Data transfer rate	
Mode 1	150K/sec
Mode 2	171K/sec
Access time	310 ms (1x)
	200 ms (2x)
Data buffer	256K
Interface card	SCSI-2
Mean time before failure	50,000

Special features:

➢ Double and single rotational speed

➢ 330K/sec transfer rate

➢ 200 ms access time

- ➤ 256K data buffer
- ➤ XA error correction code
- ➤ Built-in SCSI 2 controller
- ➤ CD DA transfer by SCSI bus
- ➤ Low electrical use
- ➤ Use with 4.75-inch (12 cm) and 3.5-inch (8 cm) CDs
- ➤ Software volume control
- ➤ Excellent dust cover
- ➤ Emergency ejection for caddy
- ➤ "Snap-On" face plate
- ➤ Function that prevents unintentional ejection of the disc
- ➤ High number of hours of operation equaling 50,000 hours
- ➤ Conforms to MPC specifications
- ➤ Kodak photo CD compatible (Multiple session)

Philips

The Philips CDD 462 is an external CD-ROM XA drive and is multiple session compatible. It's sold with the photo CD software. The internal drive is the CM 205. This drive has only single session capability in connection with the CDD 167 XA expansion card. Also, the disk drawer must be opened manually. Otherwise, it has the same capabilities as the CDD 462 drive.

Specifications	
Capacity:	
Mode 1	645 Meg
Mode 2	757 Meg
Data transfer rate	
Mode 1	153K/sec
Mode 2	176K/sec
Access time	500 ms
Data buffer	32K
Interface card	CDD167 (serial)
Mean time before failure	25,000

Features

- ➢ 153/176K/sec transfer rate

- ➢ 500 ms access time

- ➢ 32K data buffer

- ➢ XA error correction code

- ➢ Excellent dust cover

- ➢ Emergency ejection for caddy

- ➢ Discs are changed with a motorized drawer (CDD 462)

- ➢ Suitable for 12 and 8 cm discs

- ➢ Conforms to MPC specifications

- ➢ Kodak photo CD compatible (multiple sessions for the CDD 462)

A CD-ROM XA controller card is available for both drives. It provides photo CD compatibility, a cache buffer of 32K, as well as a dual ADPCM decoder for CD DA and compressed audio recording.

The CDD 167 is a controller card for CD-ROM and CD-ROM XA. Use this card to connect internal and external CD-ROM drives to IBM PCs and compatible computers.

Philips CDD 462

Sony

SCSI drive CDU 561

Sony also offers a double speed CD-ROM drive called CDU 561. This drive is connected to the computer with a SCSI 2 interface. It's compatible with both PCs and Apple computers. With an access time of 280 ms, this drive is very fast.

XA and multiple sessions capability make the CDU 561 one of the best drives to use with the photo CD. The CD-ROM drives sold by Apple Macintosh are usually Sony drives.

This drive is sold stripped. Therefore, if you don't already have a SCSI controller, you must buy it separately. We recommend using the Adaptec 1542 with Corel SCSI for optimum performance.

Installation

It's easy to install this drive. After inserting the individual components and connecting the required cables, you can start the Setup program. All the necessary drivers are automatically entered in the CONFIG.SYS and AUTOEXEC.BAT files. Conflicts with addressing rarely occur.

If a SCSI controller card is integrated in the system, you should preset the initial address from 340 hex to 320 hex. You can easily do this by adding address jumpers to the controller card. Refer to the user's manual for more information.

AT bus drive CDU 31A

The CDU 31A is Sony's version of an AT bus. This drive is less expensive than a SCSI drive and includes an interface card and photo CD software. However, it's not as fast as a CDU 561. The Sony CD 31A with the AT bus interface is about $125 less than the SCSI version.

This drive's performance isn't as good as the Sony 541 drive.

Installation

Once the drive is connected, start the Setup program with the enclosed disc. The software is then installed automatically. After rebooting the computer, you can access the additional drive.

Specifications (CDU 561)	
Capacity:	
Mode 1	599 Meg
Mode 2	683 Meg
Data transfer rate	
Mode 1	150K/sec
Access time	350 ms (1x)
	280 ms (2x)
Data buffer	256K
Interface card	SCSI 2
Mean time before failure	25,000

Features

➤ Double and single rotational speed

➤ 300K/sec transfer rate

➤ 280 ms access time

➤ 256K data buffer

➤ Excellent dust cover

➤ CD-ROM XA error correction

➤ Audio compatibility

➤ Automatic loading mechanism

➤ Emergency ejection of the CD

➤ Conforms to MPC specifications

➤ Kodak photo CD compatible (multiple sessions)

Specifications (CDU 31A)	
Capacity:	
Mode 1	599 Meg
Mode 2	683 Meg
Data transfer rate	
Mode 1	153K/sec
Access time	490 ms
Data buffer	64K
Interface card	ISA bus 8 bit interface
Mean time to failure	25,000

Features

➤ 36K data buffer

➤ Excellent dust cover

➤ CD-ROM XA error correction

➤ Audio compatibility

➤ Automatic loading mechanism

➤ Emergency ejection of the CD

➤ Conforms to MPC specifications

➤ Kodak photo CD compatible (multiple sessions)

A picture of a Sony CDU 31A appears on the following page.

Sony CDU 31A

NEC

NEC offers removable, external and internal CD-ROM drives. These drives are connected with the SCSI interface. You can use an optional NEC controller, the CDTX003, or you can attach the drive to an existing controller. NEC also provides drives with double revolutions called "Multispin" drives.

The CDR-74 is an internal drive and CDR-84 is an external drive. Both of these drives have the same capabilities.

You can also obtain transportable and optional "off the line" devices either with simple revolution (CDR-37) or with Multispin technology (CDR-38). However, you must spend more money if you want to use these devices off the line because the external battery pack isn't included in the price.

Specifications (CDR-74 and CDR-84)	
Storage capacity	680 Meg
Data transfer rate	300K/sec
Access time	280 ms
Data buffer	64K
Interface card	SCSI 2
Mean time to failure	>30,000

Features

> ➢ 300K/sec transfer rate

> ➢ 280 ms access time

> ➢ 64K data buffer

> ➢ XA error correction code

> ➢ Use with 12 cm CDs

> ➢ Mean time before failure: 30,000 hours

> ➢ Conforms to MPC specifications

> ➢ Kodak photo CD compatible (multiple sessions)

The CDR-38 has the same capabilities as the drives described above except for the high access time (400 ms).

Specifications (CDR-37)	
Storage capacity	680 Meg
Data transfer rate	150K/sec
Access time	450 ms
Data buffer	64K
Interface	SCSI
Mean time to failure	> 20,000

Features

> ➤ XA error correction code

> ➤ Use with 12 cm CDs

> ➤ Conforms to MPC specifications

> ➤ Kodak photo CD compatible (multiple sessions)

Mitsumi

The Mitsumi CRMC-LU005S is the least expensive drive available that's not only photo CD capable, but also can read multiple sessions. Although its total capacity cannot match that of the previous drives, this drive is an excellent choice for home users.

Installation

The Mitsumi drive has a 16-bit AT bus insert card that integrates audio output. Once the drive is installed, add the software with the Setup program. The installation process is performed automatically.

You'll be asked to choose whether the MTMCDE.SYS driver with a 16-bit DMA transfer or the MTMCDS.SYS driver should be installed. The user's manual recommends using the MTMCDE.SYS driver because of increased performance. However, this driver cannot be loaded with QEMM386 Version 6.0. If you try to do this, the computer will crash. To avoid this problem, add the command line after CONFIG.SYS runs the QEMM386 software. However, less working memory will be available.

A free DMA channel or a free interrupt isn't needed for the MTMCDS.SYS driver. Also, problems don't occur with the QEMM or other memory managers. The drive's performance didn't decrease during the operations. Actually the drive seems to run even faster in the normal CD-ROM mode. It doesn't matter whether you have a SCSI or an AT bus system, everything runs with this driver, even a combination of SCSI, AT bus, and an additional Mitsumi AT bus interface.

Specifications	
Access time	+/-350ms
Data transfer speed	150K
Interface card	Mitsumi 16-bit interface card (AT bus interface)
Mean time before failure	25,000
Interface	SCSI
Mean time to failure	> 20,000

Features

> Compatible with DOS and Windows 3.1

> Loading drawer in front

> CD-ROM system without use of a caddy for increased user friendliness

> Plays standard audio CDs

> Earphone jacks on the front cover with volume control

> RCA audio jack on the interface card

> Photo CD compatible (multiple session)

> Microsoft MPC (Multimedia compatible)

> Sold as a complete set

> Installation within a few minutes

> ➤ Suitable sound cards :
>
> ATI Stereo F/X CD
>
> Ad Lib Gold 3000
>
> Sound Blaster 16 ASP

Texel

Texel offers two SCSI CD-ROM drives. The internal drive is DM-3024 and the external drive is DM-5024. Both drives have the same capabilities.

The internal drive identifies and terminates the drive with a jumper. The external drive has a switch on the back of the case for setting the SCSI ID number.

The drive is connected to the existing SCSI controller with 25-pin Centronics cables. The internal connection uses a 50-pin ribbon cable. The external device has its own electrical supply.

The software for integrating the drives comes from Corel. Use an ASPI-compatible controller for trouble-free operation. A setup program installs all the necessary drivers automatically. The CDs are loaded with a caddy and ejected manually by pressing a button.

Specifications	
Data transfer rate	300K/sec
Access time	265 ms
Data buffer	64K
Interface card	SCSI-2
Mean time before failure	30,000

Features

> ➤ 300K/sec transfer rate
>
> ➤ 265 ms access time
>
> ➤ 64K data buffer

110

> ➢ XA error correction code

> ➢ Built-in SCSI 2 controller

> ➢ CD DA transfer with a SCSI bus

> ➢ Low use of electricity

> ➢ Use with 12 cm CDs

> ➢ Compatible with IBM-XT/AT, IBM PS2 Micro Channel, Apple Macintosh

> ➢ Mean time to failure: 30,000 hours

> ➢ Conforms to MPC specifications

> ➢ Kodak photo CD compatible (multiple sessions)

Matsushita (Panasonic)

Matsushita CD-ROM drives are usually sold as OEM (Original Equipment Manufacturer) products in conjunction with sound cards. Older CD-ROM drives are quite common due to their low prices. You can get photo CD compatibility in single session mode with a special driver from Totronic.

The new generation of Matsushita drives is fully photo CD compatible and runs in multiple sessions mode. The CR-532 and the CR-533 CD-ROM drives have a rapid access time of 290 ms and a double speed data transfer rate. Both drives support the SCSI 2 standard.

Specifications	
Data transfer rate	150K/sec
	300K/sec (CR-533)
Access time	290 ms
Data buffer	128K
	256K (CR-533)
Interface card	SCSI-2
Mean time before failure	25,000

Features

> ➢ Double rotational speed for the CR-533

> ➢ 300K/sec transfer rate for the CR-533

> ➢ 290 ms access time

> ➢ 256K data buffer

> ➢ XA error correction code

> ➢ Built-in SCSI 2 controller

> ➢ Excellent dust cover

> ➢ Conforms to MPC specifications

> ➢ Kodak photo CD-compatible (multiple sessions)

Hitachi

The CDR 1700 S and the CDR 1750 are stand-alone CD-ROM drives. The CDR 1700 S is connected to the computer with an AT bus interface; its XA kit supports the XA standard. The CDR 1750 is available in a SCSI version and supports DOS, OS/2, UNIX, and Apple Macintosh.

Hitachi also sells a tower system with four integrated CD-ROM drives.

The Hitachi tower system

Specifications (CDR 1700)	
Data transfer rate	170K/sec
Access time	320 ms
Data buffer	128K
Interface card	AT-BUS
	SCSI-2 (1750 S)
Mean time to failure	> 20,000

Features

> 170K/sec transfer rate

> ➤ 320 ms access time

> ➤ 128K data buffer

> ➤ XA error correction code

> ➤ Use with 12 cm CDs

> ➤ Conforms to MPC specifications

> ➤ Kodak photo CD compatible (multiple sessions)

The Hitachi 1700 S

Teac

The Teac CD-50 is the newest design of SCSI CD-ROM drives. It's well protected against dust. The CDs are loaded with a caddy and ejected by pressing a button.

Specifications	
Interface	SCSI-2
Data transfer	335K/sec
Average access time	265 ms
Data buffer	64K
Data capacity	680 Meg
Mean time before failure	30,000 hours

Features

> Photo CD compatible

> Multiple session mode

> XA standard

> Audio output

> Only internal version available

> The Teac drive is one of the fastest CD-ROM drives

Chinon

The Chinon CD-ROM drive CDS-535 supports the SCSI standard. The CDs are loaded manually with a caddy and ejected by pressing a button. This drive comes with a simple SCSI controller and is quite fast.

Specifications	
Interface	SCSI 2
Data transfer	300K/sec
Average access time	280 ms
Data buffer	256K
Data capacity	630 Meg
Mean time before failure	25,000 hours

> Photo CD compatible

> Multiple session mode

> XA standard

> Audio outlet

> Also available in external version

The Chinon CD-ROM drive is an excellent choice because of its high speed and affordability.

Pioneer CD-ROM changer

The Pioneer DRM 604 x, with Quadraspin technology, is a high speed CD-ROM drive with six-fold capacity and four-fold data transfer rate.

The main advantage of the Pioneer CD changer is its refined chip technology and the enhanced optical read head. With a rotational speed of 2,100 revolutions per minute, it can obtain a four-fold read speed. Not only is its data transfer rate of 612K per second revolutionary, the access time of 300 ms sets a new standard for speed. There is a magazine for 6 audio, video, photo, encyclopedia, and other CDs.

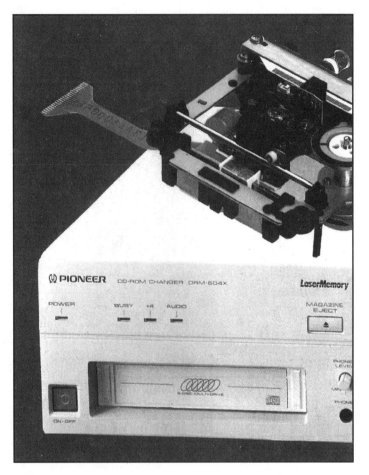

Pioneer CD-ROM changer

The DRM 604 x can be used in various ways. You can use the DRM 604 x as a universal super-fast 6 CD-ROM player (e.g., for an encyclopedia, maps, statistics, graphics, games, animation, films, or interactive media). You can also use the DRM 604 x as a jukebox for audio CDs. The JUKE utility, which is part of the package, makes it easy to do this. Since the changer also conforms to the MPC standard for multimedia applications, the system is specifically designed to work with the Kodak photo CD system. The DRM 604 x is, of course, capable of multiple sessions.

The device has a SCSI 2 standard interface and is compatible with the various standards, including DOS, Apple Macintosh, OS/2 Windows, and Silicon Graphics.

MS-DOS CD-ROM extensions support not only several drives, but also various subunits. The Pioneer device driver allows two configurations: In the first mode, separate drive names are assigned to the six CD slots of the magazine (e.g., G H I J K L). Then you can manage two CD-ROM changers and up to twelve discs simultaneously.

The second mode uses only one device, for example the device G. A help program helps you select the individual disc (e.g., you enter "disc 3" to select the third disc). This method lets you access on-line up to 7 CD changers and up to 42 discs.

These abilities make the DRM 604 x suitable for working with a network server.

The new DRM 604 x is Pioneer's design of the future.

CD writers

Currently CD writers for writing your own CDs are too expensive for most nonprofessional users. Kodak and Philips offer a CD writer for about $7,000.

The Philips CD writer CD521

The Philips CDD521 includes the operating software needed to run under Windows. This CD writer supports the CD WO technology as described in the Orange Book. The write laser burns data on the CD blank once. This complies with photo CD technology, but in order to create your own photo CDs, you need the essential software so you can convert the photos to the PCD format and record them in the required format.

This produces a CD-ROM that conforms to the specifications of the Orange Book and the ISO 9660 standard. All advantages of the photo CD technology are restricted to the Kodak Imaging Station, since Kodak sells the compression software exclusively with the Imaging Station.

The homemade CDs can be read on all CD-ROM drives. Special photo CD software isn't needed. So, you can create your own CD productions. It doesn't matter whether you write programs on the CD, record music, save picture data, or create a comprehensive backup. You have 650 Meg available for storage.

Graphics cards

The photo CD conveys pure technical photo quality to the computer. You need a suitable graphics card and a good monitor in order to display this information in true form. The minimum requirement is a fast Super VGA card, which is able to display at least 32,000 colors in a resolution of 800 x 600 pixels. A graphics card that can represent only 256 colors produces an image with noticeable lines. Therefore, this mode cannot be used for professional applications. This mode is also very slow. The picture must be recalculated to 256 colors in order to display real color images on a 256 palette, which is time-consuming.

The capacity of a graphics card also depends on the monitor that's used. The bigger the diagonal size of a monitor, the better the resolution and color display. Even the speed of the image creation is important. Graphics cards with implemented Tseng ET 4000 chips are extremely fast.

There are many fast and powerful graphics cards available that are relatively inexpensive. The latest on the market are special Windows accelerator graphics cards. They are much faster than ordinary VGA cards, but cost a little more. Although these cards are extremely fast, they are difficult to install. However, usually the extra effort is worthwhile.

Be sure to get as much information as possible before deciding to buy a graphics card.

MiroMovie

The MiroMovie meets all the basic requirements of a Super VGA card for a photo CD system. It can also accept video signals and display them. Obviously, you can also save pictures in good quality. Also, it's easy to interject TV or video images among pictures on a photo CD.

You can also use a "Video Out" box. By using the Video Out function, you can record pictures or presentations, which were processed in a computer, with a VCR and display them on a television.

MiroMovie Pro

Miro also offers the much faster MiroMovie Pro, which is also available in a VESA Local bus variation. The speed of the graphics chips has increased so much, that they are useful in video applications.

Monitors

A good Super VGA 14" monitor is sufficient for working with the photo CD. Basic requirements are low radiation according to MPRII standard and flicker-free image display. It's easier to work with larger monitors. For professional picture processing, 17" and 20" monitors are needed.

The image rescan rate should be at least 70 Hz, and the dot pitch shouldn't exceed 0.28. Miro, Philips, NEC, Sony, and Eizo are known for their high-quality monitors, but even generic monitors can be of good quality. Warrantees and service agreements are also important.

There are tremendous quality and price differences among the various monitors. For this reason, you should do some research before actually buying a monitor.

Cache controller

Accelerator cards are available for ISA as well as for EISA systems. Cards for the VESA Local bus are also available. Equipped with four to eight Meg of SIMM modules, these controllers significantly increase the system's efficiency. The time needed to load a photo CD picture can be reduced by half with a cache controller.

Cache controllers operate like a software cache. The advantage of a hardware approach is the management of the cache doesn't have to proceed as a background function of the CPU, but through a separate processor integrated on the cache controller card. This processor also has direct access to the attached drive and, therefore, can transfer data better and faster to the cache memory.

The integrated processor on the card also needs its own programs, which are stored in the card-specific BIOS, to work properly. Also, similar to all other interface cards, you need transfer addresses, called I/O ports, and interrupt cables adapted to your system, so the CPU can access data from the controller. Usually these controllers can be integrated easily into all PC systems through the controller configuration setup.

You can even regulate up to four AT bus hard drives with the DC600 controller. Two hard drives each are tied together to a volume and are formatted together. The capacity of the individual hard drives doesn't have to be identical.

For maintaining data integrity, most cache controllers contain disk mirroring. The data is simultaneously written on two hard drives. If there is a hardware defect, the second intact hard drive will hold all the data.

Because of its separate BIOS, the cache controller can also be used as a secondary hard drive controller. This can be useful if you want to boot a SCSI hard drive.

SCSI controller

The Small Computer System Interface (SCSI) is a flexible and fast interface. Adaptec is the best known manufacturer of SCSI controllers. Together with the Corel SCSI driver software, this controller provides a comprehensive and simple way to attach SCSI devices to a PC. It supports hard drives, CD-ROM drives, magnetic-optical drives, printers, and streamers.

A SCSI controller can manage up to seven devices regardless whether they are hard drives or other pieces of equipment.

Future Domain SCSI controllers are often sold together with CD-ROM drives. These 8-bit cards usually perform only one function (i.e., the connection of the special device). But similar to the Adaptec, Future Domain also conveys a comprehensive palette to the high-end SCSI controller.

A typical SCSI controller

Installing a SCSI controller into a computer system requires one or several drivers, which must be entered into the CONFIG.SYS file. Once the computer is reset, the attached devices are ready for use. Each device is connected with a 50-pin data cable. The last device must contain terminators, terminal resistance for the data circuit. Also, an identification is set on each device. This is the address with which the controller addresses the device.

SCSI adapters for the parallel interface are becoming more popular as alternatives to SCSI controllers. This adapter type has all the advantages of the SCSI interface. However, it doesn't have the data transfer speed over the parallel interface.

External SCSI adapters can be attached to any PC and are specially suitable for computers, which don't permit the installation of additional devices.

Sound cards

Many sound cards are also sold with CD-ROM drives. This makes it easy to upgrade a computer to a multimedia system. Therefore, an interface to the appropriate CD-ROM drive is integrated on the sound card.

Pro Audio Spectrum by MediaVision

A SCSI adapter comes with the MediaVision Pro Audio Spectrum sound card. Besides this card's excellent multimedia capacity and its digital stereo sound, up to seven different SCSI devices can be connected to it. This saves you a valuable expansion slot.

Trantor Systems sells drivers for the CD-ROM drives and the hard drives. It enables reliable operation of hard drives, CD-ROM drives, and cartridge drives. It also allows additional AT bus adapters and other SCSI controllers to function in the computer system.

Usually there isn't a conflict with addresses if the card is configured correctly. The card usually works with the preset values.

The PAS 16 supports all the usual sound standards. Jumpers are available for changing the addresses for Sound Blaster compatibility.

The following recommendations apply to the parameters in the CONFIG.SYS file:

```
\PROAUDIO\MVSOUND.SYS D:7 Q:15
```

The AUTOEXEC.BAT file should read:

```
SET BLASTER=A220 I7 D1 T3
SET SOUND=C:\SB
```

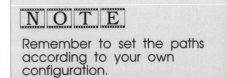

NOTE

Remember to set the paths according to your own configuration.

The jumper setting on the card is intended for the MediaVision Sound DMA 7 and IRQ 15. Different settings can be made with the Windows drivers, if necessary. However, usually this isn't necessary.

If you're interested in buying a Pro Audio Spectrum sound card, be sure that you can also get the SCSI driver from your computer dealer. You need both a CD-ROM driver and a hard drive driver. The CD-ROM driver TSLCDR.SYS must be capable of multiple sessions.

Sound Blaster 16 MultiCD by Creative Labs

Sound Blaster 16 MultiCD, from Creative Labs, includes an AT bus interface for CD-ROM drives. This sound card has excellent multimedia abilities and sound quality, but only one CD-ROM drive can be attached. The Sound Blaster card is usually sold with a Sony CD-ROM drive. This drive can read photo CDs in multiple sessions mode.

Audioblaster by CPS

CPS sells the Audioblaster to enable a connection with Matsushita CD-ROM drives. The drive becomes photo CD capable through a driver, which CPS provides free of charge to registered users. Unfortunately, Audioblaster supports only single session operations.

Mouse

A mouse can be used in all image processing programs. Therefore, if you're using one of these programs, you'll need a mouse. Use a mouse that is 100% Microsoft-compatible. This will ensure the mouse will work with all your programs.

Various types of mice are available. For example, you can buy inexpensive ones for about $16 and very expensive ones for hundreds of dollars. The less-expensive mice are usually uncomfortable to use and often contain unusable drivers.

DAT streamer

Another advantage of SCSI technology is DAT streamer technology. By using DAT streamers and the required software, you can easily save two gigabytes of data automatically and quickly. Compared to normal streamers of the QIC technology, the DAT streamer is very quiet because its recording process is similar to video technology. It uses a miniature cassette tape, which can hold up to 8 gigabytes of compressed data.

An external DAT streamer

Don't use PC Tools Backup for Windows as a background saving procedure. Effective image processing with simultaneous data backup isn't sensible, because the system is already loaded down with the background job.

In case you lose all your data (e.g., after a head crash), create a boot diskette for your system containing the SCSI driver, system files, your AUTOEXEC.BAT, and your CONFIG.SYS. This is the only way you can quickly access all existing drives, and especially the DAT streamer, to restore the data.

> **NOTE**
>
> The backup procedure under Windows as a single action is always fast. However, it's always possible to access the data during the backup process. Avoid extensive work with graphics during the backup. However, you can read the data.

Few of us think of these accidents until they have already happened. Therefore, you should create a boot diskette and store it in a safe place. By doing this, you can avoid reinstalling all your programs.

Installing CD-ROM drives and supplementary cards

Now that you know about the different devices you can use with the photo CD, we'll discuss how these devices are installed.

As you know, there are internal and external CD-ROM drives. Internal drives are usually the best option because they save space and are less expensive than external drives. However, sometimes an external drive must be used. This is true if you have a laptop computer.

Internal drives

Usually, you can easily install an internal CD-ROM drive. Most manufacturers include all the required accessories and the installation software automatically installs the new CD-ROM drive on your PC.

A controller, which forms the connection between the drive and the PC, is usually included. Originally, three methods were needed to accomplish this task:

1. Connection with a company-specific interface card

2. Connection to a SCSI interface

3. Direct connection to an existing sound card

Connecting to a sound card

To connect to an existing sound card, the card must be attached directly to the CD-ROM drive. However, this method of eliminating supplementary cards requires a compatible type of drive as well as a suitable connector cable (as a link to the sound card).

Need More Information?

For more information, refer to the sound card's user's manual or ask your computer dealer.

The easiest way to do this is probably by using a "CD expansion set", which contains, besides a CD-ROM drive, the suitable connector cable and the essential driver software.

If you don't have a CD-ROM drive or a sound card, you can purchase a multimedia package. This contains the CD-ROM drive, sound card, and all cables as well as the software. In this case, compatibility problems and installation errors are impossible, since there are also complete and comprehensive user's manuals.

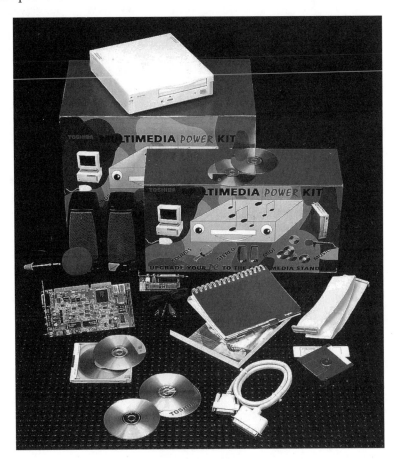

The Multimedia set by Toshiba

Installing an internal drive with an interface card

To install an internal drive with an interface card, you need a space to hold the drive and a suitable controller card, or a free slot for the included expansion card.

Before opening the computer case, switch off the computer and disconnect all the cables. Be sure that all the peripherals you detach are also switched off. Otherwise, you may encounter problems when the devices are reattached. Before disconnecting the power supply, touch the PC case to ground yourself. Then open the computer case and locate the empty shaft, which opens to the front. You may have to unscrew the face plate of your computer if you cannot insert the CD-ROM drive from the back because the power cords are in the way.

Look for a free power cord and connect the four pin plug of the cable to your CD-ROM drive. If the existing cable doesn't reach the selected shaft, or if there isn't one, you must use a Y-cable to be able to get electricity to the drive. If you encounter problems when you use the drive, first examine whether the CD-ROM drive is supplied with electricity. Unfortunately, Y cables often have contact difficulties.

Before you place the drive into the shaft, check the data plug for the side with pin number one. Usually this is marked on the plug or a "1" is imprinted on the board (this information will be important later).

Now carefully insert your CD-ROM drive into the free shaft of your computer. Screw the drive down with four screws, so it extents to the front exactly as far as the other disk drives. Sometimes rails are included to guide your drive.

Selecting the expansion slot

Usually there are two kinds of expansion slots. These slots have different bus widths. Both 16-bit and 8-bit slots are available.

A row of data cables are needed to exchange data between the central processing unit and the expansion cards. All these data cables together are called the data bus. The more cables that are arranged in parallel, the broader is the bus and the more data bits can be transferred simultaneously.

This also applies to address cables. More address cables connect to a 16-bit plug than to an 8-bit bus. This is why you have a greater option for your interrupt or the DMA channel with a 16-bit plug.

Most controller cards that are included with CD-ROM drives are 8-bit cards, because the CD-ROM drive is relatively slow and a data exchange with an 8-bit slot is sufficient. You can place these cards in any slot. However, if you want to expand your PC with other supplementary cards, you should select an 8-bit slot to keep the 16-bit slots open for the other expansion cards.

Controller settings

Your controller card must be adjusted to the computer in several ways before it can communicate with the computer. If you install the controller into a standard system that contains no other expansion cards, the preset values of the controller card are the correct selections.

However, problems may occur if other devices are installed. These devices include special graphics cards, sound cards, a scanner, or similar expansions. Normally the following parameters must be set on the card:

1. Interrupt number

2. An input and output address (I/O basic address)

3. Maybe an applied DMA channel

4. For SCSI controllers the basic address of the built-in BIOS

Let's start with the last item. If the controller card, which was included with your drive, is a SCSI controller, you must define the address, in which the BIOS on the card should be added to the CPU memory.

The SCSI controller is an intelligent interface, which means that it has its own programs for communicating with the outside world, just like your computer. These routines are called BIOS (Basic Input Output System) just like those of the computer. These BIOS occupy an address range in your computer system in the area of C800H to EFFFH. You can usually set the starting address on the interface card with a jumper. Usually the original setting is acceptable. However, if problems occur, verify, if you do not have another supplementary card, which uses the same starting address.

The controller card also needs an interrupt (IRQ = Interrupt Request). With this line, the drive asks for attention by the way of the controller. Your PC has several cables that are occupied by other hardware components, such as disks drives and an interface.

You can use the IRQs 0 to 10 only if you use an 8-bit controller card or if you use an 8-bit slot, when you have the choice of using your card between an 8 or a 16-bit slot. You can only use the other interrupts with the 16-bit slots, if your controller card is designed that way.

If you don't know which channels are occupied, you can use a program, such as Norton Utilities or PC Tools or the MS-DOS 6 command MSD to determine this.

IRQ0	System timer	IRQ8	Real time
IRQ1	Keyboard	IRQ9	By-pass IRQ2
IRQ2	Interrupt controller	IRQ10	Free
IRQ3	Free/COM2	IRQ11	Free
IRQ4	COM1	IRQ12	Free
IRQ5	Free/LPT2	IRQ13	Math coprocessor
IRQ6	Disk controller	IRQ14	Hard drive controller
IRQ7	Free/LPT1	IRQ15	Free

Interrupts

An interrupt (IRQ = Interrupt Request) is the name for a signal that is sent from a device, with a defined line, to the CPU. This occurs so the device can perform its functions. So, instead of the built-in CPU determining whether one of the connected drives has a task that should be performed, the devices are linked with these lines to the CPU. The CPU can perform its work without checking the attached devices.

However, when one of the seven available hardware interrupts change the condition of the line, the CPU stops whatever it's doing and first checks what devices wants something. When the CPU has recognized the device, it's available to the requesting device. Actually, the CPU jumps to the address belonging to the interrupt, which was occupied by the calling peripheral device during its installation. Now if two devices use the same interrupt, it's possible that a device asks for the service of the CPU and the CPU springs to the program of the other device, which is currently idle. This can cause a system crash. In this case, you must reset the computer.

Therefore, you must ensure that while using several peripheral devices like a scanner, sound cards, a mouse, or video cards, the interrupts of the individual devices don't overlap.

Also, ensure the preset interrupt doesn't overlap with that of a different device and, if necessary, change the settings on the controller card.

Always write down all the settings of the different expansion cards and keep the note near your computer. Then you'll always know what settings you can use for other expansion cards.

I/O base address

Besides the interrupt number, the controller cards also need the memory addresses, in which the data transfer proceeds. These are called port addresses. These addresses are at the beginning of main memory and consist of a list of memory addresses.

With these addresses, the communications components are controlled and also the data are transferred. Since the new controller card isn't the only card exchanging data with the computer, conflicts can occur. The following is a list of some typical port addresses:

Components/cards	Port addresses
DMA controller	000-01F
Interrupt controller	020-03F
Clock	040-05F
Keyboard	060-06F
Real time	070-07F
DMA side register	080-09F
Interrupt controller 2	0A0-0BF

Components/cards	Port addresses
DMA controller 2	0C0-0DF
Math coprocessor	0F0-0F1
Math coprocessor	0F8-0FF
Hard drive controller	1F0-1F8
Game port	200-207
Sound Blaster (standard)	220-237
2nd parallel interface	278-27F
2nd serial interface	2F8-2FF
Network card	360-36F
Scanner card	300-307
Screen machine (standard)	300-307
1st parallel interface	378-37F
Sound Blaster (FM)/ AdLib card	388-389
Monochrome monitor card	3B0-3BF
Color/graphics monitor card	3D0-3DF
1st serial interface	3F8-3FF
Floppy disk controller	3F0-3F7

DMA channel

Transferring data via the I/O port is a slow process. However, using DMA (Direct Memory Access) is a more effective way to transfer the data into the memory of your computer. To keep the CPU from exclusively transferring data to the RAM, the DMA writes the values into memory immediately, bypassing the CPU.

A special chip in the computer, called the DMA controller, controls the access of the CPU and the other cards to the RAM with the DMA channels. This ensures that conflicts don't occur between the CPU and the controller card. To avoid accidents, only one card can access the RAM with a particular DMA channel. You can assign this channel when you install the controller card.

Some controller cards let you use DMA access. You must define the desired channel for these cards either with a jumper or DIP switch on the card or you can select the needed channel with software during the installation. Then a parameter in the CONFIG.SYS file passes the setting to the driver program. We'll discuss this in more detail later.

If you want to change the settings, write them down first. During the software installation you'll be asked whether the driver programs are adjusted correctly to the hardware.

Installing a controller card

Now let's return to the installation process. Loosen the cover of the selected slot and remove it. Insert the controller card into the slot of your motherboard and screw down the card with the screw you've just removed.

Then connect the cables. First connect the data cable and then the drive with the interface card. Notice the color coding on the edge of the cable. Pin 1 of the card must correspond to pin 1 on the drive. If you aren't careful you may damage both the drive and the card. Pin 1 is also marked or a "1" is printed on the controller card. There may be a socket on the controller card, which lets you insert the plug of the cable only in one direction. The plug and socket for the power cord of the drive are a plug-in connection that can only be joined incorrectly by force.

If you have an audio line, you should connect it now. Either fasten it to the interface card of the CD-ROM drive or join the audio cable directly to an existing sound card. Although the latter option is simple, you cannot link every drive with every sound card. Refer to the user's manual and determine whether a direct attachment is possible between drive and sound card.

Before reconnecting all external cables to the computer, close it again for safety reasons. If all junctions fit correctly, you can switch on your system again. Then insert the enclosed installation diskette and start the Setup program.

Usually you're lead through an installation program, that asks only a few questions, which can generally be answered without previous knowledge and with the written down parameters.

After rebooting the system, you can use your CD-ROM drive. It can be accessed like a normal disk drive. The name of the drive is the next highest drive letter. For example, if you previously had drives A:, C:, and D:, the CD-ROM drive is now called "E:." Insert your photo CD, start your access software, select the CD-ROM drive, and look at your pictures.

Occasionally problems can occur. If something doesn't work, first examine the cable connections, then try checking other changes which were made. Check whether the Setup program altered your system files correctly.

Low level driver in CONFIG.SYS

A new device driver must be entered in the CONFIG.SYS file. This file should contain a line that looks similar to the following:

```
DEVICE=C:\MYPATH\DRIVER.SYS /D:CDNAME
```

Usually the Setup program creates a new directory on your boot drive (i.e., drive C:), into which the necessary drivers are installed. "MYPATH" must coincide with the name of this directory. "DRIVER" is then the name of your driver in this directory.

The most important parameter is the name of the new device. This name is the connection to the MSCDEX.EXE driver, which is linked to the AUTOEXEC.BAT file. The most familiar drivers use the /D switch for identification of their name and generally use the name "MSCD000."

After these parameters, you can add other switches, which switch on or switch off certain features of the driver. Refer to the user's manual for more information about your driver.

The MTMCDE.SYS driver, which is included with a Mitsumi drive, is entered in the CONFIG.SYS file as follows:

```
DEVICE=C:\DEV\MTMCDE.SYS /D:MSCD001 /P:300 /T:5 /I:10 /M:20
/X
```

The /P parameter defines the port address in hexadecimal form. The /T parameter defines the DMA channel. The /T:S parameter suppresses the DMA transfer and a DMA channel isn't assigned. /I defines the fixed interrupt. With /M, you assign the number of 2K data buffers, which you can move to extended memory with the parameter /X, if you've installed an extended memory manager like HIMEM.SYS before the device driver in the CONFIG.SYS file.

High level driver MSCDEX in AUTOEXEC.BAT

As we mentioned, a new program call is added to the AUTOEXEC.BAT file. Since DOS doesn't support any CD-ROM drives, you need an extra program, called MSCDEX.EXE, to handle this omission. This program contains all the routines that are needed in order for the CD-ROM drives to operate properly. The following line should be in the AUTOEXEC.BAT file:

```
C:\MYPATH\MSCDEX /V /D:CDNAME /M:8
```

The /V parameter indicates a list of the memory sections at the start of the program. The /D:CDNAME parameter contains the name, with which the CD-ROM drive is called. You can change the name as desired. However, if you do this, remember to change the name in the CONFIG.SYS file accordingly. The /M:8 parameter describes the number of read buffers. The higher the assigned value, the less often the CD is accessed for reading and the faster the access to continuing data. However, there are disadvantages. Therefore, the driver program reserves about 2K of RAM for each buffer.

If you want to have expanded memory for the driver, you can do this by adding the /E parameter. In this case, the main memory is relieved. However, if you work with Windows, don't install expanded memory.

As we described, your CD-ROM drive will be assigned the next free drive letter. If you want to give your drive a special drive letter, you can do this with the /L parameter. In the form "/L:F", the CD-ROM drive is called the F: drive.

However, you cannot simply address any number of drives. DOS contains a table that assigns certain IDs to each drive. DOS supports only drives A: to E: to keep from wasting memory space. If you've installed more drives or partitions or if you want to assign a higher letter to your CD-ROM drive, you must convey this to DOS. Do this by using the LASTDRIVE command in the CONFIG.SYS file. If you enter the following, DOS will support all drives from A: to P:

```
LASTDRIVE=P
```

MSCDEX.EXE also provides the /K switch. This switch is only needed if you want to read Japanese CDs.

Parameters	Use
/D:CDNAME	Is used once for each CD-ROM drive in your system. This name has to match the name, which was assigned to the low level driver in CONFIG.SYS.
/E	If you've installed expanded memory in your computer, you can instruct MSCDEX to set up the buffers there.
/L: drive letter	This parameter determines the letter, which MSCDEX should use for the assignment of the drive letter. If this parameter isn't specified, MSCDEX uses the first free available drive letter for the address.
/V	Use this switch to have MSCDEX list memory statistics after the installation.
/M:Number	Assign the number of the sector buffers you want to set up. 2K are set aside for each buffer. If you don't establish this parameter, 8 buffers are established.
/K	This switch allows processing of Kanji file structures.

Installing SCSI drives and connecting them to SCSI controllers

With SCSI technology, it's possible to connect up to seven peripheral devices to a controller. Therefore, you don't need a special interface card to install a CD-ROM drive into an existing SCSI system. Instead, you can simply connect the drive to the SCSI cable. Unfortunately, this process isn't as easy as it sounds.

If you want to connect an internal CD-ROM drive to your SCSI adapter, you must loop or attach it to the internal SCSI bus. This bus is the 50-pin ribbon cable, which leads from the controller to the individual devices. However, the existing SCSI cable may not have an additional plug available. Although your computer dealer probably has 50-pin ribbon cables, they usually have only two plugs. If your CD-ROM drive is the third device, you must either create a cable yourself or keep looking for one with more than two plugs.

If you decide to make a cable, you'll need 50-pin plugs and a 50-pin ribbon cable. You can find these in a computer or electronics store. You should buy several 50-pin plugs. You should have some extras in case something goes wrong. Also, you need a special pair of pliers for attaching the plug. If you don't want to buy the pliers, a good vice is usually sufficient.

Making a SCSI cable

After detaching all exterior connections, grounding yourself by touching the case, and opening your computer, remove the SCSI cable so you can add the plug. Do this very carefully. Ensure the plastic leader on all the plugs points in the same direction. On the plugs themselves is a mark indicating the side with pin 1. Push the lower part of the plug under the cable and place the upper part on top so the plug can still be moved easily. Now be sure the new plug sits straight and with the correct pins on the cable, before you tighten it with the pliers. Ensure that every metal contact is on top of a line. Then close the pliers. If you make a mistake, a short may occur. In this case, more than just the attached devices could be destroyed.

After you've examined the cable again, you can begin installing the drive.

Installing the drive

Before installing your CD-ROM drive, you must determine the position at which it will connect to the SCSI bus. If you don't connect it as the last device, which is attached at the end of the cable, you must deactivate the terminators on the CD-ROM drive.

The SCSI bus transports data at a very high frequency (5 MHz or more). With these high frequencies, the cable has not only resistance, but also acts as a condenser. To keep the line losses as small as possible and to maintain a clean signal, the ends of the SCSI cable must be closed with terminators.

Jumpers or DIP switches are responsible for switching these terminators on or off. You may also have to take out or insert these terminators. Refer to the CD-ROM drive's user's manual for information on how to deactivate the terminators.

If you connect the new CD-ROM drive as the last drive to the SCSI bus, normally you don't have to change anything on the drive, since the terminators are activated as part of the preset options. However, be sure to read your documentation, because you'll have to change the settings on the device which used to be at the end of the SCSI bus. For this device, you must deactivate the terminators.

Check another setting before actually installing the CD-ROM drive. Each drive has its own identification number, since the SCSI controller can access several devices. Ensure the number fixed for your CD-ROM drive isn't used on any other device. If necessary, change this number. You can do this by moving the particular jumper at the back of the CD-ROM drive.

Now insert the drive into the free drive shaft of your computer and screw it down, so the face plate of the device extends as far to the front of the case as that of the other disk drives. Then connect the power cord.

Next connect the SCSI cable to all existing SCSI devices. Make sure the pins match correctly. The color coding has to be at pin 1. The individual devices have a plug shoe with a groove in the middle, so an unmistakable plug direction is indicated.

Before you attach the power cord to the computer, reconnect all external cables and close the case for safety. Now start your computer.

Watch the messages on the monitor during the boot process. If the new drive is recognized, the installation was successful. Otherwise, you must switch off your computer and open it again. Now determine whether all the power cords and data cables are connected to the devices correctly. Check if an identification number is set on your CD-ROM drive, which is also used for another drive. Ensure the terminators are switched on only at the last device.

If your CD-ROM drive isn't the last drive in the chain and all other devices on the SCSI bus work normally, the error cannot be in the data cable and the controller. The cause of the problem can only be with the CD-ROM drive itself. If the connections to the data cable and the power cords are in order and the ID number is correct, but the device still isn't recognized by the controller, then the drive is probably defective. In this case, contact your computer dealer.

Installing the software

If the CD-ROM drive is recognized, which is normally the case, then the software installation begins. You need two programs to be able to connect the CD-ROM drive to your system; this even applies to devices that are accessed with their own controller. For one, you need the appropriate low level driver and the MSCDEX program. The low level driver comes with your device and should be compatible with your SCSI controller.

The current standard is the ASPI standard from Adaptec. In this case, the low level driver is realized with two drivers. One is the operating system-specific driver that extends the appropriate ASPI interface. For DOS and an Adaptec controller, this is the ASPI4DOS.SYS driver. This driver must be linked to your CONFIG.SYS file before device-dependent drivers. If you use other SCSI devices on an Adaptec controller, this driver is already linked to the CONFIG.SYS file.

As a device-specific driver, you still need the ASPI driver for your CD-ROM drive from the manufacturer of the drive. This drive should be on the installation diskette. You can also refer to your drive's user's manual for information about any special parameters.

NOTE

If you work with a Trantor driver, the Trantor 130B is called MA13B.SYS and the name of the Trantor T348 is MA348.SYS.

Another option for accessing your CD-ROM drive are the universal drivers that support the ASPI interface of the particular SCSI controller. Here it's important to load the ASPI driver of the SCSI card into the CONFIG.SYS file first and then all other necessary SCSI drivers. There is always an ASPI driver on an installation diskette of the controller.

The Corel SCSI package from Corel and SCSI Works from Trantor are the most familiar universal drivers. Both packages are easy to install and provide helpful information about use and installation. During the setup, all existing drives are recognized and included in the starting files, if desired. Each package also contains additional programs for error detection and optimizing.

It doesn't matter whether you own or want to buy an Adaptec, 3+, or perhaps an Ultrastore controller. Once the ASPI drivers have been activated, these SCSI adapters support any universal driver software. The only difference is the price; otherwise, these controllers are easy to use and have the same capabilities.

After you've installed all the drivers, restart your computer to activate the entries in the CONFIG.SYS and AUTOEXEC.BAT system files. Now you can access the new drive.

Test this by entering something similar to the following at the DOS prompt to see if you can access the drive:

```
DIR D:
```

If you can, then start Windows and your photo CD program. Insert a photo CD and look at the contact print.

External drives

Connecting an external CD-ROM drive with its own controller card is usually a simple process since it only involves linking a cable to the computer and starting the installation program. The controller card is installed the same way as we explained above with internal CD-ROM drives.

If your computer has existing SCSI adapters with an external interface, you can also connect the cables between the external socket of the controller and a SCSI socket of the drive. However, first you must remove the terminators on the SCSI card if a device hasn't already been connected to the plug for external devices. This ensures the adapter works properly.

Also, you must ensure that you set a free identification number on the external CD-ROM drive.

External and internal drives and accessories

The drivers are lined to the SCSI interface just as they are with any internal drive. Hardware address conflicts shouldn't occur, if all the other SCSI devices worked properly before.

Possible problems:

The drive isn't recognized

First check all connections. Be sure that all the cables are attached properly and the power cord is connected.

If other SCSI devices also aren't recognized, the error lies with the data cable and its connections.

If the CD-ROM drive isn't recognized, the drive itself causes the error. Check if the power cords and the data cables are attached correctly. Pay close attention to the pins of the data cable. If you don't find any problems there, the drive is probably defective.

The CD-ROM drive is recognized, but the communication with the drive is flawed or not possible.

Check whether all the drivers are installed correctly.

Read the messages on the monitor during the boot process. A new drive letter should appear after the message of the Microsoft CD-ROM extensions.

If this message doesn't appear, this is caused by either a false command line or incompatibility with a memory manager. With SCSI drives, false ID or termination can lead to errors. A hardware memory conflict could be the final cause.

First check whether the command lines in the starting files are correct. Refer to the user's guide and compare the recommended entries with your own. The slightest deviation can cause the CD-ROM drive to be ignored.

If the error still isn't corrected, the memory manager could be at fault. Not all CD-ROM drivers can be loaded into High or Expanded memory.

Start your computer with a "simple" combination of the CONFIG.SYS and AUTOEXEC.BAT files. Don't include the memory manager and use only essential drivers.

Don't delete any command lines. Instead, simply place a "REM" statement in front of it.

If this fixes your error, your drivers are incompatible.

To the CONFIG.SYS and/or the AUTOEXEC.BAT file, gradually add the driver and supplementary programs, that you've temporarily eliminated, and always ensure the CD-ROM drive still works correctly.

Examine the cause of the error, if you find it in a driver and supplementary program. It's usually caused by assigning an interrupt or I/O port twice. If this is the case, change the settings in the program to eliminate the overlapping.

If your memory manager is causing the problems:

Try to reinstall the memory manager after your CD-ROM drive is attached. To do this, use the included installation and optimizing program of the memory manager. For more information, refer to the memory manager's user's manual.

If your PC denies access to the new CD-ROM drive even after you restart using a simple system configuration, it will probably take you a while to find the cause of the problem. In this case, it's probably a hardware conflict.

Remove all the unnecessary cards from your system and then restart the computer.

For an existing problem:

Alter the address area of your controller card. Refer to the user's manual to determine the correct order of the jumpers. Some cards are also configured with micro switches; even software configuration is provided for some products.

If your CD-ROM drive is recognized and works properly, reinsert the removed cards into the computer. Then, if a problem occurs, you'll know which card is causing the problem. Examine the interrupt settings and the input and output addresses of both cards. If you notice a clear overlap, change the parameters on the card to eliminate the overlap and try again.

Unfortunately, if there are still conflicts even though there aren't any obvious overlaps of interrupt and I/O addresses or memory addresses, you must experiment to find the cause.

Although the problem can be a combination of all the causes listed above, this isn't very likely. If you try these hints and solutions, your drive should be recognized eventually.

Apple Macintosh Systems

If you want to use an Apple Macintosh system with photo CDs, you'll need the same hardware as described for PC systems. However, remember that Apple computers aren't as expandable as PC systems. Therefore, before purchasing an Apple computer, it's important to determine what your needs are and what capabilities the computer should have.

Unlike a PC system, an Apple system cannot be expanded by exchanging the motherboard. However, you can install accelerator boards, expand the working memory, and even exchange the graphics cards.

External devices, such as cartridge drives or CD-ROM drives, are limited to SCSI connections. So, unlike with PC systems, there are less photo CD-capable CD-ROM drives to choose from for Apple Macintosh systems.

The minimum configuration needed is an Apple Macintosh LCII with 4 Meg of RAM. However, as with a PC system, loading an image in full resolution is very slow. The optimum configuration is the Apple Macintosh Quadra 950. This computer is extremely powerful.

Between these two configurations, Macintosh offers various photo CD-capable computers. These computers are less expensive and less powerful:

> ➤ The Apple LCII 16 MHz, 4 Meg of RAM, expandable to 10 Meg, internal 40 Meg or 80 Meg hard drive, internal CD-ROM drive

> ➤ The Apple LCIII 25 MHz, 4 Meg of RAM, expandable to 32 Meg, internal 40 Meg to 160 Meg hard drive and built-in CD-ROM drive

The Performa group has similar capabilities and equipment. The Performa 200 cannot be used with photo CD technology because the efficiency rating doesn't meet the minimum requirements. The Performa 400 16 MHz, 4 Meg of RAM, expandable to 10 Meg, is the simplest system that's suitable for use with photo CDs. The Performa 600 32 MHz, 4 Meg of RAM, expandable to 68 Meg with integrated CD-ROM drive is comparable to the LCIII.

The next group of Apple systems consists of the Macintosh IIvx, the Centris 610, and the Centris 650. The IIvx 32 MHz, with coprocessor and 32K cache memory, 4 Meg of RAM expandable to 68 Meg, integrated CD-ROM drive, and a possibility for installing a 5.25-inch drive, is sold with the Apple Centris devices specially for photo CD technology. The Centris 610 and 650 are equipped with the powerful 68040 Motorola microprocessor and have capabilities similar to that of the IIvx.

The Quadra group represents the most powerful and versatile systems. They have a 68040 processor with integrated coprocessor and 33 MHz clock speed. With a hard drive capacity of at least 230 Meg, you can easily use desktop publishing applications. Memory expansion is possible to 256 Meg and there is enough room in the midi tower case to add supplementary devices. A CD-ROM drive is built-in. Even the built-in graphics adapter is capable of representing up to 16 million colors. The Quadra 800 and the Quadra 950 cost about $6,000.

Since Apple computers don't have the memory problems encountered with PC systems, you can easily load a photo CD picture if enough RAM is installed. Computers with less than 20 Meg of RAM must temporarily store the image data on the hard drive. In this case, remember to configure your system accordingly.

NOTE

Remember the easiest way to expand an Apple computer system is to expand RAM.

MiroMotion

MiroMotion is the Macintosh version of the Miro Movie for PCs. The Macintosh version has similar qualities, but this overlay board also offers flicker-free video. The MiroMotion with 24-bit color depth provides excellent picture quality. It can be used with all Apple computers from Mac II to Quadra. In order to install MiroMotion, you need a Nimbus socket.

External CD-ROM drives

With some of the Apple computers it's impossible to install an internal CD-ROM drive. In these instances, you must use an external drive. As we mentioned, the external SCSI devices we've described can be attached to Apple Macintosh computers. The only difference is that these devices use special drivers for the Apple operating system.

If you have older CD-ROM devices, you can obtain photo CD capability inexpensively by purchasing special drivers. FWB offers a CD-ROM tool kit (CDT) that contains drivers for almost all CD-ROM drives. These drivers let you read the Kodak photo CD on all CD-ROM drives. Another special feature of the CDT is the increased speed during data access.

Output Devices

When using the photo CD, you'll need a color printer to determine how your images look on paper.

Various printers are available, from the inexpensive dot matrix printer to the expensive thermal sublimation printer. Because of its excellent picture quality, the thermal sublimation printer is the only printer that's suitable for professional use.

Dot matrix printers

The most inexpensive way to produce a color printout is by using a dot matrix printer. Unfortunately, this printer doesn't provide the best print quality. Therefore, usually the printout appears "striped." Also, the brightness of the colors is usually diminished because of dirty color ribbons.

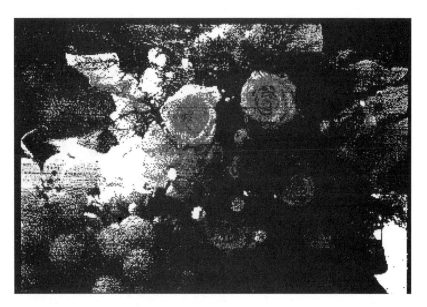

Printout from a dot matrix printer

Ink jet printers

Ink jet printers provide much better print quality than dot matrix printers. These printers are also just as affordable as dot matrix printers.

Two different print techniques are used with these printers: Piezo and bubble jet. Both methods use the "drop-on-demand" technology, which sprays individual ink drops on paper in controlled movements.

With the piezo process, a crystal is disformed by using electricity. This changing form presses on the ink and ejects it through the jets. With the bubble jet process, the thermal element heats the ink. A gas bubble forms and the resulting pressure forces color through one or more jets onto the paper. The more jets, the better the print quality.

There isn't a big difference between these two methods, except the ink can be refilled with the piezo process, while the entire print head must be changed in the bubble jet process.

When you buy a printer, you should purchase one with separate cartridges for color and for black and white. This provides a better picture quality and conserves expensive ink, since the color black doesn't have to be created from the other colors. In general, color printouts on ink jets are relatively expensive.

Printout from an ink jet printer

Thermal transfer printer

This type of printer uses heat to bring color particles suspended in wax onto the paper. The wax is removed from its carrier foil by the print head, which is heated to three hundred degrees Celsius, and is transferred to a shiny special paper. The print process is repeated three or four times, depending on whether you use a three or four color carrier foil. The printer pulls the paper several times past the print head. Regardless of how much is printed on one page, a complete carrier foil section is always needed.

The print quality is much better than with ink jet printers, but these printers are much more expensive.

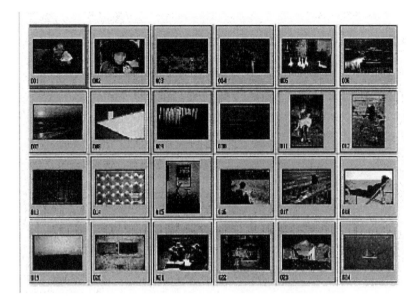

Printout from a thermal transfer printer

Dye sublimation printer

The technology used in a dye sublimation printer is similar to thermal transfer technology. The dye sublimation printer can vary the temperature in 256 steps, so you can transfer, as desired, many or few color particles to the shiny paper. This results in a color layer of fluctuating thickness, which approaches photo quality. This printer can represent 16 million colors. Unfortunately, these printers are very expensive.

Printer tips

➢ Two other color printing techniques are also important: The phase change printer and the color laser printer. Both varieties generate printouts of near photo quality, but such devices are still too expensive for most nonprofessional users.

➢ We recommend using the color ink jet printer if you're new to the photo CD.

> ➢ Remember the higher the resolution of the image you want to print, the better the print result. You'll obtain images of the quality of a newspaper photo. The quality of the printer paper also affects the print quality.

> ➢ Try the different options for the print settings. The printouts will be different for the various graphics programs used.

> ➢ The best printer to use for photo CD pictures is the thermal transfer printer. Although this printer is expensive, it provides excellent results.

Color copiers

By connecting a color copier to a computer, you produce a printout as a color copy. Frequently you can also scan in images. However, because color copiers are so expensive, they are mainly used by professionals.

Picture recorder

With picture recorders, you can change your processed photo CD pictures back into slides. Polaroid offers various picture recorders, which can generate a slide of your processed pictures within 90 seconds.

Regular slide film is placed in the device and the photo is controlled by software. When all the shots have been taken on the film, it can be developed and processed normally.

This process works because of the following reason: Your altered pictures are changed back into slides inexpensively and can also be processed in the conventional manner, because the old-fashioned print from the lab is still the cheapest way of producing a picture.

The picture recorder is suitable for PCs and Apple computers. However, picture recorders are mainly intended for large presentations or for scientific use.

Polaroid color picture recorder CI-1000

A big problem of the picture printout is the colors are reproduced differently from colors on the monitor. For correctly displaying the original picture, which you want to process, on the monitor, place your slide on a slide selector, load the same picture of the photo CD, and adjust the monitor until the colors of both pictures match.

Then you can be sure the end result will match the original. After the calibration of the monitor, you have sufficient control over the color output of the final product during your operations.

Software For Your Photo CD

CHAPTER 3

Software For Your Photo CD

As you learned in the previous chapter, you need certain hardware to use the photo CD in your computer system. However, you also need specific software in order to access the individual pictures. To ensure a smooth operation, the separate components of your computer (hardware and software) must work together efficiently.

In this chapter, we'll discuss your computer system in more detail and provide some tips on the best installation. As you'll see, there are many ways to adjust your system to create an optimal photo CD computer.

Besides the programs that make it possible to work with the photo CD, you need other programs that enable you to access and edit the pictures. A variety of programs in a range of prices are available. In the second part of this chapter, we'll provide an overview of these programs.

Essential Add-ons

When processing an image and reading the photo CD, your computer must rapidly process large amounts of data. As you've already read, at the highest resolution, a photo CD image requires 18 Meg of storage space. Additional space is needed to manage and process the file. Therefore, it must be possible to process a section of the picture.

Even the image processing program itself requires considerable storage space to process an image. Therefore, many megabytes of memory must be filled and managed.

Memory management in RAM and on the hard drive is controlled by DOS and Windows with the corresponding add-on programs. At the lowest DOS level, these are the memory management programs that provide the available RAM memory to the actual applications in different forms (program memory, XMS, EMS, UMB). If you use Windows, it manages the memory itself.

In addition to memory management, you need driver programs that link your CD-ROM drive to your operating system. This involves using a low level driver program that connects your CD-ROM drive to the AT or SCSI controller. This program is added to the CONFIG.SYS file with the

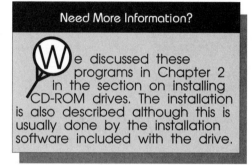

Need More Information?

We discussed these programs in Chapter 2 in the section on installing CD-ROM drives. The installation is also described although this is usually done by the installation software included with the drive.

DEVICE command. You also need the MSCDEX.EXE program, which communicates with the device driver and links the CD-ROM drive with the DOS operating system.

Memory managers

Not too long ago, a PC with 640K of memory and a 20 Meg hard drive was considered a powerful computer. Now 4 Meg of RAM and 200 Meg of hard drive space are standard, and devices with 32 Meg of memory and gigabyte-sized hard drives are common.

However, because of compatibility reasons, the DOS operating system is still restricted to the 640K memory limit. Various methods are used in order to access the memory above this limit. This is done by using the memory managers HIMEM.SYS and EMM386.EXE. This set of drivers, which is included with DOS 5.0/6 and Windows, manages memory above the 640K limit.

The HIMEM.SYS driver manages memory between 640K and 1 Meg; you need the EMM386.EXE program to manage the memory above 1 Meg. Actually this process isn't that simple. If you want to use your memory above 1 Meg as extended memory, regardless of whether you're using DOS or Windows, you need the HIMEM.SYS driver.

If this driver is used correctly, you can obtain a surprisingly large amount of free working memory, even if you're only working within DOS. This is done by moving individual drivers and memory-resident programs into the area between 640K and 1 Meg, or upper memory.

Memory above 1 Meg can be used as expanded memory (EMS) or as extended memory.

Expanded memory is based on a memory technology that originated with the XT and the 286. These kinds of computers couldn't access memory above the 1 Meg limit, or could do so only in a very roundabout way. As a result, a process was developed that enabled memory outside of the normal access range to be merged into a page frame below the 1 Meg limit. By using intelligent software (driven by a standardized interface), which continually merged the area currently being used into the page frame below the 1 Meg limit, the Expanded Memory Manager (EMM), and the corresponding application programs, these computers could use more than 1 Meg of memory. The Expanded Memory Manager of DOS is the EMM386.EXE program.

Because of the more modern architecture of the 386 and 486 series of computers, these models can use memory even above the 1 Meg limit. However, for compatibility reasons, DOS doesn't comply with this. Therefore, memory must be divided just like in the old days. However, DOS Versions 5.0 and higher include memory management programs that allow extended memory to be used. We are talking about the HIMEM.SYS driver, which includes an Extended Memory Manager.

With DOS 5.0, you still must install the driver and optimize your system manually. In particular, the optimum high-loading of memory-resident programs in the region above 640K can be very time-consuming, because the order in which the programs are loaded is important.

This is easier to do in DOS 6 because it includes an optimizing program, which makes the setup very easy.

Now let's discuss your computer's configuration. To use the memory on your 386 or 486, first you must link the HIMEM.SYS driver and the EMM386.EXE memory management program in the CONFIG.SYS file. To do this, add these lines at the beginning of the CONFIG.SYS file:

```
DEVICE=HIMEM.SYS
DEVICE=EMM386.EXE
```

157

You can optimize the EMM386.EXE memory manager with parameters.

In the form indicated above, the entire memory above the 1 Meg limit would only be available as expanded memory, which would be wasted memory especially if you mainly work with Windows.

Windows doesn't use any expanded memory. Instead, it expects as much extended memory as possible, which is optimally used by Windows' own memory manager and which can also be made available as expanded memory in a DOS application under Windows.

If you use DOS programs that work only with expanded memory, you must set the amount of memory that should be made available as EMS here. Now the disadvantage of DOS's own memory manager is obvious. You must always indicate the amount of EMS memory beforehand. Other memory managers, such as QEMM or 386MAX, divide the memory at run-time based on the requirements of the application program. The value listed is in kilobytes and should be a multiple of 16, since only 16K blocks can be used as EMS. To reserve half of a Meg as EMS, enter the following:

```
DEVICE=EMM386.EXE 512
```

If you work with Windows (almost all programs that access the photo CD run under Windows), you shouldn't reserve any EMS. You can do this by using the NOEMS parameter. However, even if you prevent the use of EMS by this parameter, DOS still reserves 64K of memory starting at E000H for a page frame, in which the EMS pages are to be merged. You can prevent this from happening by using the I (Include) parameter. The new lines in the CONFIG.SYS file should look as follows:

```
DEVICE=HIMEM.SYS
DEVICE=EMM386.EXE NOEMS I=E000-EFFF
```

With these lines, you must set the conditions that make it possible for DOS and Windows to access the memory above 640K.

To free the working memory, move memory-resident programs from working memory below 640K into the area between 640K and 1 Meg. You should begin with DOS itself. Use the following command to remove the biggest portion of DOS from conventional memory:

```
DOS HIGH, UMB
```

In the CONFIG.SYS file, you can load other drivers into extended memory by changing DEVICE to DEVICEHIGH.

Start a line with LOADHIGH (or LH) to move other programs, such as the mouse driver or the MSCDEX program, into upper memory. The result can be up to 630K of free conventional memory.

However, remember that the area between 640K and 1 Meg isn't limitless. Loading all programs high isn't sufficient if you have a lot of memory-resident programs or especially if you have add-on cards (such as a SCSI adapter or network cards) in your computer that also use memory in this range. This will mean an extended optimization process.

First, arrange the areas that your add-on cards use so there aren't a lot of little segments of free memory, but only one large one. Refer to the add-on's user's guide for more information. Usually you can change the starting addresses to different addresses using jumpers.

To examine your memory usage, type the following command at the DOS prompt:

```
MEM /C | MORE
```

A complete listing of your memory usage and a report of free memory areas, which takes up several screens, appears.

One problem with loading programs high is that when you start the program, you need much more memory than you've assigned. Therefore, it's possible that a program won't load in extended memory even though there seems to be enough room for it. It might help to load the program high before another program, as long as there is enough room for initializing.

By continually rearranging the programs and rebooting you can find the best arrangement.

If you use DOS 6, you don't have to go through this time-consuming procedure. Instead, your memory will be organized automatically with an optimization program.

QEMM-386

QEMM-386 is an expanded memory manager for 386 and higher computers. After asking you a few questions, the program is installed automatically. This program examines the memory and finds the optimal arrangement of the programs to be loaded high into upper memory.

Compared to DOS, QEMM does more than simply make the free memory between 640K and 1 Meg available. QEMM uses "stealth" technology to make it possible to use areas of memory that are normally occupied by ROM memory, such as the region between F000H and FFFFH, where the system ROM of your computer is located.

Another advantage is that QEMM makes memory above 1 Meg available as either extended or expanded memory, depending on the requirements of your application program.

If you use QEMM, you won't need the HIMEM.SYS file any more, since QEMM includes its own Extended Memory Manager. Unless you specify otherwise, QEMM only makes a maximum of 12 Meg of memory available for Windows. So, if you have 32 Meg installed in your system, this would be an annoying limitation. Therefore, after you activate QEMM in the CONFIG.SYS file, use the parameter EMBMEM=nnnn ("nnnn" is the amount of memory that must be made available for Windows to use).

In order for QEMM to work with Windows in Enhanced mode, the memory range B000H-B7FFH must be untouched. Also, if you're using a high resolution graphics card, you should exclude the memory block of C000H-C0FFH; this is where the BIOS of the graphics card is located.

You should also use the RAM parameter. This forces QEMM to fill the entire region between 640K and 1 Meg with RAM and make it available as the upper memory region.

To free the most working memory, start OPTIMIZE after you've set up all drivers in the CONFIG.SYS and AUTOEXEC.BAT files. This program then tries to move as many programs as possible into upper memory. QEMM provides two additional parameters during optimization: Stealth M and Stealth F.

ST:M transforms ROM areas into available RAM. The result is a maximum of free working memory. The disadvantage is that frequently one or more programs no longer function properly. For example, the graphics in some programs might be scrolled slightly, some Windows programs might not start any more, or the PC might suddenly crash. If you encounter these kinds of problems, you'll have to experiment by excluding certain memory regions and changing the sequence of the drivers in the CONFIG.SYS file until all the programs work together properly. If nothing helps, you can still use the other method, which is set with the parameter ST:F. Although this method is easy to use, at least 20K of working memory will be lost.

To obtain a report of all of the programs loaded in extended memory, enter "LOADHI" at the DOS prompt. You'll see a list of all loaded programs as well as areas of memory that are still free. With this information, you can try additional optimization.

Disk caches

Unless you have a hardware cache (controller), you should install a suitable disk cache program. Using these programs speeds up the data access time of your hard drive. Although the access time usually remains the same, by caching the necessary data, they can be transmitted faster the next time they are accessed. This is possible because the data are taken from the fast disk cache instead of from the hard drive. Therefore, using a disk cache always saves time.

Some disk cache programs are included in larger applications, such as PC Tools and Norton Utilities, while others are shareware, such as Hyperdisk. The easiest method is to use the SMARTDRV program, which is included with Windows and DOS. When Windows is installed, SMARTDRV.SYS is copied automatically into the Windows directory if your computer meets all the necessary requirements.

If you want to use SMARTDRV, simply insert the following line in your AUTOEXEC.BAT file:

```
DEVICE=C:\WINDOWS\SMARTDRV.SYS 1024 256
```

The first value (1024) indicates the storage capacity used by SMARTDRV. The second value (256) indicates the memory requirement with which SMARTDRV should work. This means that a 1 Meg read cache has been created. Windows will reduce this cache by a half a Meg if you run low on

161

memory. The values 1024 and 256 are simply frequently used standard values. With older computers or high-end models, change the values accordingly. For more information, refer to your DOS or Windows user's guide.

Windows

To load a photo CD picture in full resolution, you need sufficient memory and an adequate swap file.

Even if you have more than 20 Meg of working memory, you must create a swap file. This is necessary because, regardless of which program you use to load the PCD files, without virtual memory, the message "Not enough memory" or "Cannot open file" appears. This occurs because, in order to edit an image, memory is needed not only to load the image into memory, but also to process and manipulate it. Creating a swap file solves this problem.

There are permanent and temporary swap files. Since, in our case, we're interested in the optimal processing speed, we'll use the permanent swap file, which guarantees fast access under Windows.

With a permanent swap file, Windows creates a hidden file that occupies a specific area of the hard drive. Since Windows makes sure that this file is complete within itself, it can quickly access the individual sectors and manage them. Also, a lot of data can be read or written at once, since the individual data blocks are sequential. The disadvantage of a permanent swap file is obvious if you don't work exclusively with Windows, and use memory-hungry DOS programs as well. As its name implies, a permanent swap file always occupies valuable hard drive space, even if you don't work with Windows. Therefore, when you're using a DOS program, this area lies idle and cannot be used.

A temporary swap file is created each time you start Windows. Therefore, it can consist of many separate sectors, depending on how full your hard drive is and how it's organized. When you write to or read from a file like this, first the system always looks for the appropriate addresses on the hard drive, and the read and write head must be moved there. This is time-consuming, especially with the large amounts of data that are involved.

Before setting up a large temporary swap file under Windows, first establish the parameters for it at the DOS level. You must have enough contiguous free space on your hard drive so Windows can generate this continuous swap file. Since the file management system of your computer always puts files wherever there's enough space, a hard drive, on which data are frequently saved and deleted, quickly becomes a disorganized mess.

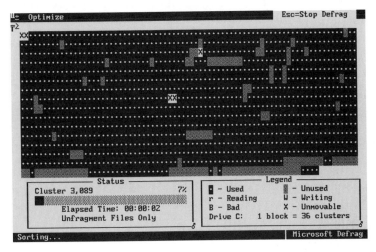

A fragmented hard drive

When you delete a file, the area that it occupied is freed. If you now copy another file to your hard drive, it probably won't have the same size as the deleted file. As a result, part of the file is written to the region that was just freed and the rest is written to another free area on the hard drive. This also occurs when you delete and copy files. Eventually, your hard drive becomes fragmented.

Fragmented hard drives negatively affect the performance of your computer because large files can be split up into dozens of segments that are spread all around your hard drive. To read a fragmented file, the read/write head of the hard drive must travel all around the disk. This slows down the access speed of the computer.

This problem becomes worse when you read from the hard drive. In this case, an entire track can usually be read in one step during a rotation of the hard drive. Therefore, if the desired data are located in one track in continuous sectors, only one rotation of the hard drive is needed to read all the data. However, if the data are spread out over several tracks, the read/write head not only has to travel to the appropriate track, but this track must go through one more rotation before the data are read. In other words, it takes two times as long to read a file split between two tracks.

Hard drive optimizers are needed to defragment the data on the hard drive. This process places all files one after another and makes the free area that's left available as one large block. Optimizers are included with Norton Utilities and PC Tools. Also, DOS 6 includes a defragmentation program.

So, organize your hard drive and start Windows again. Open the Control Panel in the Main group of the Program Manager by clicking on its icon.

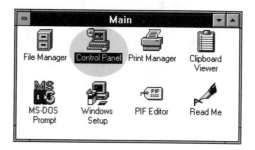

Control Panel icon

In the window that appears, click on the 386 Enhanced icon.

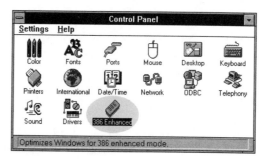

Contents of the Control Panel window (the 386 Enhanced icon is highlighted)

A window appears with information about the configuration of your computer in Enhanced mode.

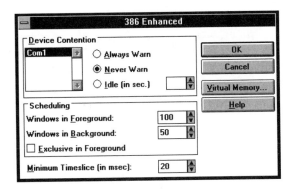

Enhanced mode dialog box

Click on the [Virtual Memory...] button to open the next dialog box.

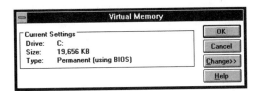

Virtual Memory dialog box

This dialog box shows the current settings for virtual memory. Now click on the [Change>>] button.

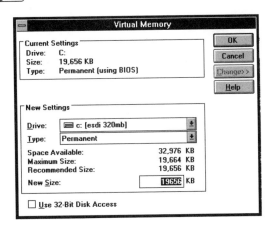

Changing the virtual memory settings

The "Virtual Memory" dialog box expands so you can make the necessary changes in the settings. Windows suggests a size for the swap file, consisting of the free hard drive memory and the installed RAM.

Normally virtual memory shouldn't be larger than twice the amount of installed RAM. For example, if you have 8 Meg of RAM installed in your computer, you shouldn't use more than 16 Meg of virtual memory. If you try to use more than this, Windows warns you that it won't use this "surplus" memory.

It's important that you have a total amount of memory of over 32 Meg available in Windows after you set up virtual memory. In order to do this, you may have to adjust the settings a few times.

If you set up the virtual memory on an AT bus hard drive, you can speed up access of the swap file even more, if you allow 32-bit access to the swap file. Windows provides this option in the bottom part of the dialog box. When this option is activated, for many operations Windows accesses the file directly, without activating the corresponding BIOS functions.

However, you can only use this setting with standard AT bus drives. If you try to use these settings with SCSI hard drives, data loss may occur or the complete data structure may be destroyed. Activate the "Use 32-Bit Disk Access" option even if you're setting up a permanent swap file. This improves the working speed.

Once you've confirmed your settings with (OK), reboot your system in order to activate your settings.

After rebooting you can examine the memory settings by activating the **About Program Manager...** command in the **Help** menu of the Program Manager. The window that appears shows you the Windows working memory.

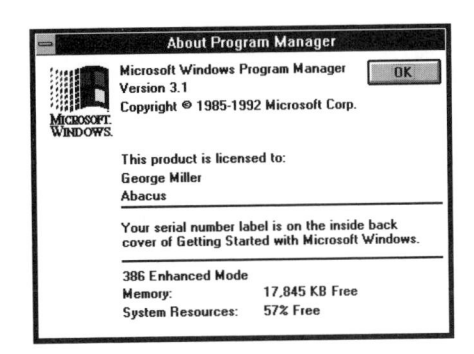

Memory information from Windows

This is basically the most important setting in Windows. Once you've set up the amount of memory required, you can immediately try to use your photo CD program to load a picture in high resolution.

Once you have 8 Meg of RAM, it doesn't matter whether you prefer to use virtual memory or physical memory. The time it takes to load a picture in memory isn't affected by this choice. Only the processor speed and the speed of the CD-ROM drive can improve performance.

We'll illustrate this with an example. A 486 50 MHz computer loads an 18 Meg picture in 3 minutes. However, a 386 40 MHz computer takes about an hour to load the same picture. Photo CD-specific settings aren't needed in the SYSTEM.INI and WIN.INI files. However, if you want to speed up this process, eliminate any unnecessary information in these files.

The simplest way to find the best configuration is to reinstall Windows. Although you're probably reluctant to do this, you could install a second version of Windows temporarily. Then compare both versions and optimize your original Windows environment according to the test version. Then you can delete the test version.

The following are guidelines you should use when working with Windows:

> Always exit any programs you no longer need.

> Avoid using large background pictures and clean out the Clipboard if possible.

> Remove any unnecessary memory-resident programs.

Image Processing Software

Besides the programs and tools that provide direct access to the photo CD, you also need image processing programs to edit photo CD pictures.

Programs are available for the Macintosh and PC. The functions provided by these programs range from simply

> **NOTE**
>
> Unfortunately, a detailed discussion of each program in this section is beyond the scope of this book. For more information about image processing software, refer to magazines and specific books on image processing software.

cutting out desired picture areas, to adjusting the color and brightness, to complex processing using filters and creating color separations.

The PhotoStyler and PhotoShop programs are extremely powerful and are suitable for professional use. However, there are also less expensive programs that offer various functions at an affordable price. Also, some software packages, like CorelDRAW!, include image processing programs.

True Photo CD programs

In this section, we'll discuss programs that are specifically designed for the Photo CD and can only read in pictures from the Photo CD.

Kodak Photo CD Access

The Photo CD Access program from Kodak provides only the necessary functions for loading a photo CD picture in order to save it in another format on the hard drive. However, Access does this at very high speed. Most current graphics formats are supported. Therefore, you can easily use another program for additional processing.

Besides saving an image in a different format, it's possible to exchange entire pictures or sections of them using the Clipboard. However, the Clipboard only lets you export pictures with a maximum of 256 colors. This can be an advantage if your computer doesn't have a lot of memory. It's possible to load a picture at low resolution and reduce this picture to the desired section. Then, if you select a higher resolution, Access only loads the section in the desired resolution. Therefore, even if you have only 4 Meg of RAM, you can use the high resolution of the photo CD.

Kodak Photo CD Access features

Access also provides the following features for manipulating images:

> ➤ Scroll the picture

> ➤ Zoom the picture

> ➤ Rotate the picture

> ➤ Mirror the picture

> ➤ Image cropping (You can specify a section that can be loaded in a higher resolution.)

> ➤ Copy to the Clipboard

> ➤ Export in another graphics format

Access is available in versions for PCs and Macintosh computers. Besides the Windows version, there is also a DOS version, which has similar features. However, currently this version is more expensive. Usually a Kodak photo CD with pictures and the Access program are included with photo CD-compatible CD-ROM drives.

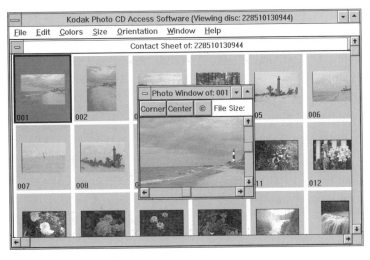

Access from Kodak

Kodak PhotoEdge

Kodak PhotoEdge is a small image editing program. This program contains the same functions as Photo CD Access except for the ability to load only sections of a picture in high resolution. However, unlike with Access, formats can be exchanged using the Clipboard with more than 256 colors.

Kodak PhotoEdge features

This program also has the following features:

> Scan brightness and color values

> Filter functions like smoothing, sharpening, contour emphasis, inversion

> Color correction

> Brightness correction

> Change contrast

Kodak PhotoEdge is available for PCs and runs under Windows. This is an excellent program to use with a simple image editing program.

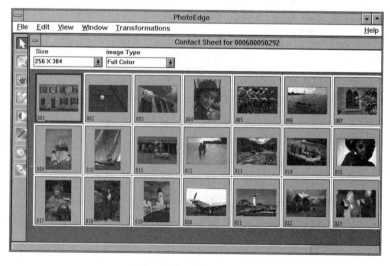

PhotoEdge from Kodak

Kodak Shoebox is a Windows application which allows you to organize photos, comment them, and even add sound, creating a multimedia extravaganza. Perhaps you kept your old photos in shoeboxes in the old days - hence the name for this product.

Kodak Shoebox features

Kodak Shoebox has the following features:

> Create multimedia catalog files (no limit), with 30,000 items stored in each catalog

> Create keyword (caption fields) of up to 32,000 characters in length

> Generate 100+ fields per catalog file

> View, zoom, crop and export images

> Create slide shows

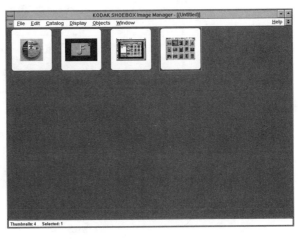

Kodak Shoebox

Simple image processing programs

You don't have to spend a lot of money to get a powerful image processing program. Actually, there are many affordable programs that offer a lot for a little money. These programs include features that are more extensive than simply improving images and modifying colors. Usually a specific feature, which isn't included in professional programs or is difficult to use in these programs, makes these programs especially attractive.

Paint Shop Pro

Paint Shop Pro is a shareware program that is currently available in Version 2.0. This program not only accesses the photo CD, but also supports several other graphics formats that can be read and written. It's an ideal conversion and viewing program for almost all picture files. Besides converting formats, you can also manipulate the picture data.

Paint Shop Pro 2.0

You can perform the conversions in a batch process. By doing this, you can easily select the source picture and determine where the new pictures should be stored.

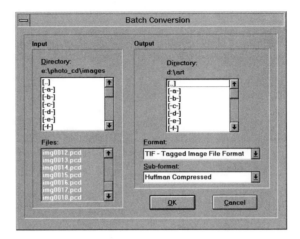

Converting formats in a batch process

Besides pure conversion, Paint Shop Pro 2.0 also has several image processing features that aren't available in many commercial (i.e., more expensive) programs. For example, the color reduction options are extensive and allow you to make optimal adjustments to suit every target application.

It's also possible to recalculate for the optimal setting for other picture sizes. Besides the "normal" optimization methods, such as contrast, brightness, and color correction, you can also directly access the palettes of the pictures or process the pictures with various filter functions.

Also, you aren't restricted to the many predefined filters. Instead, you can create and process filters yourself.

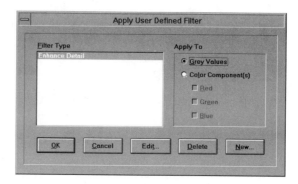

Defining your own filters

Obviously, you can also edit and cut sections of pictures. Unlike programs that are strictly image editing programs, Paint Shop Pro 2.0 lets you define only rectangular areas. However, this is enough for processing pictures.

Paint Shop Pro 2.0 is also a complete OLE server. Therefore, you can easily link and process photo CDs and other pictures in any applications.

Also, Paint Shop Pro 2.0 has a user-friendly Capture command. You can capture sections of the screen, individual windows, or only the client area, which is the window without the frames and the menu bar.

Paint Shop Pro 2.0 features

The following is a summary of Paint Shop Pro 2.0's features:

> Load pictures in many different formats

> Load photo CD pictures

> Scroll the picture

> Zoom the picture

> Rotate the picture

> Mirror the picture

> Create sections (You can define a section which can be processed separately.)

> Copy to the Clipboard

> ➢ Export in another graphics format

> ➢ Color correction

> ➢ Brightness correction

> ➢ Change the contrast

> ➢ Filter functions like blurring, sharpening, contour emphasis, inversion

> ➢ Special filters like relief, various contour filters, mosaic filters, posterizing, etc.

> ➢ Define your own filters

> ➢ Color reduction

> ➢ Calculate a new picture size

> ➢ Screen captures

> ➢ Full OLE server

Paintbrush

The Paintbrush program that's included with Windows and a true drawing program are very different. Paintbrush is mainly used to add drawn objects and text to pictures. However, you can still use Paintbrush to make minor changes to your pictures. For example, you can paint, add text, or change the background.

A disadvantage to using Paintbrush is that you cannot load a complete picture, in high resolution, with a file size of 18 Meg. However, this isn't a significant problem, since you would need a powerful image processing program to process pictures at this resolution anyway.

Graphic Workshop for Windows (GWS)

This is a well-known shareware program. Recently it was equipped with the ability to read and convert PCD files. Graphic Workshop for Windows is an inexpensive way to start using photo processing.

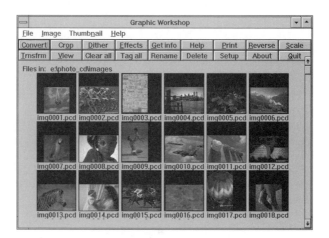

Graphic Workshop Version 1.1

GWS lets you view, convert, and print pictures in different formats, including conversion of PCD files into all popular picture file formats. This eliminates the problem of first viewing the pictures on a photo CD.

The latest version of GWS includes support for the JPEG format, color reduction, new dithering options, better memory management, and a thumbnail image mode so you can quickly examine the photos in miniature format.

If desired, the program immediately recognizes whether a photo CD has been inserted in the drive and immediately changes to the Images subdirectory. If you've activated the **Thumbnail/Use Thumbnails** command, the program displays the contents of the CD, as contact prints, in a window.

Graphic Workshop for Windows is mainly used to convert and print out pictures in a batch process. This is the program's most powerful feature.

Graphic Workshop for Windows features

Graphic Workshop for Windows has the following features:

> ➢ Load thumbnails

> ➢ Load individual photo CD pictures

> ➢ Load pictures in other formats

> ➢ View pictures

> ➢ Zoom the picture

> ➢ Rotate the picture

> ➢ Mirror the picture

> ➢ Crop the picture

> ➢ Dither pictures in many variations

> ➢ Export in another graphics format

> ➢ Color correction

> ➢ Brightness correction

> ➢ Change contrast

> ➢ Color reduction

> ➢ Calculate a new picture size

Advanced image processing programs

In this section we'll discuss programs that include features that are more advanced than simply processing pictures. These programs let you mix different pictures and include extensive highlighting features.

Corel PHOTO-PAINT!

This image processing program is included with CorelDRAW!. A Macintosh version will be available soon.

Corel PHOTO-PAINT! includes all the features that a serious image processing program can offer. It has functions for improving a picture: Sharpening, smoothing contrast, diffusing screen, section functions, inserting, color gradients, painting functions, linking text, etc.

However, processing pictures at high resolution takes a long time. Therefore, it's very difficult to use this program to process pictures at this resolution.

177

Corel PHOTO-PAINT!

Version 4.0 of this program contains even more features for processing pictures. For example, it has filters that transform your photo CD pictures into a painting on a background you select.

Corel PHOTO-PAINT! features

The following summarizes Corel PHOTO-PAINT!'s main features:

> ➤ Load individual photo CD pictures

> ➤ Load individual pictures in different formats

> ➤ Scroll the picture

> ➤ Zoom the picture

> ➤ Rotate the picture

> ➤ Mirror the picture

> ➤ Mark selected areas of the picture in different forms

> ➤ Automatic selection of certain picture areas

> ➤ Copy into the Clipboard

> ➤ Export in another graphics format

➤ Filter functions like blurring, sharpening, contour emphasis, inversion

➤ Color correction

➤ Brightness correction

➤ Change the contrast

➤ Flexible painting features

➤ Easy-to-use text features

➤ Special filters like relief, diverse contour filters, mosaic filters, posterizing, etc.

➤ Special filters for artistic design

➤ Addition of different backgrounds to the picture

➤ Color reduction, increasing colors

➤ Calculation of a new picture size

➤ Full OLE server

PhotoMagic

PhotoMagic, from Micrografx, is a powerful but moderately-priced program. It's very similar to Picture Publisher, also from Micrografx, but it doesn't include all the features found in a professional image processing program.

Since PhotoMagic can read PCD files, you don't need a special photo CD-loading program. However, it takes longer to load a PCD picture with PhotoMagic than with a pure photo CD program. But PhotoMagic's wide range of features compensates for this minor disadvantage.

The program's interface is very different from those of similar programs. With PhotoMagic, the picture to be processed is framed like a painting by different elements. A toolbox is located on the left, other elements appear along the top, and elements for managing the loaded pictures (size adjusters and icons of loaded pictures) appear to the right.

An information window is located at the bottom. This window provides information about the elements located under the mouse pointer.

It's also possible, during each loading process, to open a picture from a miniature image, through the ImageBrowser. This is possible even when you aren't accessing the photo CD, which makes it easier to select a picture. The ImageBrowser is used not only to load the individual pictures, but also manage all the pictures.

PhotoMagic

PhotoMagic provides many effects that can be used in various ways in your pictures. After activating **Effects...** from the **Image** menu, a dialog box appears in which you can select and assign the desired effect.

Selecting the effects

For each effect, you can display a brief explanation and preview the effect. With an entire series of effects, you can use several settings, which you can activate in the middle section of the dialog box.

PhotoMagic also contains other tools you need for extensive image processing. Various highlighting tools are also available. This means that automatic highlighting according to similar color values is possible. However there are differences between the corresponding tools in professional image processing programs.

Using a TWAIN interface, you can also read in pictures from other devices, such as scanners or video-grabber cards, that support this interface standard. It's also possible to convey pictures via OLE. PhotoMagic is a full OLE server and sets itself up in your Windows environment when you install it.

Since PhotoMagic cannot work with color printers, it isn't suitable for professional users who must create color printouts of their work.

PhotoMagic features

The following summarizes PhotoMagic's main features:

> ➢ Load individual photo CD pictures

> ➢ Basic image processing like rotating, mirroring, and recalculating the picture

> ➢ Export in another graphics format

> ➢ Generate sections: Rectangular, freely with a lasso function, automatically on the basis of color similarity

> ➢ Highlighting regions of color

> ➢ Color correction

> ➢ Brightness correction

> ➢ Change the contrast

> ➢ Color reduction

> ➢ Basic filter functions, such as blurring, sharpening, contour emphasis, inversion

> ➢ Special filters like relief, various contour filters, mosaic filters, posterizing, etc.

> ➢ Cloning tool

> ➢ Monitor calibration

> ➢ TWAIN interface

> ➢ Full OLE server

Professional image processing programs

In this section, we'll discuss the programs that are suitable for professional image processing. As the power of these programs increase, so does their price. In return, these programs provide features that make it possible to process photo CD pictures so they can be displayed or printed with professional tools. This means that you can create files that can be further processed by layout studios.

182

Picture Publisher

Picture Publisher, from Micrografx, is a professional image processing program. Its graphical interface is very similar to that of PhotoMagic, which is also from Micrografx. Picture Publisher's range of features will meet the needs of any professional user. In addition to all the options for improving or changing an image, which PhotoMagic also provides, all modules are designed for continued processing, such as printing and creating images.

Picture Publisher from Micrografix

As with PhotoMagic, in Picture Publisher the image files can be easily loaded with the help of thumbnails, as shown by Picture Publisher's own ImageBrowser.

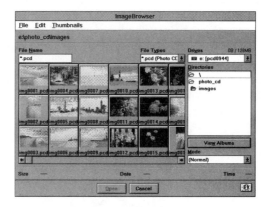

Picture Publisher's ImageBrowser

The Picture Publisher interface is easy to use and provides quick access to help information.

Besides extensive filter features, this program also has many options for changing the color of the images. You can easily change the individual color channels and color areas by using the 3-dimensional dialog boxes.

Image areas of different images can easily be mixed using variable transparency and, at the same time, the edges of the different areas can be blurred so they blend into one another.

When you're finished processing an image, Picture Publisher provides various options for outputting the image professionally. For example, you can create a color separation according to the RGB or CMYK format by simply clicking the mouse. Then you can easily merge the individual components back together again.

Picture Publisher's features

The following is a summary of Picture Publisher's features:

> Load individual photo CD pictures

> Basic image processing, such as rotating, mirroring, and resizing the picture

> Export to other graphics formats

➢ Create sections: Rectangular, with lasso function, or based on similarity of colors

➢ Mask areas of color

➢ Color correction

➢ Brightness correction

➢ Change the contrast

➢ Color reduction

➢ Fundamental filter functions like smoothing, sharpening, edging, inversion

➢ Special filters like embossing, different contour filters, mosaic filters, posterizing, etc.

➢ Cloning tool

➢ Monitor calibration

➢ Printer calibration

➢ Various color filter features

➢ Color separation by RGB and CMYK

➢ TWAIN interface

➢ Full OLE server

Aldus PhotoStyler

Aldus PhotoStyler is one of the most popular image processing programs for both the Macintosh and PC. Designed for professional applications, PhotoStyler provides problem-free data exchange between the different systems.

Currently PhotoStyler is one of the most powerful image processing programs available. Since it includes numerous features, it takes some time before you can master the program.

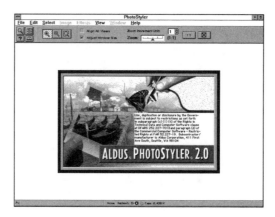

Aldus PhotoStyler

PhotoStyler's add-in utility ImagePals Album (which is also available as a stand-alone product) provides an easy way to archive your images. We'll discuss this program in more detail later in this chapter.

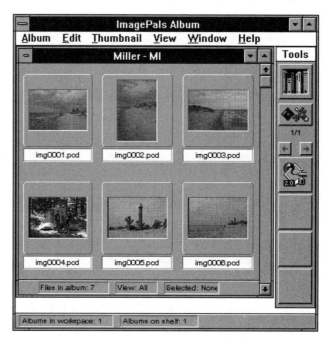

Contact print from PhotoStyler

For image processing, PhotoStyler provides all the features that you need for professional applications. In addition to many filter functions you'll find in the other programs, PhotoStyler also provides several options for combining pictures and inserting selected areas in other pictures.

For additional processing, color separation by different color models is available. You can separate and recombine the image according to the RGB, HSB, HLS, or CMYK color models.

PhotoStyler features

PhotoStyler has the following features:

> Load individual photo CD images

> Fundamental image processing like rotating, mirroring, and recalculating the image

> Export in another graphics format

> Generate sections: Rectangular, using the lasso feature, automatically on the basis of color similarity

> Color correction

> Brightness correction

> Change the contrast

> Color reduction

> Basic filter functions like blurring, sharpening, contour emphasis, inversion

> Special filters like relief, various contour filters, mosaic filters, posterizing, etc.

> User-defined filters

> Various functions for mixing images and sections

> Cloning tool

> Monitor calibration

187

> ➢ Printer calibration

> ➢ Various color filter functions

> ➢ Color separation by RGB, HLS, HSB, and CMYK

Adobe Photoshop

Adobe Photoshop is a popular Apple Macintosh program that is now available for Windows. It's a powerful program that is very similar to PhotoStyler.

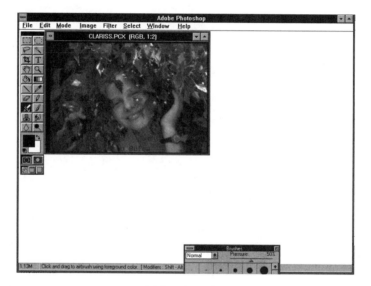

Adobe Photoshop

You can manipulate half-tone images, bitmap graphics, grayscale images, and color images with this program. The latest version of Photoshop contains more features than its competitor, PhotoStyler. However, this will probably change when PhotoStyler releases a new version. Several new features are included in the latest version of Photoshop. Many of these features have never been available in Windows. For example, the CMYK mode is new on the PC. With this mode, you can transport the image into the color area, which can be printed later. By doing this, you can discover any discrepancies between the display on the screen and the printout before you actually print.

Another new feature is the CIE-LAB color mode, which was developed specifically for electronic processing. This new standard insures the color fastness from the scan to the printout, regardless of the device that's used.

Photoshop features

The following is a summary of Photoshop's features:

> Load individual photo CD images

> Basic image processing like rotating, mirroring, and recalculating the image

> Export in another graphics format

> Generate sections: Rectangular, using the lasso feature, automatically on the basis of color similarity

> Color correction

> Brightness correction

> Change the contrast

> Color reduction

> Basic filter functions like blurring, sharpening, contour emphasis, inversion

> Special filters like relief, various contour filters, mosaic filters, posterizing, etc.

> User-defined filters

> Various features for mixing images and sections

> Cloning tool

> Monitor calibration

> Printer calibration

> Various color filter functions

> Color separation by RGB, HLS, HSB and CMYK

189

Related programs

Now we'll discuss some programs that aren't directly related to image processing, but can be used in conjunction with image processing.

Aldus Gallery Effects

Gallery Effects, from Aldus, is a constantly growing collection of various filters that make it easier to manipulate an image artistically.

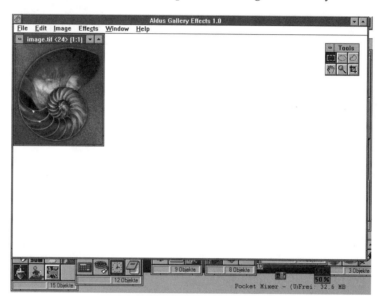

Aldus Gallery Effects

The basic package in this family, Classic Art, Volume 1, contains 16 special effects that you can apply to your images; the images are automatically transformed into the desired style.

Gallery Effects is available as a stand-alone application or as an add-on to image processing programs for both the Apple Macintosh and PC. You can easily create very expressive images with Gallery Effects.

Volume 2 offers 16 additional effects which you can use alone or combined. With the second volume, images can be changed with photographic effects; textile patterns and additional artistic effects are also included.

Gallery Effects features (Macintosh)

Plug In support for:

- Aldus Superpaint
- Aldus Digital Darkroom
- Adobe Photoshop
- Adobe Premiere
- Color Studio 1.5
- Pixel Paint Professional
- Fractal Design Painter
- Stratvision
- All programs that use Photoshop-compatible plug-in filters

File formats:

Gallery Effects for Macintosh can open and save in the following file formats:

- TIFF up to 24-bit
- PICT up to 32-bit

Images that are modified with Gallery Effects can be imported into any application that supports the Copy and Paste functions.

Gallery Effects features (Windows)

Plug In support for:

- Aldus PhotoStyler
- Fractal Design Painter
- Programs that use PhotoStyler-compatible filter

File formats:

Gallery Effects for Windows can read and save in the following file formats:

- ➢ TIFF up to 24-bit

- ➢ TGA up to 24-bit

- ➢ Windows BMP up to 24-bit

As with the Macintosh version, the modified images can be imported into any program that supports the Copy and Paste functions.

System requirements:

- ➢ A Macintosh or PC that is capable of rapidly processing images.

PhotoMorph

PhotoMorph, from North Coast Software, is a morphing program. These are programs that enable you to create animated sequences from individual pictures.

The term "morphing" is a new technology that's being developed in the computer world.

Unlike image processing programs, the morphing software that's available doesn't include the popular paint and manipulation tools. For morphing, one or two images are needed; individual points are designated where the images melt or merge into one another or are distorted.

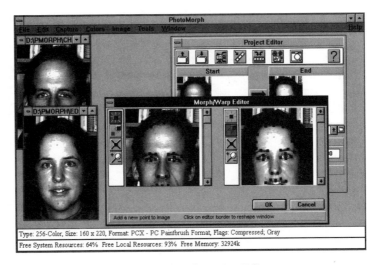

The PhotoMorph Project Editor

To use morphing software, you need a powerful computer and a lot of memory. To morph images, first you must mark the source image (in the left working window of the Morph editor) with points by using the mouse. Correspondingly, in the right window, the appropriate contours must be marked on the target image.

The program then creates a sequence, during which the images merge into one another. This makes it possible to digitize segments in videos or to change people's faces magically.

If you work with images on a computer, you'll probably be interested in this new technology, especially if you're using photo CD technology.

The hardware that's used determines whether an acceptable working speed is possible when using high resolution. However, usually the morphing process, or the actual computation by the program, takes at least five minutes for a small video sequence that's approximately ten seconds long.

In addition to morphing, PhotoMorph is also capable of "warping." In this process, instead of merging two images, an individual image warps within itself. This makes it possible to completely change a person's facial expressions.

Warping an image

It's also possible to produce different dissolving effects. These effects are perfect for scene changes within a video.

You can save the results of your transformations as AVI movies, single images, or image sequences in different formats. You can view the sequences using a built-in AVI player.

The entire program fits on a single 3.5-inch diskette. A Video for Windows Runtime module is included, so you can view your results immediately.

You'll Find It On The Companion CD ROM!

We've included some sample movies in the \WORKSHOP\PMORH directory.

Overview of image processing programs

Program	PCD	Image Manipulation	Options	Other
Picture Publisher	Yes	Total	Preview	
PhotoMagic	Yes	Good	Graphic editing	Preview
PhotoStyler	Yes	Total		
Photoshop	Yes	Total		
Paint Shop Pro	Yes	Satisfactory	Screen captures	
PhotoPaint	No	Good	CorelDRAW!	
CorelMOSAIC!	Yes	None	CorelDRAW!	
Paintbrush	No	Satisfactory	Windows	
Kodak Access	Yes	None		Sections are loadable

Desktop publishing programs

In this section, we'll discuss some desktop publishing programs you can use with the photo CD. These programs are available in both PC and Macintosh versions. Similar programs are available for both systems and most programs are capable of exchanging data between the systems.

CorelDRAW!

CorelDRAW! is a program package that consists of several components. As we mentioned earlier, Corel PHOTO-PAINT! is included with CorelDRAW!. CorelMOSAIC! is also included.

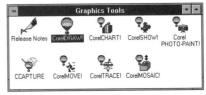

A Corel group

This program, which lets you load, save, and manage images and PCD files, is very important to photo CD users. The package also contains CorelCHART! for creating presentation graphics, CorelSHOW! for creating presentations, and CorelTRACE! for vectoring bitmap images.

CorelDRAW! itself is a professional desktop publishing program, with an emphasis on creating vector-oriented objects. It's designed primarily for professional users.

However, anyone can use it to create posters, pamphlets, invitations, business cards, articles, and even entire books. CorelDRAW! contains all the tools a graphic artist needs.

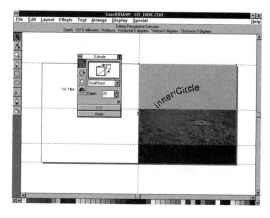

CorelDRAW!

CorelDRAW! is available in PC and Macintosh versions.

Aldus FreeHand

Aldus FreeHand is a powerful professional desktop publishing program that's used by many graphic artists. This program is now available in a Windows version.

Although FreeHand is designed for professionals, it's so easy to use that even nonprofessionals can quickly learn how to use it. However, because FreeHand is so expensive, usually only professionals can afford it.

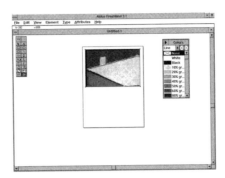

Aldus FreeHand

FreeHand is unique because of its many import and export formats and its precision. When positioning an object, the precision can be measured in 1/10,000 of a PostScript point. Like other DTP programs, FreeHand lets you work with different layers. You can edit and print up to 200 layers individually or in groups. It's also possible to sort the layers in any order.

Since FreeHand is a professional system, you can work with various color definitions and also perform color separations very easily.

We cannot list all of FreeHand's features in this limited space. However, this program is considered a standard of desktop publishing programs. It would be difficult to find another DTP program that has as many or more features than FreeHand.

Microsoft Publisher

Microsoft Publisher is a Windows program you can use to create cards, advertisements, transparencies, brochures, newsletters, business forms, and other publications easily and inexpensively. For example, if you want to create a calendar, the program provides an "assistant" who guides you through each step by asking questions.

Starting Microsoft Publisher

The basic functions of the program are located in the icon bar. Simply click on the appropriate icon to design texts, tables, diagrams, and graphics.

Simple layout

You can simply type in text or copy text from other files. By clicking the mouse, you can quickly format your document. Borders and shading help you create professional-looking documents.

Graphics

Microsoft Publisher also includes an extensive clipart library of graphics and figures. You can easily import images and then specify the size and position of the images.

BorderArt

The BorderArt library provides various types of borders for invitations, announcements, cards, etc. To select a border, simply click on it with the mouse.

Photo CD user package

The photo CD user package is a special product that's available for those interested in professional desktop publishing. This package includes the book *Photo CD & Desktop Reproductions*, which provides helpful information about using the photo CD with desktop publishing.

Use the examples in this book to compare the result of printing photo CD pictures on different types of paper, from newspaper print, to recycled paper, to high quality photographic print paper.

In addition to different dpi settings, picture sizes, and grid sizes, the quality of photo CD pictures and high-end EBV images are compared.

Currently 300 dpi is the standard output resolution for pictures. You can see for yourself which dpi resolution is needed with which grid sizes. From grid sizes of 20 to 80, all resolutions from 350 dpi to 72 dpi and their results are presented in the book.

You'll also find information on how to solve the problem of color variations between the screen display and the printed copy.

The photo CD user package for the Macintosh includes the following components:

➢ The book *Photo CD & Desktop Reproductions*

➢ Plug-in software for PhotoShop

➢ Demo CD

➢ Hue software for checking and adjusting the monitor

Presentation programs

In this section we'll discuss some programs that can be used to create presentations with your photo CD pictures.

Microsoft PowerPoint

Microsoft PowerPoint is a simple and powerful presentation package that makes it easy to present your ideas in a professional presentation.

Microsoft PowerPoint

First use the Outline feature to record your ideas and then arrange them on slides. Use the mouse to move or copy the text and pictures among the overheads. It's also easy to import photos and text. Simply click the mouse to display the desired file. Besides your own photos and drawings, there are also hundreds of clipart images, which are included with the program, that you can use.

A presentation is organized using templates. Once you've created these templates, you can use them for numerous presentations. To make it easier to create a presentation, PowerPoint also includes over 160 templates.

There are also 45 fading effects, text animation, and 256 colors with 16 million hues.

Working with PowerPoint has one disadvantage. You can display the presentation by using the included run-time module. However, this requires long waiting periods because the entire publication must be loaded into memory. This is especially noticeable if you are working with large true-color pictures. Therefore, before displaying your presentation, convert the pictures you want to use into a format that take up less memory.

CorelSHOW!

CorelSHOW! is included with CorelDRAW!. This program's interface is very similar to that of CorelDRAW! and it provides all the features that you need to create a professional-looking slide show.

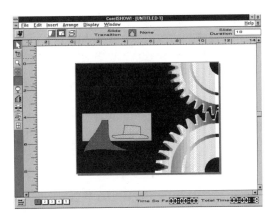

CorelSHOW!

Pictures can be imported in two ways. You can import the pictures from the Clipboard or you can link the pictures as OLE objects. Text or graphics can be input using CorelDRAW! or another OLE server. Simply select the appropriate icon from the tool bar and create a box at the point where you want to place the object. The corresponding OLE server starts and you can paste in any items.

You can also link sound, music, and video in your presentation in the same way and produce a multimedia presentation.

A show can consist of any number of slides that have a common background. As with a light table, you can rearrange the individual slides in a special window. You can also copy and delete slides.

Besides the content of a slide, for each slide you can select a transition effect and you can determine how long the slide should be displayed.

Image management programs

As your collection of pictures and photo CDs grows, it's difficult to keep track of all your images. Although the prints of the pictures supplied with each photo CD can help you locate a photo, once you have more than ten CDs, it's difficult to get a complete overview of the pictures. Also, you must search through all the prints to find a specific picture. This process can be very time-consuming.

To solve this problem, several software manufacturers have developed image management programs that help you organize all your photo CD pictures so you can locate a picture in a large collection quickly and easily. Once you've found the desired picture, these programs usually ask for the photo CD on which the picture is stored.

These programs usually allow you to apply search parameters to each picture. This makes it easier to find a picture by limiting the amount of pictures that are included in the search. We'll use an example to demonstrate how to use search parameters.

First, you must assign hierarchical key terms to each picture. For example, you could use the following key terms for your vacation pictures from Spain:

```
Spain/Granada/Alhambra
```

To locate all the pictures of Spain, use "Spain" as a search parameter. If you want to locate only pictures of Granada or Alhambra, use either "Granada" or "Alhambra" as a search parameter. As you can see, using search parameters is an efficient way to locate images in your collection.

Now we'll describe some programs you can use to organize your photo CD pictures.

ImagePals Album

This image management program is included in the Aldus PhotoStyler package. You can use this program to manage all types of pictures.

ImagePals Album

Individual pictures or entire directories can be read into the album at once. The pictures are stored in albums, which can be managed separately from the shelf. You should create albums for different criteria. Within the albums the pictures are displayed as small slides, in a size you determine. To move albums to another shelf or place pictures in several shelves, simply slide the images around. The location of the album, the file size, and the file name are automatically stored for each picture. This makes it very easy to locate a specific picture again.

The program also provides a dialog box in which you can enter specific search information applying to each picture. This dialog box appears when you select **Thumbnail/Search....** This information can include file name, date, and other criteria.

Since this program does more than just manage pictures from the photo CD, you can also directly access the files of the selected pictures and copy, move, and delete them. You can also convert selected pictures into other file formats or print them.

Besides managing pictures, ImagePals Album also lets you edit selected pictures. You can link your image processing programs to ImagePals Album. The programs are represented as buttons in the tool palette. Then you can start the program by pressing a button or, by including the name of the desired file, you can start directly with that file.

ImagePal features

The following summarizes ImagePals' main features:

- ➢ Load pictures in many different formats

- ➢ Create areas (You can define a section, which can be processed separately.)

- ➢ Copy to the Clipboard

- ➢ Export in another graphics format

- ➢ Produce and manage photo albums

- ➢ Look for pictures by entered data and by technical data

- ➢ Sort by different criteria

- ➢ Copy and move selected pictures

- ➢ Print pictures and albums

- ➢ Transfer pictures to other programs using Drag & Drop

PixFolio

PixFolio Version 2.0 is a shareware program that offers several features. Unfortunately, the current version of the program cannot access PCD files. So it cannot be used to manage original pictures on the photo CD. However, PixFolio reads almost every graphics format currently used with the PC. It also supports some Macintosh formats.

PixFolio

This program not only catalogs and manages your pictures, but also lets you convert the pictures or sections of them into other formats. It also provides detailed information about the individual pictures.

By clicking the mouse, you can search entire drives for pictures and include them in a catalog. You can add other information in addition to the size, format, and path of the picture, which the program provides. You can also include picture titles and key words, as well as a description.

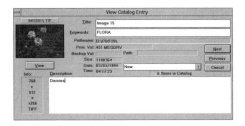

PixFolio data

You can quickly search by using key words and picture data, such as format or size, and then select the pictures that are found. Selected pictures can be copied, deleted, printed, moved to other catalogs, or displayed as a slide show on the screen.

The cataloged pictures can be displayed as miniature pictures like on a contact print. To keep better track of the collection, you can change the sequence very easily by moving the pictures with the mouse.

This program also has a Snapshot function. You can take a snapshot of the screen, individual windows, or just the active area of a window (Client Area) and store it as a file on your hard drive.

So you can immediately start organizing your picture collection, we've included this program in the \SHAREWAR\PIXF20 directory on the companion CD.

PixFolio features

The following is a summary of PixFolio's features:

> Load pictures in many different formats

> Create sections (You can define a section, which can be processed separately.)

> Copy to the Clipboard

> Export in another graphics format

> Rotate the picture

> Mirror the picture

> Produce and manage photo albums

> Look for pictures according to user-defined information and by technical data

> Sort by any criteria

> Print pictures and albums

> Complete OLE server

PhotoStar

This is a new image management program from Microtek. A version of this program is included on the companion CD.

PhotoStar

PhotoStar uses electronic photo albums to organize your pictures. Information about the picture is automatically stored with each photo and you can add information at any time. PhotoStar provides a user-friendly dialog box, which contains miniature versions of the pictures, for this purpose. Simply edit the data fields in table format.

A well-designed Search function helps you locate the individual photos. The Sort function lists the photos by title, date, and any comments you entered.

A built-in Security function determines when the hard drive is full. If this occurs, you can use this function to transfer your pictures to other storage media and then delete the files from the hard drive. The archived mini-pictures remain intact, so it's easy to reconstruct your photos. In this way, you retain the space on your hard drive as well as your overview of your collection of pictures.

PhotoStar provides different ways to read in a photo. The PCD format is fully supported, so all loading functions and the conversion of the pictures from the photo CD are easily executed. The integrated support for a scanner makes it possible to read scanned pictures directly into the program. Also, programs can be integrated into the working environment of PhotoStar, and can be immediately started using drag & drop.

The Enhancer provides the most important picture processing functions. You can use it to correct brightness, contrast, shade, sharpness, and color saturation. If these editing features aren't sufficient, you can also link your favorite image processing program and transfer the pictures to this program with drag & drop.

A presentation feature lets you create slide shows. You can use transitions to blend one image into the next when changing scenes. Even inscriptions and sound can be linked in a presentation.

You'll Find It On The Companion CD ROM!

 A demo version of this program is in the \PSTAR directory. Chapter 5 contains information and instructions for operating the program.

PhotoStar features

The following summarizes PhotoStar's main features:

➢ Load pictures in many different formats

➢ Load photo CD pictures

➢ Read in pictures from scanners

➢ TWAIN interface

➢ Create sections (You can define a section, which can be processed separately.)

➢ Copy to the Clipboard

➢ Export in another graphics format

➢ Color correction

➢ Brightness correction

➢ Change the contrast

➢ Create and organize photo albums, which can be organized in different catalogs

➢ Sort by desired criteria

➢ Look for pictures by user-input data

➢ Transfer pictures to other programs

> ➤ Print pictures and albums

> ➤ Slide show with selected pictures with sound support

Kodak Shoebox

Shoebox from Kodak is an image management program for both Macintosh and IBM-compatible computers. With Kodak Shoebox, you can organize digitized pictures and other multimedia items. You can easily locate your pictures, Apple Quicktime files, and even audio data. Shoebox recognizes both PCD files and all popular graphics formats.

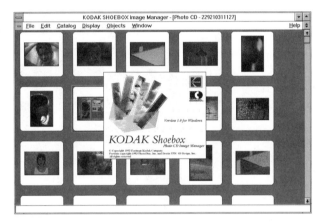

Kodak Shoebox

Detailed, user-definable indexes let you enter your individual search parameters in each database to make the search as simple and easy as possible. The picture Search tool can contain several criteria, and all pictures that match these criteria are displayed. It's also possible to search for individual pictures.

The located pictures appear on a contact sheet. Select the desired picture by clicking with the mouse. Then the picture is displayed in full resolution. You can then copy the picture to the Clipboard, convert it, or process it in other applications.

To play a Quicktime Movie or an audio file, click on the appropriate icon. The program also has a Print feature. It's also very easy to enter the information. You can add information to individual pictures or to all selected pictures.

209

We'll give an example to demonstrate how you can use the program. After the program starts, activate **File** in the main menu. Use **Load Contact Sheet** to display the contents of the inserted photo CD. Only a portion of each picture may be displayed, depending on how many pictures will fit in the window.

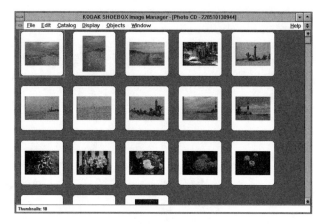

Kodak Shoebox with loaded contact sheet

If you want to include the contents in a catalog, store the thumbnails under **File/Save As...** and indicate the name of a catalog.

By doing this, you can locate your pictures on the photo CD again if you open a catalog and activate the highlighted picture by double-clicking. The program then asks you to insert the appropriate CD.

This is the easiest way to use this program. It provides a good overview of your collection. You don't have to look through all the different CDs to locate a picture; the program tells you where you can find it.

However, Shoebox also contains all the other functions you should expect in an image manager. Each picture is easily located by using indexes and keywords after they have been input. You can automatically view a list of all keywords that have been used and you can select one from the list by clicking with the mouse.

The ability to print all the pictures on the photo CD directly as contact prints is especially useful. As an added benefit, Shoebox also includes a slide show feature. You can even assign sound files using pre-settings.

Click with the mouse on Display, Select, Select All, and all the pictures on the CD will be highlighted and can be displayed. In the same pull-down menu, activate **Start Slide Show**.

The slide show starts running after you click on the button.

Slide show with Kodak Shoebox

Shoebox features

Shoebox contains the following features:

> Load and archive pictures in many different formats

> Load and archive photo CD pictures

> Load and archive animations

> Load and archive sound files

> Create sections (You can define a section, which can be processed separately.)

> Copy to the Clipboard

> Export in another graphics format

211

- ➢ Create and organize photo albums

- ➢ Add data in user-definable fields

- ➢ Look for pictures by previously entered data and by technical data

- ➢ Sort by various criteria

- ➢ Print pictures and albums

- ➢ Transfer pictures to other programs

A Photo CD Workshop

CHAPTER 4

A Photo CD Workshop

So far you've learned which hardware and software can be used with the photo CD. In this chapter we'll discuss the different ways you can use the photo CD system. As you'll see, it can be used for more than simply displaying photos on a monitor. In the following sections, we'll use examples to demonstrate the various ways to use the photo CD.

Modifying Photos

Unfortunately, sometimes the photos you take don't turn out perfectly. They may be blurry or have some other flaws. Until now, there wasn't much you could do to fix these photos. However, with photo CD technology, it's possible to improve almost any picture by touching up defects from the exposure. There are simple photo CD programs for touching up pictures or for making simple corrections. You can even find suitable shareware programs for correcting pictures.

We'll use the PhotoEdge and Paint Shop Pro programs to describe simple picture enhancement functions. Obviously, these kinds of picture manipulation features are also included in professional image processing programs.

Start by making changes to pictures in low resolution. By doing this, it won't take too much time to process the change and the end result can be easily evaluated on the screen. Because of the tremendous amount of data, it takes a long time to work with a high resolution picture (18 Meg). Even a powerful computer can take up to 20 minutes just to sharpen a picture.

215

Correcting photos

The picture correction features that are usually needed to improve picture quality are brightness control and picture sharpening. We'll introduce these functions using PhotoEdge.

Because PhotoEdge is reasonably-priced, it receives wide use. PhotoEdge provides both beginners and professionals with the tools they need to work efficiently with the photo CD system.

If you already own a high-performance image processing program that doesn't support photo CD access, use PhotoEdge to convert the photo files to a format your image processing program supports. Then you won't need to update your original program to a newer version. PhotoEdge can be used to perform preliminary work for more complex image processing.

PhotoEdge

You'll Find It On The Companion CD ROM!

The images for this section and a sample picture in TIF format (LORI.TIF) are located in the \WORKSHOP\PEDGE directory.

Place the photo CD, which contains the photo to be edited, in your CD-ROM drive. If you don't have your own photo CD yet, you can also use the Windows BMP pictures on the companion CD. Then start PhotoEdge.

You have two ways to load a photo from the CD:

1. Load an individual picture by name.

2. First, load a contact sheet of the entire CD and choose the picture you want from that contact sheet.

For individual pictures, the first method is much faster but not as convenient as the second method. If you want to edit several pictures, the second method is better because you only have to load the contact sheet once. The main disadvantage to the contact sheet lies in the amount of time spent redrawing the thumbnail images; slower computer systems take quite a few seconds for a total redraw of the small images.

Loading a picture

In the menu bar, activate the **File** menu and then select **Load Photo...**. The following dialog box appears:

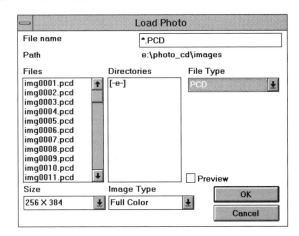

Load Photo dialog box

You can select the file name, the picture size, and the picture format in this dialog box. Also, the picture you selected is displayed as a small slide if you've activated the Preview option.

You can also use this dialog box to load pictures in other formats from the hard drive. You must specify the desired format under "File Type." Then you can input the file that you want to load by using the Directories and Files lists.

Select the file you want to load and select the picture size and format. Confirm this by clicking OK.

Loading pictures using the contact sheet

The contact sheet method makes it easier for you to select a picture, because all of the pictures on the CD appear on the screen as thumbnail images. To load a picture, double-click it. You'll be asked which resolution you want. Select **Load Contact Sheet** from the **File** menu.

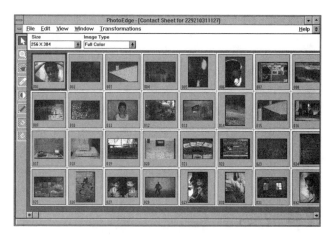

Loading a contact sheet
(\WORKSHOP\PEDGE\PEDGE1A.BMP)

Now select a picture and load it into memory by double-clicking it. Before it's loaded, you can determine the picture size and format in a dialog box.

Loading a source picture
(\WORKSHOP\PEDGE\PEDGE2.BMP)

Now the actual image manipulation begins. First, let's brighten the picture.

Underexposure is a problem that often occurs with pictures. This is especially common if there are significant contrasts and variations in brightness in the area of the field of exposure. This results in obvious underexposed areas. Either the entire picture is too dark or individual regions can barely be recognized.

Usually the source of these kinds of errors is the automatic exposure, which doesn't function properly under difficult lighting conditions. It tries to use an average value to make the best it can out of the exposure. However, then the picture seems too dark or too bright.

Unfortunately, to solve this problem, you must have some experience with photography. You must know how to trick the automatic exposure or adjust the manual settings.

However, you can use the photo CD and a computer to correct many exposure problems; this is much easier than experimenting with all the settings when taking the picture.

Changing the brightness

When the picture appears on the screen, activate the **Transformations** command. Then select **Brightness/Contrast...**.

A dialog box with two scroll bars, one for brightness and one for contrast, appears. If you move the upper scroll thumb to the right, the picture becomes brighter. To check the effect before saving the picture, click the Preview button.

Making the test picture brighter
(\WORKSHOP\PEDGE\PEDGE3.BMP)

219

Now do the same thing to correct the contrast.

Sharpening the contrast of a picture
(\WORKSHOP\PEDGE\PEDGE4.BMP)

Always use the Preview feature. Once you've saved the picture, you can't modify it as easily as you could before you saved. However, if you notice a problem immediately after performing an operation, you can still cancel the last procedure. To do this, press ⌥Alt + Bksp or select **Undo** from the **Edit** menu.

Correcting color errors

It's as easy to correct color errors as it is to adjust the brightness and contrast of a picture. Color errors always occur when you've used a type of film that wasn't suitable to the conditions of the exposure. The film material "views" the incident light differently than your eye. That's why you need to use a different film outdoors than you do for artificial light.

If you use a daylight film in rooms with incandescent lighting, the photo will have a red tinge. Occasionally, this effect may be intentional because a slight red tinge produces a warmer effect. However, this is a problem with lighting from fluorescent lamps. The film captures this type of light as a green light instead of a white light.

You can easily correct or add these color "errors" with the computer. However, it's easier to create these effects on the monitor than to print them on paper and in color. Besides a high-quality printer, you'll also need a professional image processing program that allows you to adjust your monitor and printer.

The procedure for editing the colors with PhotoEdge is the same as adjusting the brightness and contrast. A drop-down list box appears at the top of the "Brightness/Contrast" dialog box. This is where you can set the reference for changes in brightness and contrast. In addition to the setting for all colors (RGB), you can also set the basic colors so the changes only affect the red, green, or blue sections.

PhotoEdge doesn't let you change two or three color components in one step. Although you can define different brightness and contrast values for the different color components (R, G, B) in a single step, in the preview and in the final application of your settings only the modification made to the last color changed will be considered.

Sharpening a picture

Blurriness is another problem that often occurs in photos. Even cameras with automatic focus cannot guarantee sharp pictures in every situation. This occurs because usually the field of measurement is outside of the object to be photographed. The computer can usually correct this. Cameras without an autofocus feature rely on the eye and the setting of the photographer, so blurriness in this case is usually due to human error.

However, when you're filtering with the aid of your computer, remember even the computer can't fix all problems. The computer can only work with what's available. So, you can process only the picture data that's available.

When sharpening a picture, look for differences in contrast and then enhance these differences in specific ways. As a result, you'll see an apparently sharper picture. Since this method cannot distinguish between accidental and undesirable blurriness, both types will be sharpened. This is especially noticeable with portraits.

With sharpening, every impurity in the face is made more distinct. Therefore, professional image processing programs let you define certain sections of a picture, to which the filter function should be applied. However, blurriness that's caused by a shaky hand cannot be corrected even with these programs.

Now we'll demonstrate how to sharpen a picture with PhotoVision. First select the picture that you want to sharpen. Then activate **Transformations** in the menu bar and select **Filters**.

221

Sharpening a picture
(\WORKSHOP\PEDGE\PEDGE5.PCX.BMP)

From the cascading menu that appears, select the **Sharpen** command to make your picture sharper, or select **Smooth** to create a softened effect.

PhotoEdge doesn't include a Preview feature. However, you can use the **Edit/Undo** command to cancel your last action. You can repeat the process as often as you want, which can create interesting effects. Use the **Sharpen** command until you've obtained the best result.

The sharpened sample picture
(\WORKSHOP\PEDGE\PEDGE6.BMP)

The **Transformations/Filters/Invert** command is also interesting. Use this filter to create a negative image of your picture.

The sample picture as a negative
(\WORKSHOP\PEDGE\PEDGE8.BMP)

Editing sections

You can use the **Edit/Copy** command to copy the entire image. You can also crop (trim) the image. Press and hold the left mouse button, and drag a rectangle around the part of the image you want retained. Click the [Crop] button, then select **Edit/Copy**. The cropped area is copied to the Clipboard.

Run your image processing program and create a new document (if needed). Select **Edit/Paste** to paste the complete or cropped image into the window.

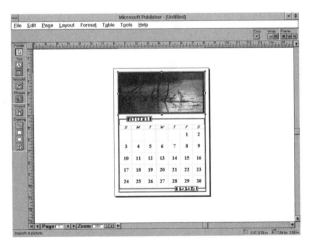

Pasting a section into the picture
(\WORKSHOP\PEDGE\PEDGE9.BMP)

223

We'll discuss working with sections of a picture in more detail later.

Paint Shop Pro

Paint Shop Pro Version 2.0 allows you to open photo CD files direct. You can also use Paint Shop Pro for simple manipulations and conversions. We've included this program on the companion CD so you can follow our examples.

There are two ways to open photo CD pictures in Paint Shop Pro. First, you can select **File/Open...**, click on the name of the .PCD file, and click OK. If you cannot open the file by this method, change to PhotoEdge, select **Edit/Copy**, switch to Paint Shop Pro, and select **Edit/Paste**.

Changing brightness

Activate the **Colors** menu and then the **Brightness/Contrast...** command. A dialog box, in which you can use two scroll bars to adjust brightness and contrast, appears. Click the Preview button to view the changes. Click OK to accept those changes, or Cancel to exit without making the change. As with PhotoEdge, you can cancel any changes with Alt + Bksp and then activate the feature again. So, you can experiment until you find the desired setting.

Changing the brightness setting

Using filters

When you activate **Normal Filters** from the **Image** menu, you'll be able to access various features that help improve your photos. These features include sharpening in different variations and softening effects. There is even a **Blur** command.

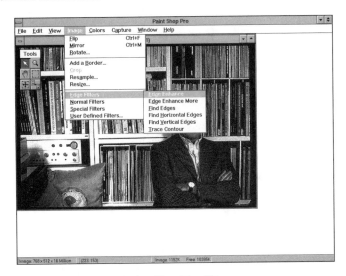

Paint Shop Pro filters

Besides selecting the desired filter, you can also define the basic colors to which the filter should be applied.

Additional Paint Shop Pro features

The **Image** menu also contains commands for rotating, mirroring, resampling, etc. You can even convert a picture to the Macintosh system.

You can also crop images using the **Image/Crop** command.

Paint Shop Pro image features

The **Edit** menu contains the commands for copying and pasting portions of the picture using the Windows Clipboard.

Special effects

You'll Find It On The Companion CD ROM!

The images for this section, and a sample picture in TIF format (LANZAROT.TIF), are located in the \WORKSHOP\EFFECTS directory.

Filters are frequently used in photography to create special effects like softening, darkening, changing colors, etc. These filters are placed in front of the lens and are used in various ways, depending on their purpose. However, there is one disadvantage to using filters. You cannot see the effect the filter creates until the film is developed. By then it's too late to fix any problems.

However, with electronic image processing, you can use filters to change a photo CD picture that is already developed. We'll use two affordable image processing programs to demonstrate how to use filters.

PhotoMagic

This inexpensive program from Micrografx Inc. includes numerous design options. We'll start with a demonstration of how filters can affect the picture.

Loading a picture

PhotoMagic lets you load pictures directly from the photo CD. Simply choose the **Open...** command from the **File** menu and select the appropriate file name. You can also select the picture from the thumbnail images by activating the "View Thumbnails" option in the "ImageBrowser Open" dialog box. In this case, simply double-click on the desired image.

Now that you've loaded the desired picture, let's add some special effects to it.

The loaded sample image

Adding noise to a picture

Select the **Effects...** command from the **Image** menu. The "EffectsBrowser" dialog box, in which you can experiment with various effects, appears.

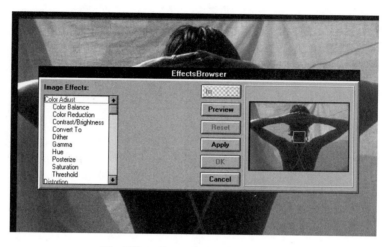

The EffectsBrowser in PhotoMagic
(\WORKSHOP\EFFECTS\PM2.BMP)

Select the effects on the left side; a small version of the picture appears on the right. A small rectangle, located in the middle of the picture, can be moved around using the mouse. The area covered by this rectangle is the area that will be edited and then displayed in a preview. Depending on the effect you selected, additional options will be available in the middle of the dialog box.

A button with the name of the selected filter is always displayed above these options. If you click this button, another dialog box appears with a description of this effect.

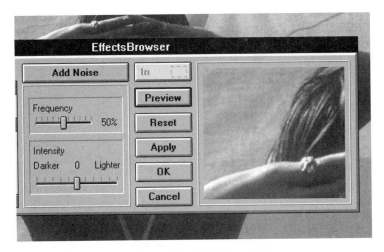

Selecting the Add Noise effect
(\WORKSHOP\EFFECTS\PM3.BMP)

Don't worry if you accidentally change the entire picture. As long as you haven't saved the picture, you can return it to its previous state by pressing Alt + Bksp or activating **Undo** in the **Edit** menu.

Select one of the effects. Try experimenting with the effects and changing the individual parameters of the filters. Always use a low-resolution image when you're experimenting.

We'll use the "Add Noise" filter as an example. When you click on Add Noise, you'll see two controls in the middle of the dialog box. You can use these controls to vary the intensity of the effect. Click the Preview button to see the results.

Adding noise to the sample picture
(\WORKSHOP\EFFECTS\PM4.BMP)

If you like an effect, click Apply to see how it affects the entire picture. This is shown in the Image window. Click OK to apply the desired effect to the entire picture.

Applying the Add Noise filter to the sample picture
(\WORKSHOP\EFFECTS\PM5.BMP)

Now you can add other effects to your picture. Keep activating the EffectsBrowser and make as many changes to your picture as you want. As we mentioned, keep trying things until you're satisfied with the result.

All the tools you need for sharpening or softening your photo are also available.

Creating a relief image from a photo

Now we'll demonstrate an interesting effect that gives a picture an embossed (relief-like) appearance.

In the "Image Effects:" list box of the EffectsBrowser, find the "Emboss" filter in the "Texture" category. You can use the control that appears to regulate the direction of the incident light, the brightness of the result, and the intensity of the effect. After you've made the settings, click Preview to see a section of the relief. If the result is satisfactory, select Apply and OK.

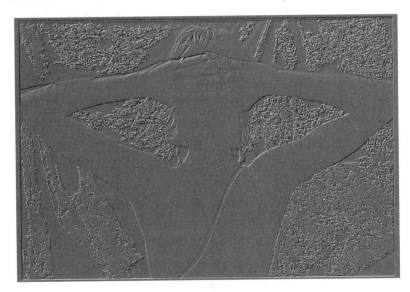

The sample picture as a relief
(\WORKSHOP\EFFECTS\PM7.BMP)

The degree of apparent depth provided by this filter depends on the contrast of the initial picture. A more pronounced embossed effect occurs with a picture that has a lot of contrast than with one that has little contrast.

231

Using the Magic Wand tool

The Magic Wand tool is an interesting tool for graphically changing a picture. For example, you can use it to edit certain areas of a picture with filters or automatically change them with colors. We'll use the Magic Wand tool more in a later example. For now, we'll use it to fill in the background.

In the toolbox on the left side of the screen, click the button with the paint can icon. A magic wand appears in the upper-left, and the mouse pointer changes into the shape of a magic wand.

Selecting colors

First select a color that you want to use to fill in areas. PhotoMagic has several ways to do this. A Color Probe tool is located on the left and two color swatches are located below, which show the foreground and the background. Simply click on one of these swatches to select the color. By double-clicking on a color swatch, you'll open a dialog box that you can use to define a color for the selected swatch.

You can also select any color that is already present in your picture. To do this, click on the Color Probe tool. The mouse pointer changes to the shape of a Color Probe tool, which you can use to pick up any of the colors in your picture.

Another method involves selecting a color from a defined palette, which is displayed below the Color Probe tool under the directory icon.

Selecting colors
(\WORKSHOP
\EFFECTS
\PM5A.BMP)

Filling in an area

Before you fill in areas of a picture with a new color, you must decide how similar these "fill-in" colors should be. Use the "Fill Range" text box above the picture to do this.

Now click on the part of the picture that must be filled in. Starting from this point, the program fills in all pixels that are in the range you specified until it comes to a color that is outside this range.

Repeat this process until you've filled in all the areas you want.

Filling part of the sample picture
(\WORKSHOP\EFFECTS\PM6.BMP)

Now we'll exit PhotoMagic and use Gallery Effects from Aldus to present some additional filter tools.

Gallery Effects

This program was designed for filtering a picture, so it doesn't have any of the painting or editing tools an image processing program usually has. However, it does contain many more filter tools. Although we can't demonstrate all these tools, we'll show you some examples.

When you start the program, a file selection window opens. Select the desired picture. Remember to use a low resolution picture for testing purposes.

Creating a watercolor painting from a photo

Activate **Effects/Gallery Effects:Classic Art**. A pull-down menu, which contains several filters, appears. Choose one of the effects from the list, or click [All Effects...].

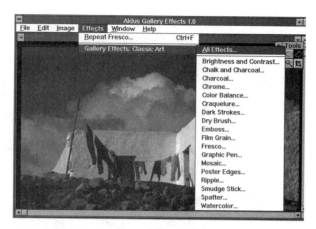

The effects in Gallery Effects
(\WORKSHOP\EFFECTS\GEFF1.BMP)

First select an effect from the menu. In our example, we used the watercolor filter. Click [Watercolor]. A window appears in which you can make changes and evaluate them using a Preview feature.

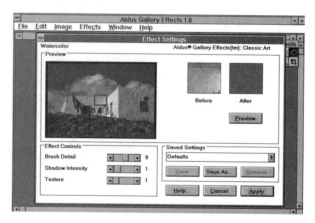

Effect Settings dialog box
(\WORKSHOP\EFFECTS\GEFF2.BMP)

Use the mouse to move the small square in the middle of the large thumbnail image to a point that will provide the best overview of the possible manipulations. This should be an area that shows a lot of details.

Positioning the detail preview
(\WORKSHOP\EFFECTS\GEFF3.BMP)

Now press the Preview button. The change is displayed in the right browse window. If the effect doesn't seem to be distinct enough, move the slider to the left and check the effect again by pressing the Preview button.

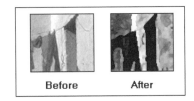

The detail preview
(\WORKSHOP\EFFECTS\GEFF4.BMP)

Once you're satisfied with the effect, click the Apply button. This changes the entire picture to match your settings. As you'll see, the result actually looks like a real watercolor painting.

The changed sample picture
(\WORKSHOP\EFFECTS\GEFF5.BMP)

If you want, continue experimenting with this effect. Once you're satisfied, save your work by selecting **Save As...** from the **File** menu.

Adding new structure to selected areas

The program provides a very interesting method for changing pictures by selecting individual sections. There is a small toolbar in the upper-right corner of the screen. Click on the button containing the dotted line. Then you can manually select an area where you want to use filters to change this area.

In the following example, the side wall of the house was highlighted.

Sample picture with highlighted area
(\WORKSHOP\EFFECTS\GEFF6.BMP)

Select the Mosaic filter as described. When you open the "Effect Settings" dialog box, the highlighted region will be displayed.

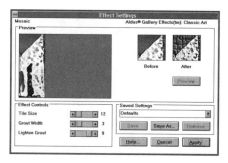

The Effect Settings dialog box for a section
(\WORKSHOP\EFFECTS\GEFF7.BMP)

Proceed as described above and apply the effect to your picture by pressing [Apply].

The picture after processing
(\WORKSHOP\EFFECTS\GEFF8.BMP)

Now the area you selected has a much more intensive structure. It's impossible to describe all the things you can do with this feature. The only limit is your imagination.

Selecting effects with preview images

Another way to select filters is by opening the **Effects** menu and selecting the first menu item, **All Effects...**. You can use the dialog box that opens to preview all the effects using two sample images.

Selecting an effect with preview images
(\WORKSHOP\EFFECTS\GEFF9.BMP)

Double-clicking opens the familiar "Effect Settings" dialog box. You can use this window to evaluate the individual filters in detail before applying them.

Changing the color balance of certain areas

We'll use the Color Balance filter in the following sample picture to change the color balance of the dark areas of the picture.

Unlike other programs, Gallery Effects lets you apply color filters to not only the entire picture or selected areas, but also to specific light or dark regions. Use the slider control to determine the color balance for the primary colors, then use the buttons to apply the effect on All, Highlights, or Shadows.

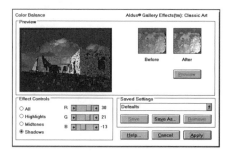

Color Balance dialog box
(\WORKSHOP\EFFECTS\GEFF10.BMP)

You can change the color of the picture using this dialog box. The best results usually occur when the colors aren't changed too dramatically.

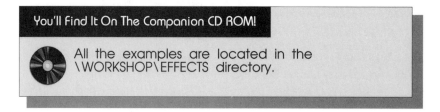

You'll Find It On The Companion CD ROM!

All the examples are located in the \WORKSHOP\EFFECTS directory.

PhotoMorph

PhotoMorph is a new program that makes it possible to generate moving sequences from individual pictures. This program uses a new technology called "morphing." You'll find several sample sequences in AVI format in the \WORKSHOP\PMORPH directory on the companion CD.

Now we'll use a brief example to demonstrate the main features of morphing using the PhotoMorph program.

Since the sequences can be stored as AVI video files, the runtime module of Video for Windows is included on the diskette with PhotoMorph. When you install the program, be sure to install this runtime module as well if you don't already own Microsoft Video for Windows.

After the program starts, the Project Editor automatically opens with its icon bar and the two working windows.

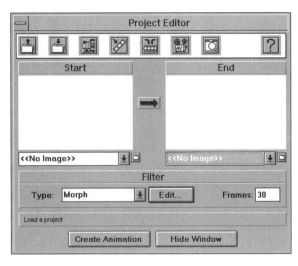

The Project Editor in PhotoMorph

Click on the working folder icon in the left image window and load your starting picture. You should use a picture of medium resolution converted to a format other than PCD. This helps with the processing speed. Now do the same thing on the right side, but, in this case, load your final picture. Now both pictures are displayed in the two working windows.

Ensure that "Type: Morph" has been selected. Then click on the ⌈Edit...⌋ button. A new working window, called the Morph Editor, appears:

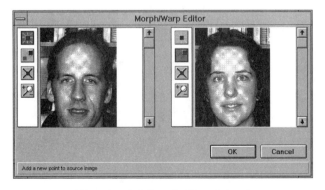

The Morph Editor in PhotoMorph

Now, in the first window, select locations at prominent points that should be transformed to corresponding points in the end picture. Then go to the second window and move the corresponding picture points so the points are approximately the same in both pictures. In our examples, the points are the hairline, the eyebrows, the eyes, etc.

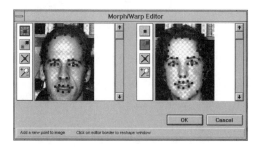

The corresponding picture points are set

Once you've set your pairs of points, click the [OK] button. Then click the [Preview] button in the icon bar. The window that appears lets you preview the individual picture and the picture sequence. If you want to save the project, do so now.

If everything is the way you want it, click the [Create Animation] button; this generates a file with the .AVI extension.

It's also possible to change the number of pictures that must be generated. You can define the form of the output file. Click the "Animation Parameters" icon (the camera icon) to display animation parameter settings in the Project Editor.

After the calculations are complete, you can view the videoclip that was just generated by using the built-in animation player.

Creating a montage

A very interesting aspect of picture processing is the ability to combine individual elements of different pictures. You can cut out interesting parts from a photo and paste them into another picture.

By doing this, you can create a completely new picture, completely unrelated to the original exposure. For example, you can place a famous person's face on another person's body. Some of these montages are so convincing that most people can't tell they are fake. This technology can be lots of fun to use; you can use your imagination to come up with amazing montages. However, don't forget about perspective. Each piece that you want to paste into a photograph must have the same dimensions as the montage photo.

You'll Find It On The Companion CD ROM!

Sample pictures demonstrating montages are located in the \WORKSHOP\COLLAGE directory.

Creating montages with PhotoStyler

In our next example, we'll use PhotoStyler to create a montage. We'll combine an image of a child and the roof of a house so it looks like the child is jumping off the roof. This is easy to do and can also be done with other image processing programs. You must have a steady hand and know how to use the available tools.

First load the picture from which you want to cut a section. To get the best possible results from editing, enlarge the picture so the object you want to cut fills the screen.

To make the copying easier and more accurate, make sure you copy the object to PhotoStyler's own Clipboard. Activate **Clipboard** from the **Edit** menu and activate the **Use PhotoStyler's** command. You must use this setting in order to paste objects, which have irregular borders, into other pictures.

Preparing to cut the child from the picture

Use the Free Selection tool to draw around the outline of the child - it looks like a lasso. When you're finished, double-click the left mouse button. Now a shiny ribbon appears around the child. Don't worry if you accidentally select too much or too little. Finish the selection process. Later you can enlarge or decrease the selection.

To enlarge the selection, simply press ⟨Shift⟩ while you trace the outline again. A small "+" appears instead of the mouse pointer when you do this. To remove sections from the selected area, select the appropriate area while pressing the ⟨Ctrl⟩ key.

When you're finished tracing around the child, select **Cut** from the **Edit** menu. The child disappears; a black outline appears in its place.

Minimize the display of the picture to keep the working screen organized. Then load the photograph in which you want to paste the cut-out section.

Cut-out of child

Use **Paste/As Selection** from the **Edit** menu to transfer the cut-out section into the new photograph.

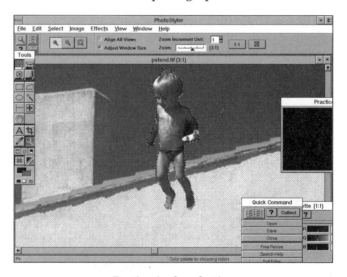

Pasting in the selection

You can move the child around in the picture by using the mouse. However, before you finally paste in the child, you must adjust its size for the new picture.

Select **Resize/Freely** from the **Image** menu. The object is surrounded by a rectangle that has handles on all four corners and in the middle of the sides. Pull on these handles with the mouse to change the object's size and shape.

After you've adjusted the size, move the object to the desired position. To disguise the fact that the object has been placed into the picture, blend it with the new background. PhotoStyler has a simple tool for doing this. Click on the tool box icon and select **Soft Edge...** from the **Select** menu. You can specify the desired width in the entry field. Enter "3" and click the "Outside" option button. Click ⌈OK⌋.

Softening the
border of the object

If there are still irregularities along the edges of the pasted object, you can remove these with the Blur tool. Activate this tool by clicking the button that contains a water drop in the image editing tool group.

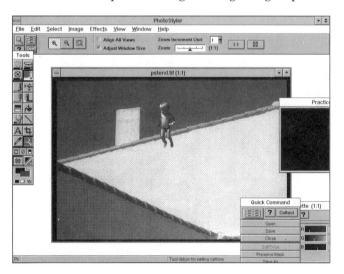

The finished picture

You must determine what you want to mix together to create an effective montage. You can also use PhotoStyler to mix several pictures with one another. For example, you can replace certain colors with contents from another picture.

243

Now we'll briefly describe how to perform similar picture manipulations by using MicroGrafx Picture Publisher.

Creating montages with Picture Publisher

Picture Publisher's low price and many features make it the application of choice among many average users.

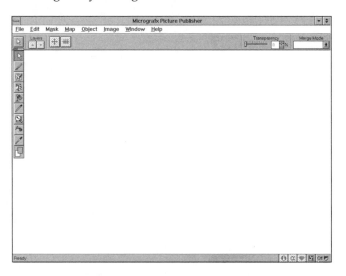

The Picture Publisher environment
(\WORKSHOP\COLLAGE\PP4.BMP)

Activate the **File** menu and select **Open....** Then select both sample pictures:

```
\WORKSHOP\COLLAGE\FLOR1.PCX
```

and

```
\WORKSHOP\COLLAGE\LESSAINT.TIF)
```

When both pictures appear on the screen, the second picture overlaps the first. Click in the title bar of the top photo, which will also be surrounded by picture handles. Drag it out of the way of the child's photo.

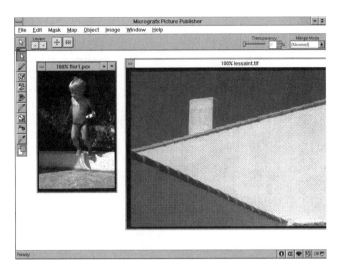

Picture Publisher and the two loaded pictures
(\WORKSHOP\COLLAGE\PP42.BMP)

Activate the picture containing the child and select the Freehand Mask
tool from the toolbar. Copy the child's image using **Edit/Copy**, then insert
the section back in with **Edit/Paste**.

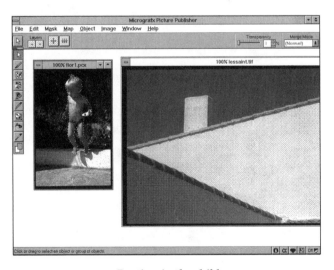

Pasting in the child
(\WORKSHOP\COLLAGE\PP43.BMP)

You can continue to edit this picture as desired. **245**

Target picture with section inserted
(\WORKSHOP\COLLAGE\PP44.BMP)

Use the paint tools to do any touch-up work. It's easy to do this if you enlarge the picture. To do that, activate the Zoom tool in the toolbar. Click on the mouse to continuously enlarge the picture.

The combined picture
(\WORKSHOP\COLLAGE\PP45.BMP)

Once the corrections are complete, save the picture as a BMP file by using **File/Save**.

As you've seen in the previous examples, most image processing programs have similar features and operate in similar ways. Obviously, professional programs, which are also more expensive, provide more layout space and convenient tools than the less expensive programs.

The professional programs emphasize the picture output. Besides being easy to use, they also allow professional color separation and support multiple color systems in order to guarantee optimal output on professional printing systems.

However, remember you don't need an expensive program to edit your photo CD pictures. Instead, the program you select should be based on your budget and the features that are provided.

Scientific applications

In this section, we'll show you how the photo CD can be used in scientific applications. This example involves using photo-imaging in the field of oral surgery. The starting condition is shown in the side view of a girl with a severe underbite.

The only way to correct this condition is with extensive oral surgery. In this case, an oral surgeon can use photo CD technology to show the girl what her jaw will look like after surgery. Until recently, trained technicians usually had to create complicated photo montages to do this. However, this procedure frequently doesn't provide satisfactory results. Therefore, the photo montage must be corrected repeatedly, which is time-consuming.

However, now the oral surgeon can use photo CD technology to show the patient the outcome of the treatment.

The procedure is relatively simple. Start PhotoStyler and open the picture of the child with the under-extended lower jaw.

The part of the lower jaw that must be modified is highlighted on the digitized picture. Use the Free Selection tool to do this. After outlining the area, double-click the mouse. A flashing line appears around the outlined area.

247

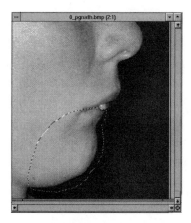

The highlighted area
(\WORKSHOP\MEDICINE\1_RECONS.BMP)

Press and hold the left mouse button and move the selected region to the desired position.

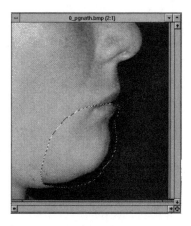

Jaw moved to the target position
(\WORKSHOP\MEDICINE\2_RECONS.BMP)

Deactivate the selected area by moving the mouse pointer to the highlighted area and then clicking the right mouse button.

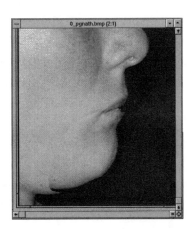

Removing the highlight
(\WORKSHOP\MEDICINE\3_RECONS.BMP)

Use the Clone and Airbrush tools to touch up the rough and cut-out areas. In PhotoStyler, the Clone tool can be accessed through the icon represented by two paintbrushes.

After you've selected this tool, hold down the Shift key and click once to define the area you want to clone. Select a point that is near the hard edge and then paint over the cut-out area.

Another way to do this is to use the Airbrush tool. Before you can use this tool, you must specify the correct color. Use the Eyedropper tool to do this. Activate the Eyedropper tool icon and pick a color near the transition area by clicking with the mouse. Now select the Airbrush tool and spray along the cut-out area.

The shape of the lips was changed and a double-chin was removed. A slight change in the area of the side of the nose completes the new profile of the patient.

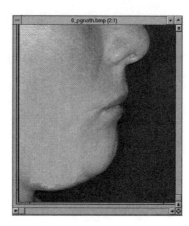

The result
(\WORKSHOP\MEDICINE\6_RECONS.BMP)

With some practice, you could perform this procedure in less than ten minutes.

Creating Different Document Types

In this section, we'll use some popular image processing programs along with layout programs to demonstrate how you can use a photo CD picture to create various types of useful documents. We'll use FreeHand, CorelDRAW!, Photoshop, and PhotoStyler to design a poster in landscape and portrait mode, an invitation, a CD cover, and letterhead.

Aldus FreeHand is very similar to CorelDRAW!. However, although these programs have the same design tools, they contain some different supplementary tools. Since they are professional image processing programs, Aldus PhotoStyler and Adobe Photoshop provide numerous tools and features. However, Photoshop currently provides the biggest selection of tools.

Designing a poster with FreeHand

First, we'll use FreeHand to demonstrate how to create posters containing photos. Since FreeHand can't read a photo CD, we must import the picture from a different format.

Converting photo CD pictures with Kodak Photo Access

Photo Access is the most affordable program you can use for photo conversions. Place the photo CD in your drive and start Photo Access. There are two ways to load one or more pictures. However, you can load a single picture by its number, which is located on the printed contact sheet. You can also use a contact sheet that you first display on the screen.

Loading the contact sheet

In the menu bar, activate the **File** menu and then select **Load Contact Sheet...**. The program checks your hardware and automatically finds all attached CD-ROM drives. The drives are displayed in a dialog box. Select the drive you want to use by clicking with the mouse. Thumbnail-sized images of all the pictures on the photo CD appear on the screen the way they look on a contact sheet.

The contact sheet

You can customize the layout of the contact sheet to a certain degree. Use **Preferences...** in the **File** menu to determine the size of each picture and the number of pictures in a row. You can also specify the number of colors or have the contact sheet displayed as a grayscale image.

Create a screen shot of the contact sheet. Simply copy the contents of the window into the Clipboard (press [Alt] + [Print Screen]). Change to the Paintbrush program and load the contents of the Clipboard with **Edit/Import**. Cut out the desired portion, save it as a file, and print the file. This is a very easy way to print contact sheets of your pictures.

All of the pictures on the photo CD probably won't be displayed because there isn't enough space on the screen. Use the scroll bars to the right and below the thumbnail images to move the page around and display the desired photograph.

Exporting a picture

To copy a picture to your hard drive in a format that can be read by your image processing program, you must click on the photo that must be converted from Photo CD Access, and then select **Export...** from the **File** menu. A dialog box, which displays a miniature version of the selected picture and provides options for defining the file format, picture resolution, and color resolution, appears.

Export dialog box in Photo CD Access

Under "Format:", select the desired file format (.BMP; .EPS; .PCX; .RIF; .TIF; .WMF) and under "Size:" indicate the desired resolution. You can choose between Wallet (Base/16 = 128x192), Snapshot (Base/4 = 256x384), Standard (Base = 512x768), Large (Base*4 = 1024x1536), and Poster (Base*16 = 2048x3072). When selecting a size, remember higher resolutions provide better quality but also require more storage space than other resolutions.

Use a lower resolution when you're experimenting with a design. The processing speed is noticeably faster. The medium resolution is best for displaying a picture on the screen, but you should use the highest resolution for printing a picture.

The last setting is for color resolution. You can choose different resolutions between 16 grayscales and true color. If you want to edit a picture, you should always select full color resolution, because that's the only way to ensure optimal editing.

After entering the name of the file without an extension (this is provided based on the file format), you can start the export process by clicking OK.

Exporting sections of pictures

Photo Access can do more than simple file conversion. You can also specify particular sections of a picture and export them. This is especially helpful if your computer doesn't have a lot of working memory (more than 4 Meg). Since it's possible to edit only sections of a picture, you can display and export portions of pictures at the highest resolution even on systems with only 4 Meg of RAM.

To define the section, use **Show Crop Window** from the **Edit** menu to open a help window that shows the selected picture in base/16 format and surrounded by a border. The dimensions of the section, in a format you can specify, appear next to and above the picture.

To move the section border, use the mouse to pull on the handles in a specific part of the picture. Then when you activate the Export function as described above, only the highlighted section will be saved at the specified resolution.

Displaying the section on the screen

To display the section on the screen, first select the resolution of the picture under **Size** in the menu bar. If you don't select a resolution, the picture will be loaded using the predefined resolution. You can change this setting by activating **Preferences...** in the **File** menu.

Load the picture by double-clicking with the mouse. You can see the size of the file below the menu bar.

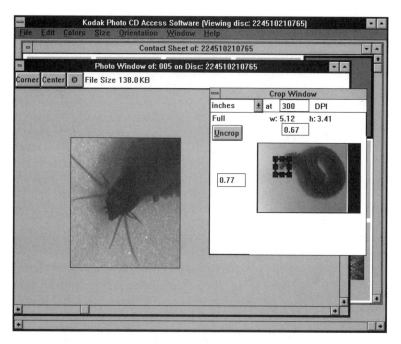

A cropped picture at high resolution and the Crop window

The picture or the section is displayed in a new window. If you've defined a very small section and you want to display the picture in a high resolution, the cropped portion may be off the screen, because the default for the display always shows the upper-left corner of the entire picture in the upper-left corner of the screen.

You can use the scroll bars to move the picture until the section appears. Photo CD Access also provides a faster way to do this. At the top of the display window you'll see two buttons:

> ➤ The Corner button lets you position the section in the upper-left corner of the window.

> ➤ The Center button lets you center it in the window.

If you trace the outline of the section with the mouse, you'll see that the mouse pointer changes into a two-headed arrow. If you press the left mouse button at this point, you can move the edge of the section, pixel-by-pixel, in the direction of the arrow.

To change the resolution in the display window, simply select the desired resolution in the **Size** menu. The picture is immediately reloaded at the new resolution.

If you press the mouse button inside the section, you can move the entire section while holding down the button.

Once you've used the options mentioned above to define the desired section, you can use **File/Export...** to store the section in another file format on your hard drive as we described. Then you can continue to edit the image using another program.

Now we're ready to create our poster with FreeHand. First activate FreeHand and then select the **New...** command from the **File** menu.

A window appears in which you can enter the size of the poster.

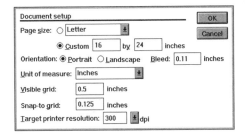

Defining the dimensions
(\WORKSHOP\GSTUDIO\POSTER1.BMP)

Enter the following:

```
Custom 16 by 24 inches
```

Then click the [Portrait] button.

```
Bleed: 0.11 inches
```

You should always indicate bleed so you have a little room for the edge of the page when you're printing a full-page picture. This way, when the film is exposed it isn't developed directly to measure. Instead, some space is left along the edge.

Confirm your settings by clicking [OK].

Activate **Ruler** in the **View** menu. Rulers appear along the left and upper edges of the screen. To display grid lines, click on the ruler; these lines can help you link text and objects.

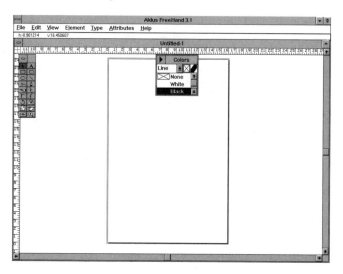

Activating the rulers
(\WORKSHOP\GSTUDIO\POSTER2.BMP)

To import a picture, activate **Place...** from the **File** menu.

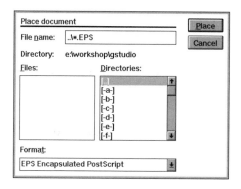

Importing a picture
(\WORKSHOP\GSTUDIO\POSTER3.BMP)

256

Indicate the format in which your picture is stored on the hard drive (TIF, PCX, BMP). Then select the directory, in which your picture is located. Double-click the desired file, and the picture is imported into the FreeHand format.

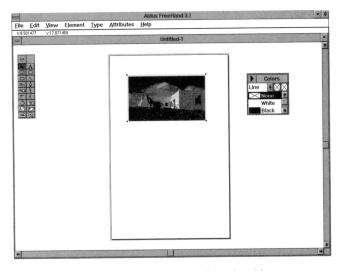

A picture was positioned on the side
(\WORKSHOP\GSTUDIO\POSTER4.BMP)

You should load the picture at the desired resolution from the very beginning so the pixels aren't visible if you enlarge the picture later. The higher the picture resolution, the better the end result.

Now you can move the picture anywhere you want with the mouse. To import text, activate the icon that contains an "A" in the toolbox.

Use the pointer, which has changed shape, to select the area where you want the text to be located. You can move this area around later. A dialog box appears in which you can type your text.

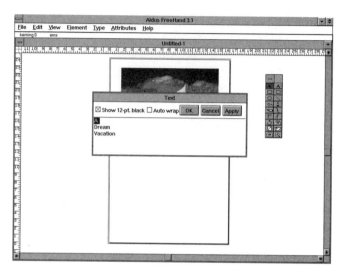

Entering text
(\WORKSHOP\GSTUDIO\POSTER5.BMP)

After you enter the text, you can change the font:

1. While holding down the left mouse button, drag the mouse across the text that must be changed. The individual characters are displayed with a black background.

2. Release the mouse button and then activate **Type Specs...** in the **Type** menu.

3. In the dialog box that appears, set the font type, size, orientation, spacing, and other individual effects that must be applied to the highlighted characters.

4. Confirm the entry with OK.

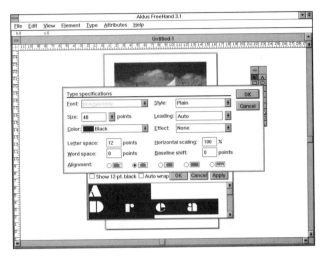

Setting the font
(\WORKSHOP\GSTUDIO\POSTER6.BMP)

Formatted text can be changed at any time. With the Text tool (the "A" icon) active, click on the text box. FreeHand displays a dialog box for you to input the text. It's usually difficult With full-page pictures to adjust the text or drawings. In this case, the Preview function is very helpful. Activate **Preview** in the **View** menu. Now it's easier to do the fine-tuning.

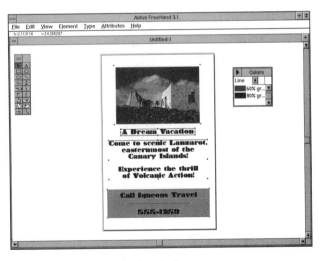

The finished poster
(\WORKSHOP\GSTUDIO\POSTER9.BMP)

259

Creating an invitation with CorelDRAW!

Another creative way to use photo CD pictures is to create your own party invitations. For example, you can use a picture of your family for a family reunion invitation.

We'll use CorelDRAW! to create our sample invitation. We don't necessarily need to use a layout program for our sample invitation.

Since we want to create a folding invitation, we must design two sides. The first side will show the inside of the invitation. We created the outside of the invitation in another file. You can see the results in the INNER.CDR and OUTER.CDR files in the \WORKSHOP\GSTUDIO\ directory on the companion CD. The picture we used is also located in this directory under the name PARTY.BMP.

Let's start with the outside of the invitation. After starting CorelDRAW! select **Page Setup...** from the **Layout** menu. Enter the size of the invitation in this dialog box.

Defining the page size

After confirming the settings with OK, draw a guideline to show where the fold should be. Drag a guideline into the working area by clicking on the ruler on the left side of the screen and drag the guideline onto the working window while pressing the left mouse button. You can define the position of the line exactly by double-clicking on the guideline. A window will appear in which you can define the position of the guideline. In our case, we need the line exactly in the middle, which, with paper 8.5 inches wide, will be 4.25 inches. Enter this value and click (Move).

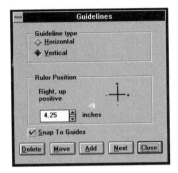

The page layout

Since the outside and the inside have the same format, save the pattern now. Then, when you're designing the inside, you don't have to define the page format and the guideline again.

After saving this data, you can start adding the text. Activate the Text tool ("A" icon) to do this. CorelDRAW! uses two kinds of text: Artistic text and paragraph text. Artistic text is suitable for short strings of text. You can enter this text immediately after clicking on a location on your page.

As its name indicates, paragraph text is suitable for longer texts. You can use more extensive paragraph formatting with this type of text. To enter this kind of text, draw a frame at the place where you want the text to be located. With either method, your pointer changes to a "+" sign while CorelDRAW! waits for your input.

After entering the text, you can change the text and the format using **Edit Text...** from the **Text** menu.

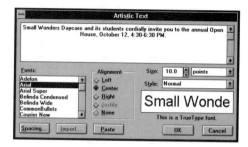

Editing the text

The **Text** menu also contains other editing options. After inputting and formatting the text, you can still use all the other design options CorelDRAW! provides. When you've finished the outside, save it under a new name.

Now let's design the opposite side. We want to import a photo on the right side of the page as part of the design. Load the layout that you just saved. Now you can import the desired picture by using **Import...** in the **File** menu. If you're using CorelDRAW! 4, you can directly import a photo CD picture.

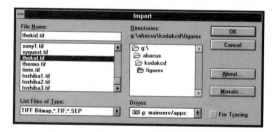

Import dialog box

Then you can adjust the picture by using the arrow pointer to move the corners in and out. If you press the Shift key while doing this, the picture won't be distorted.

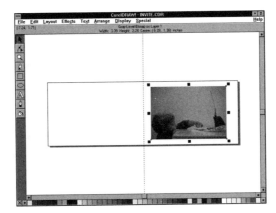

Adjusting the imported picture

Next, enter the text for the left side and format it. The invitation is finished and can be saved.

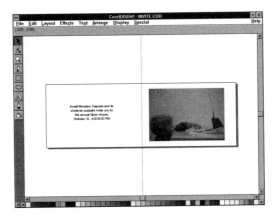

The completed invitation

Designing a CD cover

In this section, we'll create a CD cover using a landscape picture. We'll modify the picture in two different image processing programs.

Manipulating pictures with Photoshop

We'll completely change the source picture. First start Photoshop.

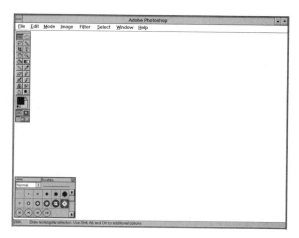

PhotoShop startup screen
(\WORKSHOP\GSTUDIO\PSH1.BMP)

Activate **Open...** in the **File** menu to load the source picture. Load the POPPIES.TIF picture.

You'll Find It On The Companion CD ROM!

You'll find this picture in the \WORKSHOP\GSTUDIO\ directory. The picture is also stored on the CD as IMG0023.PCD.

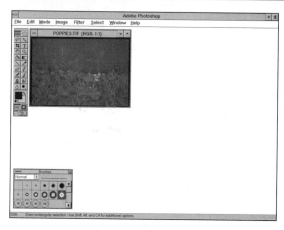

Loading the source picture
(\WORKSHOP\GSTUDIO\PSH3.BMP)

The **Filter** menu contains several options for manipulating the picture. There are filters for improving the picture and several filters that can add interesting perspectives to the picture. The **Distort** command contains filters that dramatically affect the structure of the picture. Select **Polar Coordinates...** and then "Rectangular to Polar".

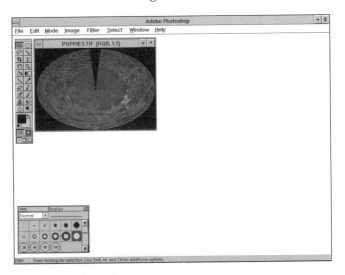

The sample picture after it's changed
(\WORKSHOP\GSTUDIO\PSH5.BMP)

The result is a variation of the picture, which is changed to a circle. Save this picture under a new name so you don't overwrite the original. You can use a program like CorelDRAW! to edit this newly manipulated image in designing the CD cover.

Manipulating pictures with PhotoStyler

Let's do a similar manipulation using PhotoStyler. Load the source picture in PhotoStyler. To create an interesting effect, activate **2D Spatial** in the **Effects** menu. Then select the **Whirlpool...** command. A dialog box appears, in which you can enter the degree of rotation.

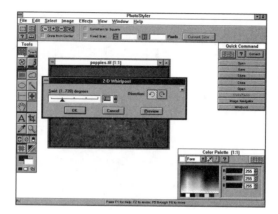

Entering the degree of rotation

The result looks different than the manipulation in Photoshop, but it shows the different features of various image processing programs.

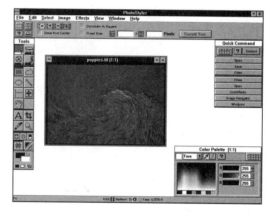

The result

Now we'll place the picture in CorelDRAW! so it can be processed further.

Although CorelPHOTO-PAINT! can also be used to manipulate pictures, we wanted to demonstrate that individual image processing programs can be combined with DTP programs, regardless of manufacturer.

Finishing with CorelDRAW!

The picture that you just modified in PhotoStyler can be imported into CorelDRAW! and arranged on the workspace, like we did in the example with the invitation.

You'll Find It On The Companion CD ROM!

The picture is in the \WORKSHOP\GSTUDIO\ directory under the name POPPIES2.TIF.

When importing, indicate the dimensions that you'll need later for your CD cover.

After you start CorelDRAW!, you must define the page format.

We want to design a slide-in CD cover to fit in a CD "jewelbox," with a picture on the front. That means we need sides that are 4.75 inches by 4.75 inches.

First, position the picture you just created using **File/Import...** in CorelDRAW!. To distort the picture further, compress it a bit lengthwise.

The page format for the CD cover

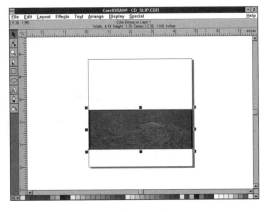

The positioned picture

267

Now create a colored background above and below the picture using borderless rectangles. Select the Box tool and draw rectangles above and below the picture. This process is much easier and more exact if you place guidelines along the upper and lower edges of the sides and on the upper and lower edges of the picture.

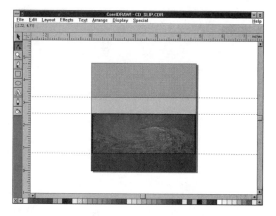

The cover with colored backgrounds

Position the text. To graphically modify the text, draw an arc along which the text will flow later. Activate the pencil icon in the toolbar. Click once just above a spiral arm of the picture and then again further right and higher, near the edge of the side. You just created a line.

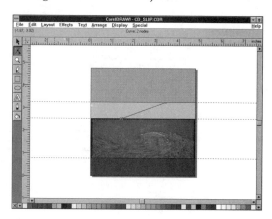

Base line for the title

Now select the tool for editing lines and double-click on an endpoint of the line. Click ToCurve in the button bar that appears; this changes the line into a curve. There is a node at each end of the line, which you can use to bend the line. Bend the line so it becomes an extension of the whirl in the picture.

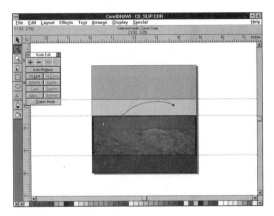

The line becomes an extension of the whirl

Now enter the title above this line, and format it using a large, rounded font. To make the font more striking, you can also extrude it. Select the pick tool and click on the text. The text will be enclosed by a selection frame. Select **Extrude Roll-Up...** from the **Effects** menu. A roll-up window, in which you can enter the necessary parameters, appears. Select "5" for the depth value.

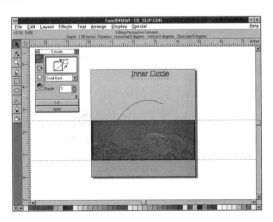

The text is extruded

269

Activate the (Colors) button, which is the bottom button in this window, to set the shading from black to white. Apply the settings by clicking the (Apply) button.

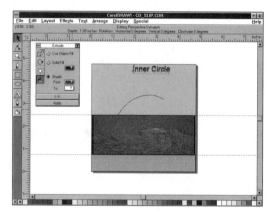

Text shading

Select the text and the curved line using the mouse and the (Shift) key. Now both objects are active. The text can be fitted to the path of the curve using **Fit Text to Path...** from the **Text** menu. First a window appears in which you can select different options for orientation of the text.

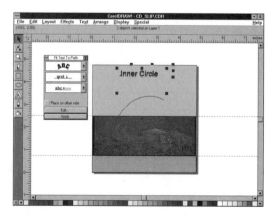

Selecting text orientation

After you've made your selection, click (Apply); the text will be fitted to the curve as desired. Now select only the curve and delete it. Then save your work and print it.

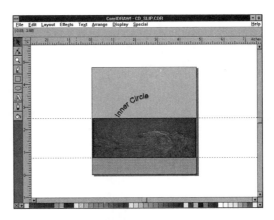

The finished cover

You'll Find It On The Companion CD ROM!

The finished picture is located in the \WORKSHOP\GSTUDIO directory under the name CD_SLIP.CDR.

Creating letterhead

In this section, we'll create letterhead containing a picture of a child. However, we'll use only a part of the entire picture. We'll use PhotoStyler to prepare the picture.

Editing the picture with PhotoStyler

Load the picture \WORKSHOP\GSTUDIO\HEADSHOT.BMP from the companion CD.

271

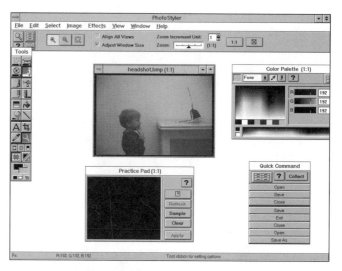

The sample picture in PhotoStyler
(\WORKSHOP\GSTUDIO\MAGIC1.BMP)

We want to extract the portion of the picture containing the child and then edit this portion so we can create a silhouette. Then we'll use the silhouette in the letterhead.

Fortunately, the background in our sample picture is quite uniform. However, for a silhouette, the background must be white and the object (in this example, the child) must appear in black.

There are several ways to extract the portion of the picture containing the child. One way is to use the Free Selection tool to trace around the child and then copy it, as we described earlier. However, there is a faster and easier way to do this. Simply color the background white and then copy a rectangular section.

First, select a white foreground color. Double-click on the rectangle that represents the foreground color. The "Color Picker" dialog box appears.

The best way to define pure white is to use the HSB (Hue, Saturation, Brightness) settings. Click the "H:" option button and type 0 in the corresponding text box. Click the "S:" option button and type 0 in the corresponding text box. Finally, set the brightness at 100% and click OK.

Now we'll use the Bucket Fill tool. You can use this to fill areas that have the same color as the foreground color.

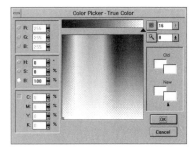

To set the color similarity, click on the icon and select the value 50 next to the "Similarity:" item. Confirm and click on the background near the child. The background is immediately filled with white. If parts of the child are filled too much, select **Edit/Undo** and click at another location.

Choosing the foreground color
(\WORKSHOP\GSTUDIO
\MAGIC2.BMP)

To fill the areas of the background near the child, which aren't filled yet, repeatedly click on these areas.

Filling the background with white
(\WORKSHOP\GSTUDIO\MAGIC3.BMP)

Then copy the child into a new picture. Use the rectangular Outline tool to draw a frame around the child, and select **Copy** from the **Edit** menu. Create a new picture containing only the child by using **Edit/Paste/As New Document**.

273

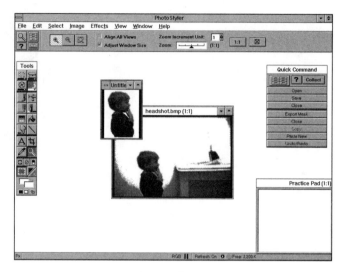

A new picture
(\WORKSHOP\GSTUDIO\MAGIC4.BMP)

Use the Eraser tool to remove any colored pixels still remaining in the background. To smooth the edges of the child, use the Blur tool on the picture.

Next, generate the silhouette by selecting the Magic Wand tool and click on the white background. The background is immediately highlighted. Hold down the ⟨Shift⟩ key and click briefly (adding to a highlighted region) on the area beneath the child's hand that is not highlighted. To highlight only the child, you must invert the highlighting. Click the ⟨Inverse⟩ button to do this.

Now it's easy to create the silhouette. Click on the upper-left Mask button (the black triangle). The white silhouette of the child appears. Select **Image/Tune/Negative** to invert the picture and produce the silhouette of the child.

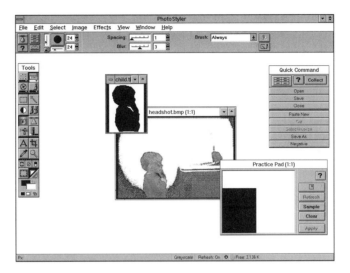

Creating a silhouette
(\WORKSHOP\GSTUDIO\MAGIC5.BMP)

Select **File/Save As...** and save the file.

Creating the letterhead with FreeHand

You'll need to create a new letter-size document in Freehand, then place the graphic using **File/Place....** To improve the letterhead's appearance, add color. Specify the colors using **Attributes/Fill & Line....**

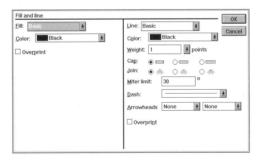

Selecting colors in FreeHand
(\WORKSHOP\GSTUDIO\FRH4A.BMP)

275

First, in the "Fill:" drop-down list box, change the setting from "None" to "Basic", and then in the "Colors:" drop-down list box, change the colors to the appropriate settings. You must specify the type of colors used (e.g., Pantone colors).

If you will be using only two or three colors, and you will be having the final product exposed and printed, then you should choose the Pantone color scale.

Use the four-color process, because it produces the least problems (magenta, cyan, yellow and black are standards). Besides, the program automatically adjusts the screen angles in the four-color process so moires aren't generated.

Another alternative is to first determine the colors via Pantone colors and then change to four-color process later. If the Pantone color selection is active instead of the full-tone color, the change is automatically made in the four-color process.

A selection window opens when you activate **Attributes/Colors....**

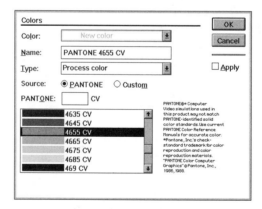

Setting colors
(\WORKSHOP\GSTUDIO\FRH5.BMP)

Click the "Custom" option button. Select the desired color and click OK.

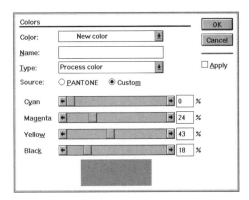

Adjusting hues
(\WORKSHOP\GSTUDIO\FRH6.BMP)

Hues can be adjusted very precisely. By using the square icon in the toolbar, while pressing the Shift key, you can fill the entire page. To make the silhouette motif visible again, activate **Element/Bring to front**.

The toolbar contains several options you can use to personalize the letterhead.

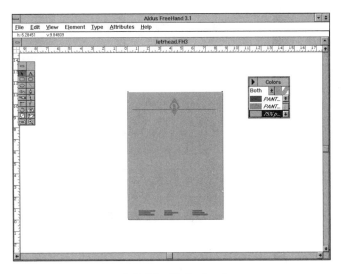

A finished letterhead
(\WORKSHOP\GSTUDIO\FRH7.BMP)

You'll Find It On The Companion CD ROM!

You'll find the letterhead in FreeHand format in the \WORKSHOP\GSTUDIO directory under the name LETRHEAD.FH3.

Creating the letterhead with Word for Windows

You don't need a professional program like FreeHand to create an attractive letterhead. You can also create letterhead with Word for Windows or any other powerful word processing program.

We'll use an example in Word for Windows to demonstrate how easy it is to link our sample picture to a letterhead. Activate Word for Windows and create a new document. Since we want to create letterhead, you should display the graphic in a header. So, select **Header/Footer...** from the **View** menu and then confirm the question in the dialog box with OK.

Now import the picture of the child using **Insert/Picture...**. In the dialog box that appears, click on the desired file and click OK. The picture is loaded into your letterhead.

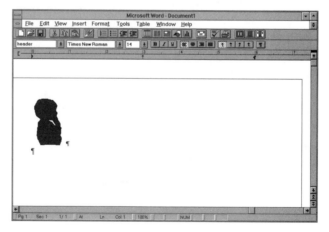

The loaded sample picture
(\WORKSHOP\GSTUDIO\BKF1.BMP)

Now click on the picture to highlight it. Then double-click the highlighted area; Microsoft Draw starts automatically. Use this program to edit the picture. For example, you can add additional graphical elements and text.

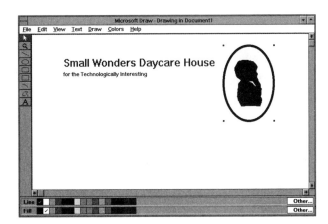

Editing the letterhead in Microsoft Draw
(\WORKSHOP\GSTUDIO\BKF2.BMP)

To exit Microsoft Draw, select **File/Exit...** to return to Word for Windows. A dialog box asks whether you want to apply the changes to the Word document. Answer yes; you'll see the following:

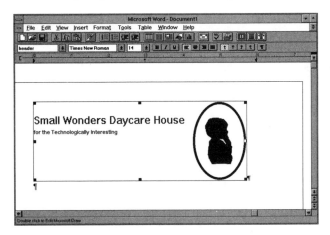

The Word document with letterhead
(\WORKSHOP\GSTUDIO\BKF3.BMP)

Now you can save this document as a new document style sheet and use it any time you need letterhead.

You'll Find It On The Companion CD ROM!

The Word for Windows document used in this example is located under \WORKSHOP\GSTUDIO\LETRHEAD.DOC.

Creating calendars

In this section, we'll create a calendar using Microsoft Publisher. This program includes a Wizard (an assisting program) that helps you design your document by asking certain questions. When the calendar is complete, you can either print it out or take the file to a professional printing shop.

First start Microsoft Publisher. A window, which provides the option of working with the assistant, appears.

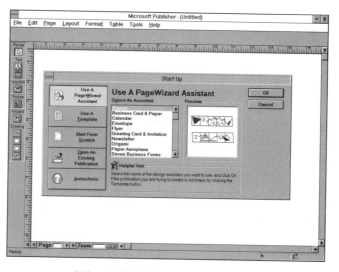

Microsoft Publisher startup screen
(\WORKSHOP\GSTUDIO\MSPL1.BMP)

For our example, select "Calendar" and click OK. After a brief pause, the logo of the calendar assistant appears.

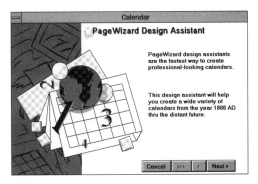

The calendar assistant
(\WORKSHOP\GSTUDIO\MSPL2.BMP)

Now click Next>. The assistant asks you some questions about the calendar's layout.

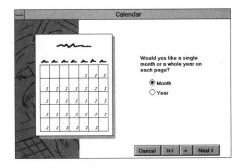

Annual or monthly calendar
(\WORKSHOP\GSTUDIO\MSPL3.BMP)

Choose whether you want to prepare a monthly or an annual calendar. Then determine the format. The layout is defined in the next window. Click on the individual options and the assistant will show you the respective layouts.

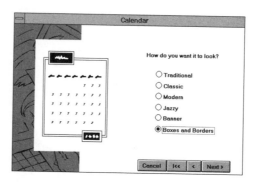

Calendar formats
(\WORKSHOP\GSTUDIO\MSPL4.BMP)

In the following dialog box, you have the option of pasting a picture into the calendar page.

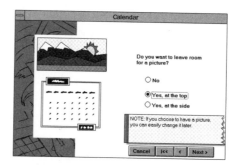

Creating space for a graphic
(\WORKSHOP\GSTUDIO\MSPL5.BMP)

The picture that's displayed can be exchanged later with a photo CD picture. You can also make additional changes in the calendar. After indicating the year, selecting the months, abbreviations and language, the assistant prepares the calendar.

A small window at the lower edge of the screen informs you of the progress. If the processing is too slow, move the scroll thumb to the right. After a short time, the calendar is finished. Now you must add your pictures. There are two ways to do this. You can link a graphic as an object via another program that supports OLE, or you can directly import the finished graphic.

Activate **Edit/Insert Object...** in the menu bar.

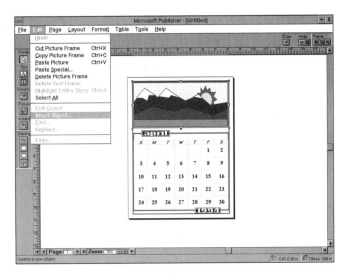

Linking your own pictures as objects
(\WORKSHOP\GSTUDIO\MSPL6.BMP)

Select the program, or the OLE server, that you want to use to insert the picture. The sample picture is IMG0009.PCD, which is on the companion CD.

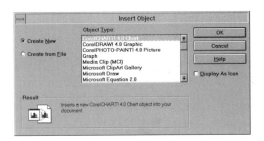

Selecting an OLE server
(\WORKSHOP\GSTUDIO\MSPL7.BMP)

As an alternative to image linking described above, Publisher provides graphic linking that is independent of other image processing programs. However, to use it, your finished calendar pictures must already be located on the hard drive.

Activate **File/Import Picture...** and look for the desired file in the dialog box that appears.

283

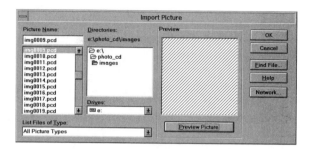

Importing graphics
(\WORKSHOP\GSTUDIO\MSPL8.BMP)

When selecting a picture, you should view it before transferring it. Click OK to incorporate the selected picture into the calendar page.

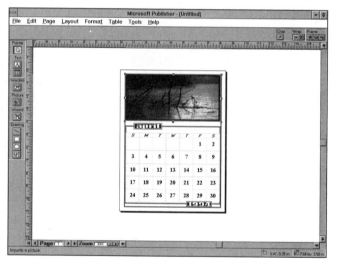

Linking the graphic

The picture is surrounded by eight small squares. You can use these squares to change the picture dimensions with the mouse pointer. By pulling on each individual square, you change the side and edge ratio of your picture until it fits exactly in the calendar page. If you click in the middle of the picture, the picture is moved as a unit.

Once the picture is in the desired location, change to page two. To change working pages, use the arrow keys at the lower-left edge of the picture. A small window shows the page number. You can also save each page separately.

A test print shows the results of your work. Now practice using the example we just described. You'll find that working with Publisher is extremely easy. It won't take long before you take advantage of all the options the assistant offers.

NOTE

Remember to use only low picture resolution when practicing.

Printing pictures

Besides printing pictures on your own printer, occasionally you may want to have your pictures printed professionally. This is necessary in order to obtain high-quality color output. In this section, we'll discuss how you can do this and explain the different types of output.

Screen printing

Besides the usual options for editing electronic pictures, many professional print shops also provide many other interesting services. For example, they can use a specific photo from a photo CD and imprint it on the following items:

> Paper prints   > Sweatshirts   > Coffee cups

> Mouse pads   > T-shirts   > Business cards

> Puzzles   > Pillows   > Canvas bags

You can also process your own photos and send the final product as a file to the printer.

Overview of the printing process

The easiest way to print a picture from a photo CD is by taking it to a professional printing company. The quality is almost as good as a print made from a slide, but it is much more expensive.

To get a printout of a picture you've modified, follow these steps:

1. Start your image processing program.

2. Import the desired picture from the photo CD.

3. Define the picture size. If you're using an existing layout, all the information will already be noted there.

4. Set the basic parameters of your image processing program based on the printer requirements. Ask the printing company about these requirements. This helps avoid problems that may occur, which add time and expense to the process.

5. Save the export format.

6. Import the picture into a layout program.

7. Match the text and the picture with each other.

8. Save the finished work and copy it to an external data storage device. We recommend using a Syquest cartridge for this purpose, since it usually provides sufficient capacity and is the most widely used medium for desktop publishing. Don't forget to include all the necessary files.

9. Include all the information that the printer will need, such as grid size, color separations, and file size.

10. Print the film.

With a thermal transfer printer, you can print your files with professional printer-like quality before the film is prepared. By doing this, you can locate and fix any errors before sending the file out. However, digital prints are usually output in three colors, but the actual printing is done in four colors. With enough practice, however, you can use the digital output as a quality control step.

The print is made from the film later. However, before you can provide the printer with the necessary information, you need proofs to show you the individual scannings and resolutions. Ask the printer for this information.

Once you've completed image processing, copy your picture in PS, TIFF, or TARGA format on a Syquest cartridge. Then bring your file to a special printing company. For approximately $20, you can have your picture printed as a miniature slide. The quality almost matches that of a photo CD picture, if you give them a 16 base file.

The slide can then be processed further just like a normal slide. This process takes about two days.

Special services from the photo lab

For a price, some printers can produce posters of a photo CD picture or of pictures you've modified yourself. At a maximum picture width of six feet (about two meters), the length of the picture is practically unlimited.

Camera equipment

An expensive method for processing your pictures further is to purchase equipment for making exposures. Polaroid, which is known for its instant photos, offers some equipment that is affordable by nonprofessionals.

Polaroid Color Picture Recorder

Polaroid produces several types of color picture recorders. The starter model CI-1000, the enhanced models CI-3000 S, CI 5000 S, and LFR, the new Personal LFR, and the new high-end model, LFR Mark II. Obviously, the more features the model has, the more expensive it is.

Quality slides can be produced even with the CI-1000. These are suitable for presentations and lectures.

Color picture recorders can also be used to create an enlargement of photo that was modified on a computer. With the exposure, you once again have a photo which can be enlarged as usual.

Ordinary film can be used in all of the color picture recorders, including Polaroid instant slide film. The possibilities for different applications are enormous.

All color picture recorders can be used on PC and Macintosh systems. The necessary software is included with the instruments, which assures extensive compatibility with common DTP and image processing programs.

287

Polaroid color picture recorder CI-1000

Color recording devices aren't intended for nonprofessionals, but some businesses, such as advertising agencies, can apply this technology. Also, these devices are extremely helpful to educational institutions because they can create their own slides for classroom presentations.

Picture output for a photo lab

We'll use Aldus FreeHand to demonstrate the procedure for sending an edited picture to a photo lab.

288

In FreeHand, the colors are defined using the **Attributes/Fill & Line...** command. When the dialog box appears, first change the setting for "Fill:" from "None" to "Basic" on the left side of the box. Then change the color setting in the "Colors:" drop-down list box. Here you have to decide between Pantone colors, four-color process, full-tone color, and hues.

If you want to use only two or three colors, and you want to send out the whole thing for exposing and printing, you should select Pantone scale.

Since the monitor isn't "true color", even at a resolution of 16.7 million colors, you should use color palettes for orientation. Otherwise, you may find the ocean blue color you wanted appears as a greenish turquoise on the print.

We recommend using the four-color process, because you won't encounter any problems with it (magenta, cyan, yellow, and black are standardized). Besides, the program automatically adjusts the screen angles during the four-color process, so there are no moire patterns. Books of color values are available. You can use these books to mix colors correctly. You probably shouldn't try to create mixtures manually because you cannot tell whether the mixture will actually correspond to what you wanted before the print is made.

An alternative method involves defining the color using Pantone colors and later changing to the four-color process. If during the Pantone color-definition process a full-tone color isn't activated, the change to the four-color process occurs automatically.

Once everything is ready, you should talk to the photographer. It's important to know which kind of camera he or she will use for the exposure. You should also determine whether the photographer's system and software are compatible with your own. Using a job sheet like the following ensures that you'll have all the necessary information.

Photographic job sheet (example)

Customer:	Neumann & Co.
Your job no.:	
Contact person:	Jerry Neumann
Extension:	
Our job no.:	

Information about the file

Program:	FreeHand 3.1 or CorelDRAW! 4.0
File name:	TESTSHOT.FH3 (an example)
Operating system:	MS-DOS 5.0 or 6.0, or OS2
Import formats:	none or exact format description
Fonts, styles:	Helvetica (Black) (an example)

Printout parameters

Printing machine:	Linotronic 500 *(frequently used color recorder)
Print made on:	Film - SV positive *(reversed positive, so the printed product appears right side up (depends on the printing process: offset or letterpress))
Resolution:	500 lines *(provides a very high-contrast print, high-quality)
Number of pages:	One or more
Format:	Letter, smaller or larger
Cut:	trim, color name *(coding the film to be exposed for better quality control after the exposure in reference to the color)
Size of print:	100%
Grid:	60 *(average grid for offset printing)
4c-colors:	Black (four-color printing)
Overprinting:	black *(you'll need to try out the combination of overprinting and leaving areas open on your own)

Deadlines:

Estimated completion date:	4/15/93
Job submitted:	3/29/93
Status:	3/30/93

If you have questions about any of the specific points, you should talk to the photographer. The photographer can complete an itemized invoice which should include the following valuable information:

- ➤ Materials used
- ➤ Materials for misprints
- ➤ Postage
- ➤ Discounts
- ➤ Exposure time in minutes
- ➤ Courier travel
- ➤ Telephone charges
- ➤ Net amount

Invoices with this information can help you calculate the costs involved in creating a print. With complicated prints using scanned and/or revised pictures, the exposure time can quickly increase. This prevents the photographer from creating other exposures. With twenty colors, this process is very expensive.

Exposing an electronic picture

Creating an exposure of an electronic picture is an extremely complicated process. It requires a lot of knowledge and experience. Although you may not completely understand this process, it does illustrate the problems associated with printing an electronic picture.

The following summarizes the most important points mentioned above:

Information about the file:	
Program	The program that was used to create the file
File name	Use an easily recognizable file name
Operating system	DOS or Mac
Import formats	Imported pictures have to be named
Font types	Describe the desired font that you used in editing your file

Output parameters	
Output device:	(For example, LINOTRONIC 500)
Output on:	(Paper or film; inverted or not; positive or negative)
Number of pages:	
Format:	Indicate a standard format (although this isn't necessary)
Print size:	100% or 200% with trim marks
Grid:	Indicate the grid
Colors:	The standard colors are cyan, magenta, yellow, and black
Decorative colors:	Pantone
Remarks:	(For example, convert from DOS to Mac)
Itemized photo bill:	(completed by photographer)
Font types:	Describe the desired font that you used in editing your file

Itemized photo bill (completed by photographer)	
Materials used:	(For example, LINOTRONIC 500)
Exposure time:	(Paper or film; inverted or not; positive or negative)
Materials for misprints:	
Delivery:	Indicate a standard format (although this isn't necessary)
Postage:	100% or 200% with trim marks
Telephone:	Indicate the grid
Discounts:	Itemized photo bill
Decorative colors:	Pantone
Remarks:	(For example, convert from DOS to Mac)

The difference between four-color printing and printing with decorative colors (i.e., Pantone colors) is the printing costs. Four-color printing consists of the four basic colors established by the printing industry:

> Magenta   > Cyan

> Yellow   > Black

Since all colors can be prepared using these primary colors, printing machines are set up for these colors. They have these colors available in large quantities and can immediately begin with the four-color process, without any other expenses, as soon as they receive your film.

The Pantone colors cost more than the primary colors since they're specially made. Part of these "decorative colors", which are already premixed, are the HLS (Hue-Lightness-Saturation) colors, which are treated like Pantone colors.

The price sets the tone. If the final result, whether it's a picture, poster, etc., can be produced more economically with comparable quality, usually the less expensive method is used. However, occasionally this means that the image processing program must make conversions.

Creating Presentations

All types of presentations can be enhanced by adding slides of photos. These slide shows support the information that's being presented and provide a visual aid for understanding the material.

With the help of presentation programs, you can use your computer to create presentations that feature slides. Although presentation programs have been available for a while, the ability to read pictures into the computer easily and inexpensively is fairly new. The photo CD makes this possible.

Microsoft PowerPoint

In this section, we'll use Microsoft PowerPoint to create a presentation. You can also create presentations with CorelSHOW! or similar programs.

Remember, for a computer presentation, the pictures you use shouldn't be processed at full resolution, since the screen doesn't support this resolution anyway. Besides, the presentation would be extremely slow because of the long loading times.

However, if you'll be using the pictures from the presentations as individual slides, you should use the 4-base or 16-base format. In this case, a high resolution produces better results.

Start Microsoft PowerPoint. In the startup screen that appears, you'll see borders around the title line and the main section below. Highlight this section by clicking the mouse in the middle of the framed field.

Since we're working with the photo CD, first load a picture. To do this, activate **Insert/Picture...**.

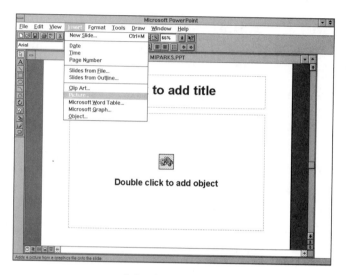

Selecting a picture
(\WORKSHOP\SHOW\PPTPARK1.BMP)

A dialog box appears in which you can select the desired picture.

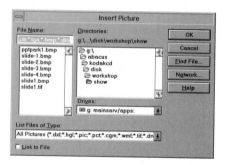

PowerPoint supports several graphics formats
(\WORKSHOP\SHOW\PPTPARK2.BMP)

Look for your picture file and click on it, then click OK. After a brief pause, the picture appears in the main workspace.

Inserting a picture
(\WORKSHOP\SHOW\PPTPARK3.BMP)

Now you can change the size of the picture. To do this, activate **Scale...** in the **Draw** menu.

Change Size dialog box
(\WORKSHOP\SHOW\PPTPARK4.BMP)

You can change the picture's size as desired.

To add text, activate the Text tool by clicking the button containing the "A" symbol in the toolbar. Then move the cursor to the place where you want to insert the text. After you've entered the text, you can change the font size, style, and color using the **Font...** command from the **Format** menu. Use the toolbar to define the text attributes.

A picture with text
(\WORKSHOP\SHOW\PPTPARK5.BMP)

After you've made all the desired changes, save the file. To do this, open the **File** menu and activate **Save As....** This also assigns a name to the presentation. Now continue with the second slide.

Click on the New Slide... button in the lower-left portion of the screen. An empty screen appears again, waiting for you to fill it with information. Now load another picture and enter the desired text. Repeat this process for the remaining slides. After saving them, you can view your presentation.

Now change to your first slide. The easiest way to do this is to move the slider bar on the left up. The status line indicates which slide is loaded. Click on the screen icon in the icon bar on the right. Your first slide now appears on the screen.

Click the mouse to change to the next picture. At the end of your presentation, you'll automatically return to the PowerPoint screen.

Usually the best screen presentations are those that run automatically. In PowerPoint, you can easily create an automatically running, non-stop presentation. To do this, select the **Slide Show...** command in the **View** menu. The following dialog box opens:

The Slide Show dialog box
(\WORKSHOP\SHOW\PPTS1A.BMP)

Click the "Rehearse New Timings" option button and start the presentation by clicking the (Show) button. When the first picture of the presentation appears, you'll see a button in the lower-left corner of the screen.

Click this button, which indicates the display time in seconds, when you think the picture should be changed. Repeat this step for each picture. At the end of your slide show, a dialog box, which recommends that you save the time settings, appears. After you've saved the settings, the show can run automatically.

You can also create a non-stop presentation. To do this, activate the "Run Continuously Until 'Esc'" check box in the "Slide Show" dialog box.

It's also possible to modify your presentation at any time. For example, you can add three-dimensional effects to your pictures. This makes your picture look as if it's lying on the surface of the screen. You can create this effect by adding shading to the back of the pictures and the text. To do this, select **Shadow...** in the **Format** menu. You can select the color of the shading in the dialog box that opens.

As you can see, it's easy to create a slide show with text and a few enhancements. However, this is just a small sample of the features PowerPoint offers.

You'll Find It On The Companion CD ROM!

 The finished presentation (MIPARKS.PPT) and the pictures that were used are located in the \WORKSHOP\SHOW\ directory.

When creating a presentation that will be used on the computer, use pictures with low resolution. The slide show should flow smoothly. So, long loading times delay the presentation unnecessarily. For the best results, use a 486/50 MHz computer to run the presentation. However, a simple 386SX is sufficient.

Also, use a low color resolution. Although true-color pictures are attractive, they take up a lot of storage space and take a long time to load. If your presentation will be run on other machines, you should reduce the number of colors to 256 for the pictures.

After Dark

After Dark is a screen saver program. The main purpose of screen saver programs is to prevent "monitor burn-in." This occurs when the same image is displayed on the screen for long periods of time. The screen saver automatically changes the screen display after a certain amount of time passes without keyboard or mouse activity.

Usually these programs aren't used as presentation programs. However, this is possible with After Dark because it has a module for linking images.

Double-click the After Dark icon. The "After Dark Control" window appears. On the left side of the window, you can select the individual modules and even combine them with one another.

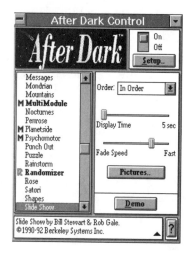

After Dark Control window

Select "Slide Show". On the right side of the window, click the Pictures... button. In the dialog box that appears, select the desired directory. After Dark displays all of the BMP files in this directory.

Besides selecting the directory, you can also determine the delay time for the pictures and specify whether the pictures should be displayed in the order they are listed in the directory or randomly.

To start a sample show, use the Demo button, which is hidden by the "After Dark Control" window until needed. There is also another way to start the screen saver. With the Setup... button, you can define a corner of the screen, in which you can start the screen saver, without a time delay, by moving the mouse pointer to that corner.

Therefore, minimize the control window and move the mouse pointer into the activating corner. You'll immediately see all the .BMP pictures in the directory you selected as a slide show.

The ability to combine several modules in After Dark is especially interesting. In the control window, you'll see some multimodules that were already created; they're indicated with an "M." You can use the empty multimodule to design new ones. Move the selection bar to that point and a New button will appear to the right, which lets you input a new definition.

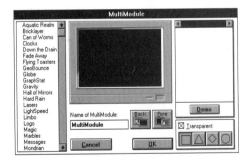

Defining multimodules

You can select the desired modules on the left side just like before. In the middle, you can determine where the individual modules will be displayed on the screen. On the right side, you see the control windows of the selected modules.

It's fun to combine messages with sounds. This is an inexpensive way to create a multimedia slide show.

Obviously, an After Dark presentation cannot be compared to one created with a real presentation program. However, by adding text to the pictures with appropriate image processing or DTP programs before linking the pictures to the screen saver, you can create a quality presentation.

Your Companion CD
Your Companion CD

CHAPTER 5

Your Companion CD

By using the companion CD, you can begin experimenting with the photo CD system immediately. However, it's not only a photo CD. It also contains programs and pictures in other formats.

You can insert this CD in your photo CD player like a normal photo CD and view it on a television. If you insert the CD in the CD-ROM drive of your computer, you can use your photo CD Access software to access the photo CD pictures and read all the other data as you normally do. However, your CD-ROM drive must support the XA standard.

Contents of the CD

Besides sample pictures in the photo CD format and other formats, the companion CD also contains all the examples from Chapter 4. There are also shareware programs that can be used with the photo CD, a demo version of PhotoStar from Microtek, and more on the CD.

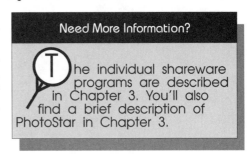

Need More Information?

The individual shareware programs are described in Chapter 3. You'll also find a brief description of PhotoStar in Chapter 3.

Directories

The following is an overview of the directories located on the CD:

Directory			Files and Information
BOOKFIGS			Contains figures from the book
	256_COL		256-color versions
	TRUECOL		True Color versions
CDI			Contains the files that are needed to play this CD with CD-I players
COREL			Sample photographs from the COREL photo collection
PHOTO_CD			Contains Kodak Photo CD system files
	IMAGES		Contains image packs
	RIGHTS		Additional information for the images
PSTAR			PhotoStar from Microtek
	IMAGE		PhotoStar image information
	DATA		PhotoStar data
	CLIPART		PhotoStar clip art
SFW			Seattle FilmWorks materials
SHAREWAR	ALCHEMY		Alchemy Mindworks shareware
		GWS11F	Graphic Workshop v.1.1f for Windows
		QSHOW	QuickShow
	JASC		JASC shareware items
		IMGCMDR	Image Commander software package
		PSP20	Paint Shop Pro 2.0
	PIXF20		PixFolio 2.0
	THUMBS		ThumbsUp software package

Directory	Files and Information
WORKSHOP	Contains pictures and examples from Chapter 4
COLLAGE	Picture collage (Chapter 4)
EFFECTS	Filter effects
GSTUDIO	Private graphics studio (Chapter 4)
MEDICINE	Scientific applications (Chapter 4)
PMORPH	PhotoMorph (Chapter 4)
QSSLIDE	QuickShow Light slide show
SHOW	Microsoft PowerPoint slide show (Chapter 4)

Using the CD

If you want to take a fast tour of the companion CD, we recommend you take advantage of the START.EXE interface program you'll find on the root directory of the companion CD.

To run START.EXE, select **File/Run...** from the Program Manager. When the "Run" dialog box appears, type the drive letter of your photo CD drive, a colon, and the name START.EXE. For example, if your CD-ROM drive is drive E:, you would type:

```
E:START.EXE
```

Click [OK] or press [Enter].

The main screen of the START.EXE program looks like this:

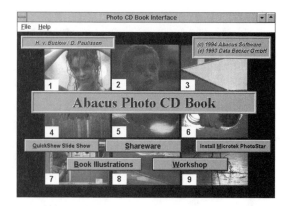

The main screen of the START program

As you can see, clicking on a button will take you through different parts of the CD. Here is what each button does when you click it:

Button	Purpose
QuickShow Slide Show	Runs the QuickShow Light Slide Show, with a set of graphics from Chapter 4 (more on this later).
Shareware	Opens a dialog box, from which you can select one of a number of shareware products.

Shareware dialog box

Button	Purpose
Install Microtek PhotoStar	Clicking this button installs the Microtek PhotoStar software.
Book Illustrations	Clicking this button displays a dialog box from which you can select figures in 256-color format or True Color format.

Throughout the book, you'll find references to pictures that are located on the companion CD. True Color pictures are stored in the \BOOKFIGS\TRUECOL directory, while you'll find 256 color pictures in the \BOOKFIGS\256_COL directory. These pictures are shown only as grayscale pictures in the book, but they are more impressive in color.

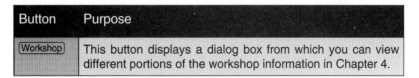

Button	Purpose
Workshop	This button displays a dialog box from which you can view different portions of the workshop information in Chapter 4.

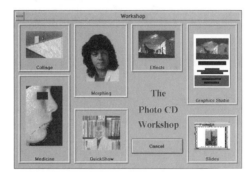

Photo CD Workshop dialog box

The \WORKSHOP directory contains the subdirectories accessed by the elements of this dialog box. To display the pictures faster on the screen, you should install the shareware program Paint Shop Pro, which is in the \SHAREWAR\JASC\PSP20 directory. Install it by copying the contents of the \SHAREWAR\JASC\PSP20 directory to a directory on your hard drive, then use **File/New...** from the Program Manager to create a group for Paint Shop Pro, and add Paint Shop Pro to that group.

QuickShow Light Slide Show

QuickShow Light, an exceptional viewer program designed by Canadian shareware author Steve Rimmer (aka Alchemy Mindworks), exists in two locations on the companion CD. You can run QuickShow Light on your own, but we took the liberty of creating a slide show using QuickShow Light.

You'll Find It On The Companion CD ROM!

You'll find this slide show in the \WORKSHOP\QSSLIDE directory. You can start the program directly from the CD or copy it to a directory on your hard drive and start it from there.

Introduction

Photographs are being used to increase the quality of multimedia shows and presentations. The Kodak Photo CD system is the ideal medium for presenting high-quality photos. Photo CD pictures can be transferred by PC systems that have Toshiba XA-compatible CD-ROM drives, so they can then be linked to other applications.

With QuickShow Light, you can easily create a multimedia show with photo CD pictures, Windows bitmaps, Wave (*.WAV) sounds, and MIDI (*.MID) music files. A photo CD slide show can be started by simply clicking a button.

NOTE

Before you begin, read the README.TXT file, located in the QuickShow Light directory. This file contains the latest program information.

QuickShow Light lets you select a desired sequence, add music to individual pictures, and save, load, and edit a slide show.

Registering QuickShow Light

Steve Rimmer describes QuickShow Light as "...neither freeware, shareware or commercial software. It's bookware." Rimmer asks that you register QuickShow Light using one of two methods:

1. Send money ($40.00 US).

2. Buy Rimmer's book - *The Order* - then photocopy the cover and receipt from the bookseller from whom you bought the book (about $7.00 US), and mail the photocopy to Rimmer as proof of purchase. This is the less expensive, more creative, and preferred method of registration.

Using your mouse

The left mouse key selects picture names, menu commands and buttons. The right mouse button stops the slide show in progress.

Using your keyboard

You can also use the keyboard to access menus and commands. To do this, press the [Tab] key to move between buttons. When you want to select a command, press [Enter]. You can also use [Alt] to access the menu bar and select menu titles and commands by pressing the key corresponding to the underlined letter of the title or command.

For example, if you want to display the information about the program:

1.   Press the [Alt] + [H] key combination to open the **Help** menu.

2.   Press [A] to select the **About...** command.

PhotoStar

 A demo version of PhotoStar from Microtek is located in the \PSTAR directory on the companion CD. Except for a few limitations, this program is the same as the commercial version. The following functions are <u>not</u> supported in this version:

➤   Loading images from the hard drive

➤   Direct scanning of images into memory

➤   Conversion of images to a different format

Introduction

PhotoStar helps organize your entire photo CD collection. This program reads the summaries of your photo CDs and stores them in an album. You can place several albums together in shelves and sort the albums by topic. At any time, you can assign the albums to other shelves.

It's also possible to add additional information to the images. Four fields are provided for this purpose. You can search for images or sort them using the contents of these fields.

You can easily print the images in the albums, or transfer them to other applications. A user-friendly image editing feature for processing the images is also included.

Installation

To install the demo version of PhotoStar, change to the \PSTAR directory on the companion CD and activate the PSSETUP.EXE program. After you specify the desired target directory, PhotoStar is installed and a new program group is created in the Program Manager.

Start the program by double-clicking the PhotoStar icon. After a brief pause, the program interface appears.

Use the menu and application icons, which are located on the left and right sides of the screen, to control the program.

File menu

Use this menu to load and print images.

New....

This command opens a dialog box from which you can create a new album. Enter the name for the new album.

Open...

This command opens a dialog box from which you can open an album. Double-click an album to open it.

Close

This command closes the active album. All images are saved when the album is closed. Use **File/ Open...** to open the album again.

The Library dialog box

Backup...

When you work with albums and images in PhotoStar, only thumbnail images of the original files are used. Each effect on the source images is indicated. The **Backup...** command backs up the original images on another disk.

After the backup process, the originals can be deleted and the storage space on the disk is made available again. The thumbnail images in the album aren't affected by this process and help manage the contents of the original images.

PhotoStar supports several types of data compression to reduce the file size during the backup process.

To backup an album, choose **Backup...** from the **File** menu. A dialog box appears displaying the following options:

Button	Purpose
Album Name	The default album name is the active album. Enter any name you want here.
Required Size	Total disk storage required by the album.

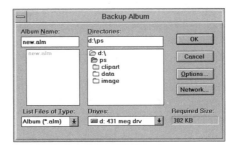

Backup options

The Options... button opens another dialog box, which contains the following options:

311

Photo Compression:

The LZW compression process reduces files to approximately half the size of the original file. The image quality isn't affected by LZW compression.

JPEG provides a more efficient data compression. However, with JPEG compression, the image quality decreases. The higher the compression factor, the more image information is lost.

Delete:

When backing up an album, all the files in the backup directory and/or the original image files and the album can be deleted.

All files in backup directory

If this check box is activated, all the files in the backup directory are deleted. Therefore, if you want to keep the files in the backup directory, don't select this option.

Original image files and album

Activate this check box to delete all the source files automatically after the backup. If you want to keep the original files, don't select this option.

You can also use **File/Backup...** with diskettes and in a network.

Restore...

This command restores the files, which were backed up using the **File/Backup...** command, to the hard drive.

Choose **Restore...** from the **File** menu. The "Restore" dialog box opens. Choose the file you want to restore. The selected file must have been created using **File/Backup...**. Click the ⬚OK button to start the process.

Open Album

If this check box is selected, the album is automatically opened after it's restored. If the album already exists in the target directory, PhotoStar provides three options: ⬚Replace, ⬚New, and ⬚Cancel.

Information

Click the ⌐Info...⌐ button to display information about the contents of the album to be restored. The only difference in backing up albums on diskettes is that you must change diskettes when they are full.

Photo CD...

If a photo CD driver is installed in your PC, place the disc, containing the images that must be loaded, in the photo CD drive. Double-click the photo CD icon or select **Photo CD...** in the **File** menu to open the "Photo CD" dialog box.

Now click the ⌐Create Album⌐ button. Enter the name of the album and choose a shelf on which the album should be stored.

Limitations on using photo CD images

1. Since photo CD images are "read only", it's impossible to edit an image unless the original photo CD image file is converted into a PhotoStar-compatible file format.

2. Although the image data itself cannot be edited, the **Edit/Edit Notes...** command can be activated.

3. The **File/Backup...**, **Edit/Check Link**, and **Edit/Relocate Photo...** commands also aren't available for photo CD image files.

Load Photo...
(unavailable in this demo version)

Select **Load Photo...** in the **File** menu to open the "Load Photo" dialog box.

Acquire...
(unavailable in this demo version)

This command installs the Scan module used by PhotoStar. For information about the installation and settings, refer to the documentation included with the scanner.

Select Source...
(unavailable in this demo version)

This command opens the "Select Source" dialog box.

Print Photo...

This command prints images from albums. Once you've set the desired printer parameters with **File/Printer Setup...**, the **Print Photo...** command can be activated from the **File** menu. The status line in the top portion of the dialog box indicates the number of images to be printed and the name of the appropriate album.

Thumbnail images, which represent the images in the album, contain a number which indicates the number of copies to be printed.

To select an image, click on a thumbnail image with the left mouse button. The selected image is displayed in the thumbnail field.

Print Photo dialog box

Click on the thumbnail image again with the left mouse button to increase the number of copies to be printed. Click with the right mouse button on the thumbnail image to decrease the number of copies.

Fit image in paper

If the "Fit image in paper" check box isn't activated, the image is printed in its normal size. If the image is larger than the paper format, it will be cut off at the edges. If this option is activated, the image will be enlarged or reduced, according to the paper format.

Preferences...

Use [Preferences...] to define attributes of the text to be printed. Click this button to open the "Preferences" dialog box.

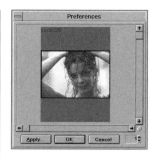

Preferences dialog box

This dialog box shows the images in the form in which they will be printed, along with any associated description. Clicking the [Apply...] button opens the "Apply" dialog box, in which you can determine how the description and images should be printed.

All

If the "All" check box isn't selected, individual attributes can be assigned to each element. If it is selected, all elements are automatically selected and cannot be modified.

PhotoStar uses the style and position of the description on the selected images in the album.

Description:

Title, Date, Place, and Description are available as description groups. Each field has options for style and position. If style or position is highlighted, the current style or position is applied to all printed images.

Click [OK] to confirm the settings. Click [Cancel] to cancel the changes and to close the dialog box.

Description Attributes

Description elements, which can be printed along with the images, include Title, Date, Place, and Description. The description itself is entered in the "Note Editor" dialog box. To change the description, open the **Edit** menu and choose **Edit Notes...**.

If a description isn't available for an image, no text is displayed with the image in the "Preferences" dialog box.

The colors and shading of the text that are displayed are the default settings. To change these settings, double-click the corresponding note text. The "Print Notes" dialog box opens.

The attributes of the description can be defined in the "Print Notes" dialog box. Double-click the text to open this dialog box.

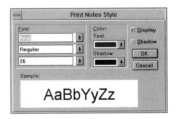

Print Notes dialog box

315

Font:

Choose a font, style, and point size for the description. A minimum point size of 10 is recommended for printouts.

Color: Text:

Choose a color for the text from the list.

Color: Shadow:

Choose a color for the shading of the text from the list.

Display:

To display the note, activate this check box. Otherwise, the note won't be printed or displayed.

Shadow:

Select the "Shadow" check box if you want the text to be printed with a background shading in the indicated color.

Click OK to confirm the selected text attributes or Cancel to cancel the changes and close the dialog box.

Print Thumbnail...

To print thumbnail images of image files, choose this command in the **File** menu. The "Print Thumbnail" dialog box opens.

Layout:

Use this command to define the number of thumbnail images to be printed on a page. The number of thumbnail images that can be printed depends on the paper size, the margin, and the description to be printed.

*Print Thumbnail
dialog box*

If the number of thumbnail images exceeds the paper size, when you click the Print button, the highest possible number will be indicated.

316

Print Border

To print a border around each thumbnail image, activate this check box.

Print Header

To print the header of an album, activate this check box. Information in the header includes the album and shelf name.

Print Notes:

Activate this group if you want to print the note along with the thumbnails.

Printer Setup...

This command sets up the printer. To select a printer, activate this command from the **File** menu. Select the desired printer and click the OK button. If you want to change the printer setup, click the Options... button.

For more information about printer options, refer to the Microsoft Windows user's guide. The changes you make in the printer options affect only printouts made from within PhotoStar.

When you exit PhotoStar, the printer settings are restored to their original state.

Exit

This command exits PhotoStar. All albums are saved, so all images are still in albums the next time you start PhotoStar.

Edit menu

This menu contains commands for deleting, copying, and pasting images. It also contains command you can use to convert images into other file formats.

Undo

Cancels the last editing step.

Cut

Cuts images from the album.

Copy

Copies images to the Clipboard.

The standard Windows functions of **Cut** and **Copy** can be executed in an album window. If an image is deleted, the space it used to occupy is freed, and the image is moved to the Microsoft Windows Clipboard in DIB (Data Image Bitmap) format. If you copy an image, the image is copied to the Clipboard in the same image format.

Paste

After using **Cut** or **Copy**, the image can be pasted into the active album. To do this, activate **Paste** from the **Edit** menu. PhotoStar inserts the image from the Clipboard in the first available position in an album window.

Delete

This command deletes thumbnail images from the album.

Search...

This command looks for images in albums. The image itself is a bitmap, which doesn't contain any identification for search tools. After you've used **Edit/Edit Notes...** to add notes to images, you can use these notes to locate the images.

To start the search process, activate **Search...** in the **Edit** menu. The "Smart Search" dialog box appears.

Find Field:

Choose one the available find fields: Title, Date, Place, Description, and All. If you select "All", a specific text can be looked for in all fields simultaneously.

Smart Search dialog box

Where:

The options in the "Where" list are Active Album and All Albums. Ensure that the desired album is opened before starting the search process.

With Text:

The "With Text:" field is used with a search by Description, Title, and Place. Enter the text to be searched for. The length of the text is limited to 64 characters for the Description, and 32 characters for the Title and the Place.

From: ___ To: ___

The "From: To:" fields can be used in the date field to search in a specific time frame.

Match case

If this check box is activated, the search text and the text you're looking for must have the same upper and lowercase letters.

Whole field

If this check box isn't activated, an image will be found if the target text is present in the field. If this option isn't activated, the search text must match the contents of the search field.

Click (Go!) to start the search process or (Cancel) to close the dialog box without starting the search process.

The images that match the search criteria are displayed. The status line shows the total number of images found and the name of the albums in which the images were located.

The images found in the Search dialog box can be displayed in a given order using Sort By. You can also indicate whether the images should be sorted in ascending or descending order.

Sort By:

Images can be sorted according to one of the following fields: Name, Date, Place or Comments.

Ascending:

If this check box isn't activated, the images are sorted in descending order; otherwise they are sorted in ascending order. If the sort key is the date, PhotoStar recognizes the sequence independent of the date format used. **319**

Locate

Click the (Locate) button to start the search process. The images that are found are highlighted with color in the album windows.

Find only looks for images. If there are several selected images, the name of the image is displayed with a dotted frame.

Collect
(unavailable in this demo version)

Collect lets you arrange the images that are found in a new album. Select the desired images in the "Smart Search" dialog box and click the [Collect] button. The link between the thumbnails and the image files will be transferred to the new album, and the thumbnails in the original album will be deleted.

Edit Notes...

Use this command to edit comments. In PhotoStar, a note can be included with each image so it's easier to find the image later. This note can then be used with many PhotoStar features, such as **Locate**, **Sort**, **Collect**, **Print** and **Associate/Photo Show....**

Select **Edit Notes...** in the **Edit** menu. The "Note Editor" dialog box opens.

If you want to add a note to an image that isn't currently in the dialog box, click on this image or scroll with the slider bar to find it. Thumbnail images of the images are displayed in the "Note Editor" dialog box.

Edit Notes dialog box

To finish editing the note, click (OK) to confirm or (Cancel) to cancel the changes.

Select All

This command selects all the images in the album.

Invert Selection

This command inverts the current selection of the images.

Discard Selection

This command discards the current selection.

Squeeze

This command moves the images in the album to empty places. When you rearrange images in an album, occasionally this creates empty areas in the album. Use this command to fill these empty areas.

Check link

This command checks the link from the thumbnail image to the original image file. Sometimes you may have to examine the connection of the thumbnail images to the original image files. The images in your album file might have been changed in the image editing module or in another image processing application like ImageStar II or PhotoStyler.

Although the thumbnail image is displayed, the original file may not be available if you didn't use **Check link** beforehand. Select an image and select the **Check link** command from the **Edit** menu. PhotoStar re-reads the image source file.

Remember, you must select the images before using **Check link**. If you don't do this, this command cannot be selected.

Convert Photo...
(unavailable in this demo version)

This command changes the format of the image file. In PhotoStar, images can be converted into different file formats. Select the files you want to convert in the opened album and then activate **Convert Photo...** in the **File** menu to start the conversion.

Relocate Photo...

This command moves an image file to another directory. Images can be moved between the albums that are available. It's also possible to move original image files to other directories. Open an album and select some images by clicking on them. To select groups of images, hold down the Ctrl + Shift keys while clicking the mouse. Then select **Relocate Photo...** from the **Edit** menu. The "Relocate Photo" dialog box appears.

321

To Directory

Select a directory or enter the name of a directory for an image file transfer. If you aren't sure about the desired target directory, click the [Search All] button to select a directory. If the directory doesn't exist, PhotoStar creates it. The default name of the directory is IMAGE, which is a subdirectory under the PhotoStar directory.

Delete original files

"Delete original files" can be used to copy or move image files. If this option isn't selected, the source files will be copied. If this check box is selected, the source files will be deleted from the source directory after they have been copied.

To Album:

Select an album for the transfer. To find the desired album, open the selection list and select an album.

Keep original link

If this check box isn't activated, the thumbnail image and the photo files will be transferred to a new album. If it's selected, the thumbnail image remains in the original album.

Duplicate files for destinate album

If this check box isn't selected, the thumbnail image and the image files will be transferred to a new album. If it is selected, the image files will be copied to the pre-determined directory in a new album. The default directory is defined using **Directory...** in the **Configure** menu.

View menu

This menu contains commands that define the size and order, in which the thumbnail images in the album will be displayed.

Full Page

When this command is activated, the album window is displayed in its maximum size. If only part of the images can be displayed, **Entire Album** displays reduced versions of the images.

Huge View

This command sets the thumbnail image display size to the maximum size.

Large View

Sets the thumbnail image display size to "large".

Normal View

Sets the thumbnail image display size to the normal size.

Small View

Sets the thumbnail image display size to "small".

Sort By

Sort By changes the order of the images in the active album. Four key fields are available for the sort process: Title, Date, Place, and Description. Select one of the key fields. Text for the sort fields is added using **Edit Notes...** from the **Edit** menu.

The images can be sorted in ascending or descending order. The default setting is ascending. If "Date" is the key field, PhotoStar will recognize the order regardless of the date format used.

Hide Index

This command hides image numbering in the album.

Hide Album Status

This command hides information about the images in the status line of the album.

Associate menu

You can use the commands in the **Associate** menu to add additional application icons to the working area in PhotoStar.

Photo Show...

This command creates a slide presentation. If images have been loaded into an album, they can be displayed using **Photo Show....** This command supports colored text, different transition effects for notes and images, and manual or automatic image changing.

If a sound card is installed in your PC, sound files can be linked with each image.

Photo Show... displays images in normal, reduced, or enlarged sizes. If images were selected in an album, only the selected images will be displayed. If none of the images were selected, all of the images in the album will be displayed, one after another.

Select **Photo Show...** in the **Associate** menu or double-click the "Photo Show" icon. The "Photo Show Preferences" dialog box appears.

Fit image in screen

If this check box isn't activated and the image is smaller than the size of the screen, the image is displayed in its actual size. If the image is larger than the screen, PhotoStar reduces it to the size of the screen. If this check box is activated, PhotoStar enlarges or reduces the image to adjust it to the size of the screen.

Time Interval:

This text box is only used with automatic photo shows. It determines how long each image is displayed.

Depending on the size of the image file and the speed of the microprocessor, it can take several seconds to load an image. Decreasing the "Time interval:" setting doesn't decrease the load time. If a sound file is loaded with an image, PhotoStar waits until the file has finished playing before loading the next image. In a manual photo show, you flip from image to image using the left and right mouse buttons. In this case, the settings for "Time interval:" are ignored.

Preferences...

You can use this button to define text attributes, transition effects, and the sound file for each image. Click the [Preferences...] button to open the "Preferences" dialog box.

Notes

The notes on each file consists of the following elements: Title, Date, Place, and Description. The default colors are used for text and shading. Activate the **Edit Notes...** command in the **Edit** menu to create or edit the description. To change other attributes, double-click on the text you want to change. Then, enter the changes in the "Photo Show Notes Style" dialog box.

Font:

Use this command to specify the font name, the style, and the point size. One inch equals 72 points. You should use point sizes of 14 or more for displaying images on the screen.

Color/Text:

Select the desired text color from the list.

Color/Shadow:

Select a color from the list for shading.

Transparency/Text:

Define the degree of transparency. 0% means opaque, 100% means completely transparent.

Transparency/Shadow:

Define the degree of transparency. 0% means opaque, 100% means completely transparent.

Display

If this check box isn't activated, the note texts won't be displayed in the photo show. Activate this check box if you want the text to be displayed in the photo show.

Shadow

If this check box is selected, the note will have a shaded background.

Transition Type:

Select the transition type for the display of the images from the list.

Click OK to confirm the settings for photo show notes, or Cancel to exit the window.

Photo Show Style

To define the styles used for displaying the images in the photo show, double-click in the image area. The "Photo Show Style" dialog box appears.

Transition Type:

Define the transition type for the display of the images using the drop-down list.

Sound

If this check box is active, a sound file can be played with each image. Select the desired sound file from the list. In order for this option to work, a compatible sound card must be installed in your PC.

Load...

Clicking the Load... button loads a sound file for the image. The audio format in PhotoStar corresponds to the Microsoft Windows MPC standard. Refer to the Microsoft Windows 3.1 user's guide for more information.

Current:

Shows the current image number.

Hide

Hides the control window and changes to Presentation control in the background mode.

Stop

Click the [Stop] button to stop the playback. The presentation doesn't end; instead, the current image is frozen on the screen.

Back

Click the [Back] button to display the previous image.

Playback

Hides the control window and starts the presentation.

Press [Enter] to display the control window again. To pause the presentation, press [Spacebar].

Forward

Click [Forward] to display the next image.

Loop

The presentation starts with the current image. When the last image is displayed, the presentation starts over from the beginning. The images in the loop will be displayed until the [Esc] key is pressed or until you click the [Loop] button again.

Selector triangle

Move the selector triangle to the desired image number. This is equivalent to Display Current, except that the display is done in real time. When you move the triangle, the number in the Current window is updated to reflect the change. When you release the mouse button, the presentation will continue from the point of the selected image number.

Total:

Shows the number of images in the active album.

Exit

Switches back to the album window. You can also do this by pressing the [Esc] key.

327

Controlling the photo show in the background

To select the background mode for controlling the photo show, either click the [Hide] button or press the [Enter] key.

To exit the background mode and return to the "Photo Show" window, press [Enter]. Pressing the [Esc] key exits the photo show and returns you to the album window.

Clip Art

This command adds clip art to an image in the album.

The "Clip Art" window shows the thumbnail images of the available clip art. To load graphics into the "Clip Art" window, click the [Add Clip Art...] button. The "Load Image" dialog box appears.

The format of the clip art image file is limited to 24-bit true colors or 256 grayscale shades. If you want to add images in a different format to the "Clip Art" window, you must convert them beforehand. The size of the clip art shouldn't exceed the size of the target image. In this case, it would be rejected by the image processing module.

Loading clip art into the "Clip Art" window

Images are loaded into the "Clip Art" window using a method similar to loading images into an album. However, the images in the clip art window must be converted to the JPEG format, regardless of their original format. The converted image files are saved in the clip art directory, which was defined in the **Configure** menu with the **Directory...** command.

Add clip art to an image

Move the selected clip art to one of the following:

1. A thumbnail image in the opened album.

2. An image in the opened window of the Photo Enhancer window.

If you drag a clip art over an image, it becomes a movable area in the Photo Enhancer module. If you drag a clip art to an opened album, the image will automatically be opened in the Photo Enhancer module.

Move the clip art to the desired location in the working window, scale it if needed by dragging on one of the eight handles on the clip art, and click somewhere outside of the selection area to insert the clip art.

Rename an image in the clip art window

Click on an image and, while holding down the [Alt] key, press [Enter] to open the "Object Properties" dialog box. Enter a new name for the image and click [OK] or press [Enter] to complete the process.

Deleting an image in the "Clip Art" window

Drag the image to be deleted to the "Accessory Box" icon or the "Accessory Box" window.

Accessory Box

Use the Accessory Box to delete images from the album. This can be used as temporary storage for the following objects:

1. Empty shelves

2. Unopened albums

3. Thumbnail images (in an album or on the desktop)

4. Clip art

To dispose of material in the Accessory Box, double-click the "Accessory Box" icon to open the "Accessory Box" window. Click the [Empty] button to empty the contents of the "Accessory Box" window.

Use one of the following procedures to place objects in the Accessory Box:

1. Drag the objects to the "Accessory Box" icon. You can examine the contents of the "Accessory Box" window by double-clicking on its icon.

2. Open the Accessory Box by selecting **Accessory Box** in the **Associate** menu. Then drag the objects to the "Accessory Box" window.

3. Open the "Accessory Box" window by double-clicking on its icon. Then drag the objects to this window.

329

If the Accessory Box contains objects, its icon's appearance will change to indicate this.

To permanently delete shelves, unopened albums, clip art, and thumbnail images from the Accessory Box, click the Empty button in the "Accessory Box" window. Before it deletes the images, PhotoStar asks for confirmation. Click Yes to delete the original image file and the thumbnail image. If you click No, only the thumbnail image is deleted and the process is aborted.

"Apply To All" means that the choice of Yes, No, or Cancel will be applied to all the other images in the album.

Photo Enhancer

Images in albums can be edited by using the Photo Enhancer in PhotoStar. If you need advanced image processing functions, use the **Plug In...** command in the **Associate** menu to add an image processing application to PhotoStar.

The Photo Enhancer loads images from albums in the working area of PhotoStar. There are several ways to open images in the Photo Enhancer:

1. If the album is open, double-click on an image.

2. Drag an image to the "Enhancer" icon.

3. Double-click the "Enhancer" icon without first selecting a image. The Photo Enhancer loads the first image in the album.

4. Double-click the Thumbnail icon on the desktop.

5. If you're in the Photo Enhancer, double-click on an image in the album to load the newly selected image. PhotoStar will ask if you want to save the changes to the current image.

If your image file is a read-only file or if it was loaded from a photo CD, the Photo Enhancer commands aren't available.

Photo enhancement

After you've loaded an image into the Photo Enhancer, the image can be edited and touched-up. The Photo Enhancer has eight tools on the left side of the window:

- ➢ Undo
- ➢ Zoom in
- ➢ Zoom out
- ➢ Cut
- ➢ Copy
- ➢ Paste
- ➢ Paste Control
- ➢ Optimize

To edit only a specific area of a image, drag the mouse pointer across the area and then select one of the eight tools. If a specific area isn't specified, the changes affect the entire image.

Undo tool

This tool restores the last editing operation that took place. Only the last editing step can be restored. So, you cannot cancel any editing steps that occurred before the most recent one. To determine the most recently restored step, move the mouse pointer to the Undo tool icon and press the right mouse button. Some of the editing processes that cannot be undone are:

- ➢ Scale selection
- ➢ Select new area
- ➢ Enlarge display
- ➢ Reduce display

Zoom In tool

Each click on the Zoom In tool enlarges the display by 200%, up to a maximum of 800% of the original image. The image itself isn't enlarged; instead, only the display is enlarged.

Zoom Out tool

Each click on the Zoom Out tool decreases the display by 50% down to a minimum of 25% of the original image. The image itself isn't reduced; instead only its display is reduced.

Cut tool

Select a rectangular area and click on the Cut tool to copy the selected area into the Clipboard of Microsoft Windows. The section that was cut will remain blank.

To cut out the entire image and paste it in another image, leave the Photo Enhancer and execute this function in the album window.

Copy tool

Select the area of the image to be copied by dragging the mouse over the image. You can adjust the size of the selected area by pulling on the handles of the object frame. Then click on the Copy tool to copy the selected area into the Clipboard. The area that was copied doesn't change.

To copy the entire image into another image, exit the Photo Enhancer and use the **Copy** command inside an album window.

Paste tool

The Paste tool pastes the image from the Clipboard into the image in the Photo Enhancer. The image that is pasted was copied to the Clipboard using **Cut** or **Copy**.

You can move around the pasted image as much as you would like until you click once with the mouse outside the selected object.

Paste Control tool

Before an image is pasted from the Clipboard into the target image, the blending of the two images can be defined. Click on the Paste Control tool to open the "Paste Controls" dialog box. The paste control settings aren't applied until you actually paste the image.

The "Paste Mode:" drop-down list box determines how the fill color or the fill pattern will be mixed with the selected area of the target image.

Select one of the four Paste modes:

> ➤ Normal
>   This is the default setting; the entire selected area is replaced by the new image.

> ➤ Darken Only
>   This compares pixels in the selected area with those of the image in the Clipboard. If the pixel of the Clipboard image is darker than that in the selected area, the pixel in the selected area will be replaced.

This compares pixels in the selected area with those of the image in the Clipboard. If the pixel of the Clipboard image is darker than that in the selected area, the pixel in the selected area will be replaced.

➤ Lighten Only
Lighten Only compares pixels in the selected area with those of the image in the Clipboard. If the pixel of the Clipboard image is lighter than that in the selected area, the pixel in the selected area will be replaced.

➤ Color Only
Color Only (only for 24-bit true-color images) replaces the color and saturation values of the pixels in the selected area with the color and saturation values of the pixels in the Clipboard image.

Optimize tool

The Optimize tool optimizes the color, saturation, and brightness of the selected image. Click on the tool to optimize the image. The Optimize process can be used repeatedly on the same image, although the result will not be as optimal as it was the first time.

Image Effects tools

In the lower part of the window, the Photo Enhancer has five Image Effects tools for fine-tuning the image: ➤

➤ Brightness   ➤ Contrast

➤ Hue   ➤ Saturation

➤ Blur/Sharpen

To toggle display of the Image Effects tool icons, click on the Toggle icon (an icon of a hand holding a handle) in the lower-left corner of the Photo Enhancer's window.

To use one of the fine-tuning tools, click on the icon of the desired tool and adjust the slider. The further you move the slider, the more pronounced the changes will be in the image.

To change only a selected area, use the mouse to draw a rectangle inside the image. You can adjust the size of the rectangle by pulling on the sizing boxes. If an area has not been selected, the tool settings affect the entire image.

Slider

Adjusts the intensity of the effects.

Toggle icon

Displays/hides Image Effects tools.

Brightness

Make the image brighter or darker.

Contrast

Change the image contrast.

Hue

Adjust the hue of the image.

Saturation

Change the intensity of the colors.

Blur/Sharpen

Reduce or increase the sharpness of the image.

Information...

In the Photo Enhancer, you can obtain information about the image from the Control menu of the window.

Exiting the Photo Enhancer

After you've edited the image, select **Close File** from the Control menu of the Photo Enhancers or double-click the Control menu. The "PhotoStar" dialog box opens, asking if you want to save changes before closing.

Click [Yes] to save the changes in the image, or [No] to exit the "PhotoStar" dialog box without saving the changes, or [Cancel] to return to the Photo Enhancer. If you save the changes, the original image file will be changed and the thumbnail image in the album will be updated.

Plug In...

Plug-in associates expand PhotoStar by using additional applications. The icon for each Windows application can be anchored in the PhotoStar workspace, like the default icons present in PhotoStar. The expansions are performed by using the **Plug In...** command in the **Associate** menu. Up to 16 additional applications can be added at the same time.

Loading other applications

To add an application icon to PhotoStar, do the following:

1. Open the **Associate** menu and select **Plug In...**.
   The "Plug-In Association" dialog box appears.

2. Click the [Add...] button in the "Plug-In Association" dialog box.
   The "Associate Properties" dialog box appears.

3. Click on the [Browse...] button.
   The "Browse Associate" dialog box opens. The "List Files of Type:" drop-down list contains two options: Program and All Files. The Program option only shows files with the .EXE or .COM extension. The All Files option lists all of the files in the current directory.

4. Use the "Browse Associate" dialog box to find the directory for your application and the .EXE startup file. Double-click on the .EXE file to select it.

5. Click [OK] to load the application.

6. Click [OK] to close the "Associate Properties" dialog box.

   Properties
   Clicking the [Properties...] button opens the "Associate Properties" dialog box.

Description:
This text box contains the name of the application that is represented by the application icon. Use the name that is shown or enter a new one.

Command Line and Working Directory:
These two text boxes are displayed as soon as you select the program name in the "Browse Associate" dialog box.

Show associated Icon
If this text box is activated, the icon for the application is displayed in the PhotoStar workspace. If this check box isn't selected, you can only access the plug-in programs using the **Associate** menu.

7. The icon for the new application appears on the right side of the screen. The name of the application is added to the **Associate** menu.

Starting the plug-in

To start an application, double-click its icon. The easiest way to start image processing programs is to drag the selected image from the album to the application icon. The selected image will be opened in that application. If it's supported by the application, several can be opened simultaneously.

Configure menu

The commands in the **Configure** menu define the default setting for the display of the application icons, the size of the album, and the JPEG compression factor.

Device Icon...
(unavailable in this demo version)

Use this command to arrange the application icons.

Directory...

This command defines default directories. The "Directory Configuration" dialog box opens when you activate this command.

Default Work Path:

The work path is the directory in which PhotoStar and the working files are stored. The name of the default working directory is defined when you install PhotoStar. PhotoStar creates some system files and temporary files when it's running. Temporary files are deleted when you quit PhotoStar.

Default Album Path:

The album files are stored in this path.

Default Image Path:

Image files are stored in this path. Image files can be created by copying a file or importing files.

Default Clipart Path:

Clip art files are stored in this path.

Browse...

If you've forgotten the name of a certain file, click on the [Browse...] button to search for it.

Restore

Click the [Restore] button to restore the directory name back to the original name. Click [OK] to confirm the change. Click the [Cancel] button to close the dialog box and to cancel the changes.

Album...

This command defines the default configuration of the album. Use the **Configure/Album...** command to determine the appearance of the albums on the screen and the appearance of the images in the albums.

These changes don't affect the currently opened album. Instead, they define how future albums will look.

Default Photo Space:

The "Default Photo Space:" drop-down list box defines the number of lines in newly created albums. You can select from one to six lines. If you originally set the number of lines at two and you need more, the number of lines will automatically be increased.

Thumbnail Size:

This drop-down list box defines the size of the thumbnail images in the album window. The four available sizes are the same as those in the **View** menu. The file size for the thumbnail images is about 30K for color image and about 10K for grayscale images, regardless of the size of the original.

Show status line.

Select this check box to create the status line for an album. If this check box isn't activated, the status line will be hidden.

Show photo space number.

Select this check box to display a number with each image. If this check box isn't activated, the number display will be hidden.

Status Line Fields:

If this group is activated, elements of the status line can be selected. Since there is a limited amount of room in the status line, not all fields can be displayed simultaneously.

There are two kinds of status line fields: Automatic and user-defined. Information from the computer appears in the automatic field. Information for the user-defined field is entered using the **Edit Notes...** command in the **Edit** menu.

Click on the check boxes that you want to see in the status line. You can select a maximum of nine fields. If more information is available than can fit in the status line, you won't be able to see it all at one time. Use the button on the right side of the status line to scroll the fields.

For information about the individual images in the status line, click on the thumbnail image of the image. If you select several images in an album, album information will be displayed in the status line.

Title

The title of the image can be a maximum of 32 characters long. When images are inserted into an album, the original file name is used as the default title for the image. The default title can be changed using **Edit Notes...** in the **Edit** menu.

Place

This field shows the text entered using **Edit Notes...** in the **Edit** menu. Although the actual purpose of this field is to retain the name of the location where a image was made, any kind of text can be entered here.

Date

This field displays the date that was entered using **Edit Notes...** in the **Edit** menu. The format of the date is either long (Nov. 12, 1993) or short (11/12/93), depending on the setting in the "Date Format" dialog box.

Description

This field shows the description of the image that was entered using **Edit Notes...** in the **Edit** menu. A maximum of 64 characters can be used for the comments.

File size

"File size" shows the amount of hard drive space occupied by the original image.

File extension

This field shows the extension from the name of the image file. The available file extensions are: .TIF, .PCX, .JPG, or .BMP.

Image type

"Image type" describes the information in the original image data. The possible types are 24-bit true color and 256 grayscale images. To display the information in the "Image type" field, PhotoStar checks the original image file for the selected option.

Dimensions

The Dimensions field shows the size of the original image in pixels.

Resolution

Resolution shows the resolution of the original image in dots per inch (dpi).

Click OK to confirm the changes. Click the Cancel button to close the dialog box and to discard the changes.

Date...

This command defines the date format. You can choose from several formats, and from "Long date format" or "Short date format".

Order:

This group specifies the order of the three components of the date: M for Month, D for Day, and Y for Year.

Separator:

Lists all three available separators.

Leading zero

If you want to display leading zeroes (e.g., 01 to 09) for single-digit days and months (1 through 9), activate this check box.

2 digit year

If you want to display the year as a two-digit figure, activate this check box. Otherwise, you must input values for years with four digits.

This century always

If this check box is activated, it will be assumed that each year is to be associated with the current century. Otherwise, the year that is input can belong to any century.

Click OK to confirm these settings. Click the Cancel button to close the dialog box and to cancel the changes.

JPEG Engine...

This command defines the JPEG compression factor. The compression factor will be applied to all files that are saved on the disk from within PhotoStar. File compression is used during file conversion, file backup, loading image files into an opened album, and importing clip art into the clip art window.

Compression Level:

The allowable compression factors are in the range between 5 and 30. The higher the compression factor, the smaller the image file and, therefore, the more image data is lost.

Save some files and compare the loss of detail against the amount of storage space gained to determine the best setting. The default setting of 15 is suitable in most situations.

Preferences...

This command configures some of the PhotoStar options. You can configure the layout of the Clipboard and define the sound effects.

Show animation on startup.

If this check box is active, each time you start the program you'll see an animated PhotoStar startup logo. If it isn't active, the PhotoStar startup logo will be bypassed and you'll go directly to the setup of the application icons and of the desktop.

Hide library after opening an album.

Activate this check box if the library window should be closed each time an album is opened. If several albums must be loaded one after another, don't activate this option.

Sound effects enabled on Photo Show.

Activate this check box if you want sound effects to accompany PhotoStar. To hear the sound effects, a sound card must be installed in your PC. Otherwise, you must upgrade your PC to the MPC standard.

Click OK to confirm the changes. Click the Cancel button to close the dialog box and to cancel the changes.

341

Window Menu

The commands in this menu arrange the albums and icons in the work area of PhotoStar.

Tile

This command displays all opened albums in tiled format.

Cascade

This command shows all opened albums in cascading format.

Arrange Album Icons

Arranges album icons.

Close All

This command closes all opened albums.

Arrange Device Icons

This command arranges device icons.

Hide Device Icon

This command hides device icons in the working area.

Arrange Desktop Photos

This command arranges photo icons on the desktop.

Seattle Film Works

The PhotoWorks program from Seattle Film Works could be called a "frugal photo CD."

PhotoWorks is a DOS-based program that lets you view film processed to disk (rather than to film) by Seattle Film

NOTE

Seattle Film Works film roll format is incompatible with Kodak's proprietary PCD format.

Works. Once you view each file, PhotoWorks lets you convert the file to other popular graphic formats. To view PhotoWorks from DOS, change to the SFW directory on the companion CD and type the following from the DOS prompt:

```
SFWPW  Enter
```

Corel Sampler Photos

Corel, makers of CorelDRAW!, CorelPHOTO-PAINT! and other products, have provided us with five photos from their Photo Sampler CD. To install the Sampler programs, select **File/Run...**, change to the COREL directory on the companion CD and run SETUP.EXE.

Shareware on the Companion CD

Several quality shareware image processing and image organizing products exist. With the permission of their publishers, we've included some of these products on this companion CD. You can run them from the CD, or copy them to a new directory on your hard drive and run them from there. We'll tell you what each product does, how to run it, and show you a screen from it, and leave you to play from there.

Shareware runs on an honor system. That is, the author assumes that you can acquired his or her product through some distribution channel (in this case, our companion CD), and after a testing period of reasonable length (e.g., 30-60 days), you'll register your software with the author.

Registration means sending a specific amount of money to the author - usually far less than you might pay for a commercial version of a similar product. Please support these authors, if you like their products.

Graphic Workshop

We mentioned Alchemy Mindworks and author Steve Rimmer earlier as author of QuickShow Light. Graphic Workshop Version 1.1 is another graphic converter and viewer. You can view a file, change its coloration, scale and crop, and convert files to over a dozen different formats.

343

To run Graphic Workshop from the companion CD, select **File/Run...**, and type the following (replace the "x:" with your CD-ROM drive letter):

x:\SHAREWAR\ALCHEMY\GWS11F\GWS.EXE `Enter`

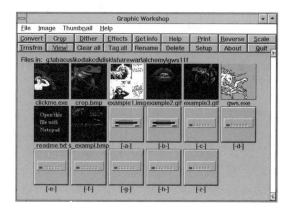

Graphic Workshop

ImageCommander

Here's another JASC, Inc. shareware product. ImageCommander lets you create albums of image files, displaying them as thumbnail images. You can also convert files into many different file formats and sub-formats.

To run ImageCommander from the companion CD, select **File/Run...**, and type the following (replace the "x:" with your CD-ROM drive letter):

x:\SHAREWAR\JASC\IMGCMDR\IMGCMDR.EXE `Enter`

ImageCommander

Paint Shop Pro

Paint Shop Pro, by Minnesota-based JASC, Inc., is a Windows program for viewing, manipulating and converting photo CD and other images. Many of the screen shots for this book were generated with the help of Paint Shop Pro.

To run Paint Shop Pro from the companion CD, select **File/Run...**, and type the following (replace the "x:" with your CD-ROM drive letter):

```
x:\SHAREWAR\JASC\PSP20\PSP.EXE Enter
```

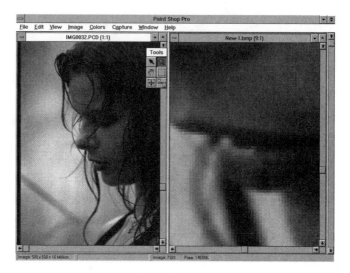

Paint Shop Pro

PixFolio 2

PixFolio 2 is another image manipulator. It will help you keep track of your image files, using the "catalog" concept. PixFolio lets you create databases of images and their diskette locations, and these databases, or catalogs, help easy retrieval of the images.

To run PixFolio 2 from the companion CD, select **File/Run...**, and type the following (replace the "x:" with your CD-ROM drive letter):

```
x:\SHAREWAR\PIXF20\PIXFOLIO.EXE  Enter
```

PixFolio 2

QuickShow Light

We mentioned QuickShow Light earlier in this chapter. QuickShow Light is a program that lets you set up slide shows quickly and easily.

To run QuickShow Light from the companion CD, select **File/Run...**, and type the following (replace the "x:" with your CD-ROM drive letter):

x:\SHAREWAR\ALCHEMY\QSHOW\QSHOW.EXE `Enter`

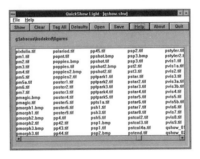

QuickShow Light

ThumbsUp

This program lets you quickly create thumbnails (small versions of images). You can convert the thumbnails to many different file formats, view them "up-close," and even assign thumbnails as Windows wallpaper.

347

To run ThumbsUp from the companion CD, select **File/Run...**, and type
the following (replace the "x:" with your CD-ROM drive letter):

`x:\SHAREWAR\THUMBS\THUMBSUP.EXE` (Enter)

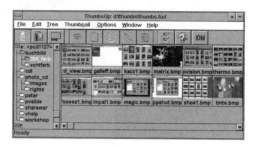

ThumbsUp

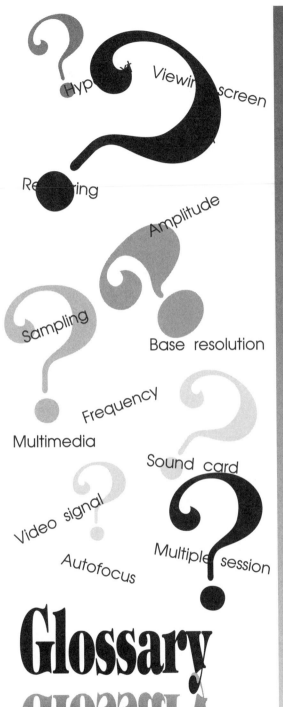

Hypertext Viewing screen

Rendering

Amplitude

Sampling

Base resolution

Frequency

Multimedia

Sound card

Video signal

Autofocus

Multiple session

Glossary

CHAPTER

6

CHAPTER 6

Glossary

Access time

Access time is a specific factor in CD-ROM, disk drive and hard drive speeds. The average access time, given in milliseconds, defines the time required to move the disk to the proper location and move the read(/write) head to that location.

Additive primary colors

On the basis of additive color mixing, you can produce the color white by mixing the primary colors of red, green and blue.

Amplitude

Amplitude is determined by the highest point along the curve of a sound wave. The higher the amplitude, the louder the sound. The physical unit of loudness is the decibel (dB). Decibels are a logarithmic unit of measure, specifying the degree of loudness of the wave.

Analog

Analog information can take on any value and is infinitely variable. Analog information is the opposite of digital information, which can only take on discrete values. An ADC (Analog/Digital Converter) is required to convert analog information to digital information.

Animation

Moving graphic images. Several frames show a progression of movement, and thereby simulate movement.

Anti-aliasing

Anti-aliasing is a technique for smoothing out jaggies - the jagged lines which result when you display slanted lines or round shapes at relatively low resolution. Anti-aliasing fills in the jaggies with pixels, which have a color value mediating between the line and the surrounding area.

API

(Acronym for Application Program Interface) Refers to a Windows interface for applications. You can call a series of system functions from the API.

ASCII

(Acronym for American Standard Code for Information Interchange) Standardized term for the coding of letters, numbers, special characters and control characters. The ASCII character set is made up of 128 characters. Each character is represented by a number between 0 and 127. The extended ASCII code developed by IBM comprises 256 characters and contains foreign characters (e.g., German umlauts) and a number of graphics characters.

ASPI

(Acronym for Advanced SCSI Programming Interface) A standardized driver that forms the interface between the operating system and the controller card. This driver provides the necessary functions for allowing device dependent drivers to communicate with the interface, and thus also with the computer.

Audio

The term audio refers to all tones that are audible to the human ear or can be measured. For example, audio includes music, speech, and all other noises. Musical tones are graphically depicted as waves. The maximum distance of an oscillation from its lowest to its highest point is called amplitude. The distance between two adjacent maximum waves is called oscillation. The unit of measurement for the frequency (the number of oscillations per second) is Hertz.

Authoring system

An authoring system is software for creating interactive tutorials, presentations and databases using multimedia components. Unlike a programming language, through which one actually programs in code, the authoring systems let the author use tools (usually accessible through icons) for adding functions to create a presentation. These functions are automatically converted to program code later. Even a non-programmer can create presentations using an authoring system.

Autofocus

This is an electronic/optical feature that automatically focuses a camera lens. The measurement of the focus usually takes place by a contrast measurement through the lens. When an object is focused, the image is at its highest contrast. In order for the autofocus to work properly, it requires a minimum amount of light to perform the contrast measurements. Also, the object in the measuring range must have contrast.

AVI

(Acronym for Audio Video Interleave) Compression procedure developed by Microsoft for software synchronous compression of live video and sound on a multimedia PC.

Base resolution

The images on the Photo CD are stored in various resolutions. Here are the formats that a PCD file is made of:

> ➢ Base/16, 128 lines x 192 pixels, resolution at 1/16 of the information of the normal image.

> ➢ Base/4, 256 lines x 384 pixels, resolution at 1/4 of the informaiton of the normal image.

> ➢ Base, 512 lines x 768 pixels, normal image.

> ➢ 4 Base, 1024 lines x 1536 pixels, resolution at 4 times the information of the normal image.

➢ 16 Base, 2048 lines x 3072 pixels, resolution at 16 times the information of the normal image.

➢ 64 Base, 4092 lines x 6144 pixels, resolution at 64 times the information of the normal image, Pro Photo CD resolution.

➢ Base, Base/4 and Base/16 images are uncompressed.

➢ 4 Base and 16 Base images are stored on the CD in compressed format.

BIOS

(Acronym for Basic Input Output System) The basic programs and functions required by a processor in order to work. A processor without basic work instructions is like a motor without a transmission. A processor BIOS is usually stored in ROM (Read Only Memory). You will find such basic programs on your computer as well as on intelligent expansion and interface boards.

Bitmaps

Bitmaps, unlike vector graphics, are images composed of pixels. Each pixel contains a color attribute which can be between one bit (black & white graphic) and 24 bits (true color image) wide.

Block matching

With block matching, data ranges are checked for similarity or consistent changes during compression, so they can be combined.

BMP format

BMP format is a bitmap format that saves images according to the bit pattern. Windows uses BMP format more than any other program. There are many different bitmap formats, but most of them are very similar. Along with the standard BMP format, there is also DIB format (almost identical to BMP format) and RDIB format, which is used by Windows Multimedia Extensions.

There has been a compression procedure for bitmap files ever since Windows 3.1 was released. RLE format is actually just a compressed version of DIB format.

Bridge disc

A bridge disc is a CD ROM which can be read by a CD-ROM XA drive as well as by a CD-I playback device. The Kodak Photo CD is a bridge disc.

Burst

1. The color synchronous signal of the PAL standard, sent at the beginning of each screen line. This signal serves as a reference for the color information.

2. Within the technical data of a CD-ROM drive you will often find a data transfer rate for Burst mode.

BUS

A collection of communication lines transmitting signals between components on a circuit board or between the circuit board and expansion or other cards.

Cache

A special area of RAM to store the most frequently accessed information in RAM. You can greatly improve the speed of your system by using cache memory because it "optimizes" the cooperation among the different components of your system.

Caddy

Many systems require a special plastic case, called a caddy, to insert a CD-ROM into the drive.

Camcorder

Integrated device for receiving and playing back video signals. The term camcorder is a compound word made up of camera and recorder. This term also does a good job of describing the function, since a camcorder is a video camera with an integrated video recorder.

CATV

Abbreviation for American cable television.

355

CAV

(Acronym for Constant Angular Velocity) This is a recording procedure, in which the rotation speed of the medium remains constant. This procedure is used with CDs, hard drives and disk drives.

CCD

(Acronym for Charge Coupled Device) The term for a chip that converts light into electronic signals. Modern video cameras use these chips for image reception, some scanners also use these chips.

CD

(Acronym for Compact Disc) Optical storage medium for receiving digitized information. The compact disc has a diameter of 3.5 inches (8 cm) or 4.75 inches (12 cm). The information is read by a laser beam in the CD-ROM drive of a computer. The CD is most popular in the world of audio, where it is replacing records. The greatest advantage of using the CD in the computer world is its high storage capacity.

CD-A

(Acronym for Compact Disc Audio) The term refers to the audio standard for a 60 minute, 4.75 inch (12 cm) CD.

CD-DA

(Acronym for Compact Disc Digital Audio) Standard for digital audio recordings on a CD.

CD-G

Term for the audio standard for analog audio recordings and digitized fixed images.

CD-I

(Acronym for Compact Disc Interactive) CD playback stations that are operated independently from the computer. Connecting a CD-I to a conventional television set allows the use of multimedia applications for the consumer market. You can play up to 90 minutes of live video with stereo sound on a CD-I player.

CD-ROM

(Acronym for Compact Disc - Read Only Memory) Term for a read-only CD containing computer and audio data. The information is read from CD-ROM drives that can be internal or external. Some drives require a caddy for the CD. You place the CD inside the caddy and then insert the caddy into the drive. CD-ROM drives are one component of the MPC Standard.

CD-ROM-XA

(Acronym for Compact Disc - Read Only Memory Extended Architecture) Audio data is stored separately. The advantage lies in the ability to read audio and video information. The CD-ROM-XA uses conventional drives.

CD-V

(Acronym for Compact Disc - Video) Term for a CD standard that contains up to 15 minutes of analog video and digital audio. However, this standard requires special hardware.

CDTV

(Acronym for Commodore Dynamic Total Vision) CD-playback station developed by Commodore for the consumer market. Using a separate Motorola 68000 processor, CDTV can be operated independently from the computer.

Chroma

Color percentage of video signal.

Chroma Key Colorkey

Special effect in video. A special color, called the colorkey, is replaced by live video. Also called the blue box effect, since a special kind of blue is normally used as the color key.

CLUT

(Acronym for Color Lookup Table) Stores the color values for pixel images with up to 256 (2^8) colors. The color values can be selected from a much larger palette, making it possible to display brilliant images with only 8 bits of color information for each pixel.

CLV

(Acronym for Constant Linear Velocity) Recording/playback process in which the medium turns at a varying speed, depending on the radial position of the information to be read/written. This way, data everywhere on the medium is read/recorded at the same density. CD-ROM drives work according to this process.

CMYK color model

Normal color model for print shops. Color tones are formed from the colors cyan, magenta and yellow. The K stands for blacK, since mixing the other three colors doesn't yield a proper black. This also explains why the HP DeskJet 500C doesn't print the color black correctly. It has cyan, magenta and yellow in its color ink cartridge, but no black.

Color depth

Color depth refers to the number of bits used to describe the color information of a pixel. A color depth of 8 bits produces 256 colors. True Color is a color depth of 24 bits (8 bits each for red, green and blue), in which 16,777,216 colors are defined.

Color extract

A color extract is an extract from a color picture that contains just the information of a color as a grayscale image. Color extracts are produced in the color separation process.

Color separation

This process is used to manufacture raster films for the various print colors in four color printing. The model is broken down into single overlays, three of which contain a complementary color (red, green, blue) and one with the color black assigned to it.

Color temperature

Color temperature is measured in degrees Kelvin. The color temperature specifies the color composition of light. The lower the value for K, the redder the light. For example, candle light has a color temperature of around 2800K. Increasing the value for K makes the light bluer - daylight has color temperatures ranging from 3000K (red sunset) and 5000K (midday sun) all the way to 10000K (clear blue sky).

Compression

Compression of *live video* and *still video* is a very important task, since there are huge amounts of data to be dealt with in this field. Depending on the color display and the number of still shots for *live video*, more than 10 Meg of storage capacity are required for a one second recording. Standard compression procedures are *JPEG* for *still video* and *MPEG* for *live video*.

Controller

A component or group of components that enable a computer to access peripheral devices. For example, the computer requires a controller for the drives (disk drives/hard drives/CD-ROM).

Convergence

In the video field, convergence means the correct intersection of the three electron beams for red, green and blue within a color picture tube. If the convergence is incorrect, the image is displayed with white lines and areas with muddy colors.

Data throughput

Data throughput or the transfer rate is the maximum number of bits that can be exchanged between the computer and the controller. It's measured in bits per second. The higher the data throughput, the better the performance of the drive.

Depth of field

The depth of field refers to the area in front of and behind the reference plane that can still be reproduced clearly. The depth of field depends on the distance, the focal length and the set f-stop. The depth of field influences the design of the image. For example, a smaller depth of field can emphasize the main motif.

Digital

Digital data can be displayed in the form of discrete values. Digital information is processed in the computer as a sequence of bits, either 0 or 1. However, information can also be present in analog form.

Digitization

Digitization is the prerequisite to storing analog information digitally. Digitization converts analog signals to discrete values. Along with digitization of audio data, called sampling, images and video signals have to be digitized before storage. The most user-friendly method of digitizing images is to use a scanner, which converts the brightness and color information to a digital format.

Dithering

With the help of dithering it is possible to display color images that have high amounts of color information with fewer colors. Colors are produced by mixing different-colored pixels.

DMA

(Acronym for Direct Memory Access) To reduce the burden on the CPU, you can exchange information between two chips in the computer. The DMA controller, a special chip, provides conflict-free exchange of data in which the CPU is not required.

Drop-on-demand process

This is a process used by inkjet printers in which droplets of ink are sprayed onto the paper. With bubble jet printers, the ink is heated by a heating element. When a gas bubble forms, one or more jets per color shoot onto the paper.

With Piezo inkjet printers, each jet has a ceramic element. The piezoelectric voltage is applied to the element, in the form of an electric impulse. Its initial state chages abruptly and it begins to oscillate. This creates pressure that ejects the ink droplet from the jet. This happens at an impulse frequency of approximately 20,000 Hertz.

DVI

(Acronym for Digital Video Interactive) Delivery and capture board developed by Intel. This DVI board lets you digitize live video and store it in compressed format on storage media of your PC. The digitization and compression of the audio and video signals occur in real time.

Dye sublimation printer

These printers currently produce the best printing results. They work in accordance to the same principle used by thermo transfer printers.

EPS

(Acronym for Encapsulated PostScript) Most word processors can read EPS format, but usually they cannot display the format on the screen. You can save images in EPS format, and then output them on a PostScript laser printer from any text program without losing much quality. Although EPS format is often used as an intermediate format for converting between different vector formats, this format is also used frequently in image processing or desktop publishing. Usually a TIFF image in lower resolution is bundled along with the EPS image so you can display it on the screen.

Expanded Memory

Expanded Memory is a memory technology that dates back from the old days of the PC/XT and 286. These computers either couldn't access memory over the 1 Meg limit, or else could only do it in a very awkward, roundabout way. To make more memory available to these comupters, a process was developed for inserting memory from outside the normal access area into a memory window below the 1 Meg limit.

Exposures

You can use special equipment to expose digitized photos, graphics or text in files as a print, a slide or an overhead transparency. High quality imagesetters achieve resolutions of up to 8000 lines per inch and a color spectrum of up to 16.7 million colors.

F-stop

F-stop is defined as the focal length divided by the widest aperture of the lens. With zoom lenses that have a fixed f-number (e.g., 1:1.2/9-54mm) the aperture must adjust to changes in focal length.

A lens with an f-number of 1.2 allows almost twice as much light through as a lens with an f-number of 1.6.

FBAS

Standard video signal, in which the information for color and brightness is sent from one line, in contrast to S-VHS.

Frame grabber

The frame grabber is an add-on function of overlay boards, which digitize an analog video signal of an external source and save it in real time. Most overlay boards have frame grabber options. However, only single images can be saved, not image sequences (live video).

Frequency

Frequency refers to the rate of vibration of an analog signal. How high or low a given tone sounds depends on the number of pulses per second. This number of pulses is referred to as the tone's frequency. The unit of measure for frequency is Hertz (Hz). This unit specifies the number of pulses per second that a given tone emits. The three standard Sampling frequencies are 44.1 kHz, 22.05 kHz und 11.025 kHz.

Genlock

(Abbreviation for Synchronization Generator Lock) Genlock boards are used to synchronize video and VGA signals, since the signals differ from one another due to their resolution and frequency. The mixed image can then be output on a video tape.

GIF

(Acronym for Graphics Interchange Format) GIF format is an even more versatile format than TIFF. You can use this format on various types of systems. Unfortunately, GIF can display only up to 256 colors (8 bit). CompuServe developed GIF.

Gray scales

Color pictures can be broken down into gray scales. The gray tones are produced by varying the density of black pixels in printing. The greater the density of the pixels, the darker the picture appears.

Green Book

Definition of the standard for CD-I. This format is based on Mode 2 of the Yellow Book. In addition, 8 bytes are defined for a CD-I subheader. This standard also defines coding processes for various user data (Graphics, audio etc.).

Halftone image

This term refers to a black & white image with an infinite number of gray scales.

HDTV

(Acronym for High Definition Television) A standardized high resolution type of television transmission. The image is reproduced in motion picture format with an aspect ratio of 16:9.

High Sierra Standard

Early standard for CD-ROM file system, later became the ISO 9660 standard.

HLS

(Hue, Light, Saturation) American printing standard for a color model. The color model is represented by a cube. The specification for the individual values is usually in percentages.

HSB

(Hue Saturation Brightness) American printing standard for a color model. The color model is portrayed by a sphere with the colors on the equator (Hue), the saturation on the x-axis and the brightness on the y-axis. The values are usually specified in degrees.

Hypertext

Unlike reading a text from beginning to end, hypertext gives you the option of moving around from cross-reference to cross-reference on different pages in the text and then returning to the original page. Hypertext applications are used for online Help systems and reference "book" applications.

Image Pack

Information unit on a Photo CD containing the hierarchy of components necessary for a single image. The size of an image pack can range between 3 Meg and 6 Meg.

Information terminal

An information terminal supplies information on specific topics. Using a touchscreen or a keyboard, users can call information through interaction. Information terminals frequently appear as a kiosk with an integrated screen, but usually contain a complete MPC.

Interaction

The term interaction in general has to do with the mutual actions of several persons, and is often used in reference to software solutions. The program reacts to user input and the program flow continues in a certain direction, depending on the input. For example, in a tutorial program users can review or skip chapters depending on how well they answer test questions or solve practice exercises.

Interlaced

Displaying an image using two half frames, one containing the even lines and the other containing the odd lines. Television and video use this process to achieve flicker-free playback with a lower number of images. This process is only suitable for animation. On a computer screen, which usually doesn't show much movement of images, the flickering can be irritating and tiresome.

Interrupt

(IRQ = Interrupt Request) Term for a signal sent to the CPU from a peripheral device so that a specific function of the device is carried out. A total of only seven hardware interrupts is available. If you use many different peripheral devices such as scanners, sound cards or overlay boards, make sure the interrupts don't conflict with each other.

ISO 9660

A *Yellow Book* standard for CD-ROM that describes the file system. This is a hierarchical file system like the one you are familiar with from your PC. The only differences or limitations have to do with the filenames. PCs only allow eight characters for the name and three characters for an extension. Amiga and Macintosh computers allow as many characters as you wish for filenames. To guarantee compatibility among the various computers, two levels were defined in the ISO-9660 Standard, Interchange Level 1, which accepts DOS conventions, and Interchange Level 2, which allows filenames of any length.

Special drivers are responsible for translating the file organization on a CD to the appropriate operating system. The program for MS-DOS is called MSCDEX.EXE.

JPEG

(Acronym for Joint Photographic Expert Group) This body of experts recommended a standard for compressing digitized video color images that are to be saved as *still video*. Their standard allows for *compression* up to a ratio of 50:1 without a loss of quality.

Lead In / Lead Out

Each time a CD is inscribed, the appropriate tracks are framed by a "Lead In" and a "Lead Out." These structures reveal to the drive the start and the end of the written sector of a CD. Firmware prevents other areas of the CD from being read. Drives that cannot find several sessions on a CD, with multiple sessions capability, can identify and read only the first session.

Lens hood

The lens hood protects the camera lens from stray (scattered) light that would otherwise detract from the brilliance (clarity) of the photograph. The most effective type of lens hood is an adjustable bellows.

Magneto-Optical Disk

This term refers to a magneto-optical disk in 5¼-inch format that can be written many times. Unlike conventional diskettes, the *magneto-optical disk* offers a much higher storage capacity.

MCI

(Acronym for Media Control Interface) Term for a manufacturer independent, cross-platform software interface. Microsoft and IBM collaborated in the development of MCI to create a standard for the use of multimedia hardware components such as *sound cards*, *CD-ROM* drives and *overlay boards*.

MPC

Multimedia hardware standard developed by different companies in cooperation with Microsoft. Only computers that meet minimum requirements can be called *MPC* computers. The minimum requirements are a computer with an 80386SX processor, a VGA card, a *sound card* and an MPC *CD-ROM* drive. Also, MPC standard requires that an MPC computer be compatible with *Microsoft Multimedia Extension*.

MPEG

(Acronym for Motion Picture Expert Group) A group of experts was formed to develop a standardized compression procedure for storing *live video* on normal mass storage systems. The objective of this group is a transfer rate of 1 to 1.5 MBits per second for *compression* and *storage* of live video.

MSCDEX

A Microsoft device driver for running a *CD-ROM* drive in DOS. After installing the drive, you can address the *CD-ROM* drive like a normal disk drive and read data.CD-ROM drive

MTBF

(Acronym for Mean Time Before Failure) Specification for data security of storage media. Expresses the statistical mean time before an error occurs. An MTBF of 10,000 hours is an element of the *MPC* specification for *CD-ROM* drives.

Multimedia

Generic term for the combination of language, sound output, *animation*, *hypertext* and *video* within a computer application. People also use the term *Multimedia* to refer to combinations of only two or more of these multimedia components. For example, outputting sound files for specific events that occur in the application is also considered to be multimedia. A general definition is difficult, because manufacturers have their own definitions.

Multiple session

These are numerous digitizing procedures. Pictures are randomly transferred to the photo CD. In this case, the maximum storage capacity is 100 pictures, because it must include information and control data for each session. Each session occupies about 20 Meg for informational data, which is located in the Lead In and the Lead Out, for consolidating the individual sessions.

The photo CD system uses a hybrid disc as described in the orange book in order to write data on the CD sequentially, while retaining compatibility with simple players. This hybrid disc contains multiple program areas called sessions.

The hybrid disc technology permits the creation of a photo CD as a single or a multiple sessions CD. If the user wants to add pictures to a partially filled photo CD, the subsequently digitized images are added during a later session.

NTSC

(Acronym for National Television System Committee) The American television standard, which works with 525 lines and 30 frames per second.

OCR

(Acronym for Optical Character Recognition) Optical character recognition is used with *scanners*. Initially, a scanned text is present as a graphic. *OCR* software is required to read the letters, numbers and special characters from the graphic. Barcode readers are also equipped with optical character recognition software to assign a numeric value to the scanned bar code.

Orange Book

Contains the special specifications for write-once CD-ROMs and magneto-optical drives.

Overlay Board

With the help of an *overlay board* it is possible to display signals from external video sources (video recorder, video camera etc.) on the PC monitor by overlaying the VGA image in *real time*. Most *overlay boards* have a *frame grabber* function for saving frames in digital format.

PAL

(Acronym for Phase Alternate Line) This is the standard signal output by televisions in most countries outside of North America and Japan. Works with 625 line resolution and 50 half frames (25 frames) per second.

Palette

A *palette* is a color group from which the color display of an image or graphic is taken. Each palette entry describes a color. Each pixel of the graphic is assigned an entry from the *palette*. The number of colors that can be displayed at the same time is limited to the number of entries in the *palette*.

When a graphic is imported to a program that works with a different color palette, any original colors not included in this palette are either deleted or replaced.

Pantone

To be able to produce clearly defined colors, American companies developed a color scale that contains approximately 150 labeled colors. A fixed mixing ratio of primary colors is defined for these colors.

PCX format

The most widely used format for pixel graphics is *PCX format*, which was developed by ZSoft for their Paintbrush program. While *PCX format* can be read by almost all (especially Windows) programs; this advantage is offset for professional image processors by the fact that a TrueColor display with resolutions of more than 1024 x 768 pixels is not possible. An 8 bit display is the maximum. In spite of that, *PCX format* has established itself as the PC standard.

Perspective

Depending on the position of the camera, you differentiate between the following main perspectives: worms-eye view, normal perspective and birds-eye view. In normal perspective, the camera is positioned at eye level, while in the other two perspectives the camera is above or below.

Photo CD

Photo CD is a process developed by Kodak for storing photographs taken with a camera on a *CD*. You can process the photographs with image processing programs. Then you can create prints from the *CD*.

Pixel

Refers to the smallest displayable unit on the monitor or in printer output. *Resolution* on the computer screen is measured in pixels. In printer output or scanning, resolution is measured in dots per inch.

PLV

(Acronym for Production Level Video) Process for digitizing *live video* in *real time*. In the *PLV* process, digitizing takes place at a resolution of 256 x 240 dots. Because of this resolution, recorded *live video* can be displayed in full-screen mode without sacrificing quality.

Port address

Communication between software and peripheral hardware is managed from a port. To be able to address a specific port for data input or output via software, the port is identified by an address.

PostScript

Refers to a standardized page description language in which graphical information is represented by a command set. A *Postscript* file is converted to printer output by a special *Postscript* interpreter inside the printer. *Postscript* has established itself as a widespread standard and is supported by nearly all software applications.

Presentation

A *presentation* is an audio-visual demonstration of a product or subject. Multimedia components such as *animation* and acoustical accompaniment are important aids in delivering the *presentation*.

Raytracing

To create photo-like images, it is necessary to calculate shadows and reflections that are produced by defined light sources. This process of calculation is called *raytracing*.

Real time

Real time refers to the simultaneous processing of the input signal. In the case of a live video recording, the image is compressed and saved without delay, so that no delay occurs in processing the following image sequences.

Red Book

Definition of the standard for audio CDs. A sector contains 2352 bytes of useful data. In addition, 784 bytes are required for error identification and 98 bytes are needed for management.

Rendering

To produce realistic three-dimensional animations, it is necessary to move complex three-dimensional objects through virtual space. The computer calculates the buffer images for you with the necessary software. This process is referred to as *rendering*.

Resolution

Used in conjunction with graphic cards, scanners or printers, the term resolution refers to the dithering of an image into single picture points, called pixels. The greater the number of pixels used per area unit, the higher the quality of the displayed image. Since resolution normally varies in horizontal and vertical direction, the resolution for both directions is specified per length unit.

dpi (Dots per Inch) is the unit of measurement used with printers and scanners.

RGB

Refers to the three primary colors of red, green and blue. On *RGB* monitors, colors are produced from the proportion of primary colors in the mixture according to *additive color mixture*. The term refers to a composite color signal. There are *RGB* analog signals and *RGB* TTL signals, depending on whether you are dealing with *analog* or *digital* image signals.

RLE

(Acronym for Run Length Encoding) A data compression process in which redundant sequential values are combined into data blocks containing the value and frequency.

RTV

(Acronym for Real Time Video) Digitizing process for *live video* in *real time*. The *RTV* process uses a maximum *resolution* of 128 x 120 pixels. All irrelevant information about the image is suppressed. Because of their low resolution, video sequences stored by the RTV process should be displayed only in small windows. See also *PLV*.

Sampling

The term *sampling* means converting acoustical analog signals into digital values that can be stored as a sequence of bytes. Sampled tones can be modified and played back as sound files. The quality of the *sampling* is determined by the *sample depth* and the *sample rate*.

Scanners

Scanners are devices that use a light reflection process to scan images and store them on the computer as files. Depending on the type of scanner, you can scan artwork with color information or convert the colors to *gray scales*. Scanned images and graphics can be edited by image processing programs. With the help of *OCR* you can also convert text to text files.

Scanning frequency

Scanning frequency describes the representation of single frames within a unit of time. In describing monitors, scanning frequency is the number of lines illuminated on the screen per second. The unit of measurement is Hertz. Normal monitors work with a scanning frequency of between 50 and 60 Hertz.

SCSI

(Acronym for Small Computer System Interface) Standardized interface for various devices such as hard drives, *scanners*, *CD-ROM* drives etc. You can connect as many as seven devices to a controller.

Because it's possible to hook up different end devices to a SCSI controller like hard drives, CD-ROM drives, scanners etc., you need a different driver for each device. Data is transferred at 9 bit width (8 data bits and one stop bit). *SCSI* interfaces can be operated both in serial and parallel operation. Data transfer occurs in blocks.

Sound card

A *sound card* is a card that can be installed in a free slot of your computer. *Sound cards* are used to play back sound, but you can also use them to record and save sounds, speech etc. *Sound cards* have a number of ports for connecting speakers, headphones, *stereo* equipment and *microphone*s. Some *sound cards* have a port for a *CD-ROM* drive. *Sound cards* are a component of the *MPC* standard. Sound cards also have an internal *synthesizer* for addressing *MIDI* data.

TGA format

TGA format is a graphic format that allows saving and conversion of true color graphics between PC and Macintosh. The US uses this format more than other parts of the world.

Thermo transfer printers

Thermo transfer printers print images by transferring color to the paper. A foil covered with colored wax is used for the colors. The individual colors are arranged in layers. A strip of elements heat up the foil, melting the wax on the paper. By varying the temperature, the right amount of wax goes on the paper.

Thumbnail

A small version of an image. Many image processing programs let you preview images in thumbnail size before opening them for processing.

TIF format

(Acronym for Tagged Image File Format) TIF (also called TIFF) format is a frequently used graphic file format. The big disadvantage to TIF lies in the many different versions of TIF that exist - there is no one "true" TIF format. Uncompressed TIF files require large amounts of memory, so a compression option exists. However, some programs do not support compressed TIF images.

Touch screen monitor

This type of monitor has a touch-sensitive surface. By touching a specific location on the screen with his or her finger, the user can select options displayed on the screen. Information kiosks often have these touch screen monitors.

True Color

This refers to a type of graphic image, displayed in 24-bit format, using up to 16,777,216 colors.

Vector graphics

These graphics are defined using vectors rather than pixels. For example, a line definition consists of the starting point, ending point, and the line thickness. An enclosed object would include the type of fill. Vector graphics are easily resized without degeneration of the image.

VHS

Frequently used video format. Most home VCRs are VHS.

Video

General term for conveying visual information.

Video signal

A video signal passes visual information using electronic means, from a video recorder or a video camera. Television stations transmit video signals for you to view on your TV at home. Many different types of video signals exist: NTSC, PAL and SECAM. Information can also be generated as a composite signal (sometimes called FBAS).

Videodisc

Videodiscs contain a great deal of graphic information (e.g., IBM tutorials) because they have such a high memory volume. Videodisc players also provide direct access anywhere on the disc. Video data is recorded in analog format and sound is recorded in digital format.

Viewing screen

Viewing screens are often used to display a presentation. The viewing screens consist of a number of monitors. A special process makes it possible to split up a frame by segments on the individual monitors. By controlling each monitor, you can produce many special effects.

WORM

(Acronym for Write Once Read Many) Unlike the standard CD-ROM, WORM lets you write to a CD just once. This is useful for archiving data (e.g., registration information) for later recall.

XA

(Abbreviation for Extended Architecture) A new standard stated in the Yellow Book. The most important factor in XA is the coexistence of music, video and graphic data between tracks on a CD. The XA standard basically follows the Mode 2 sectors of CD-ROM standards. XA standard offers two types of program data in Mode 2 - Mode 2 Form 1 and Mode 2 Form 2. An eight-byte subheader indicates the use of each form.

YCC standard

Kodak-defined standard for displaying True Color graphics from binary formats. This color system uses the RGB color scheme (eight bits for each primary color), within the components chrominance and luminance, similar to YUV coding. Photo CD pictures use YCC color coding.

This 24-bit system divides each color pixel into two components: Eight bits of luminance (256 degrees of brilliance), and eight bits of chrominance (the color components). These components ensure optimal display of natural color. Critical colors (e.g., red) have more color hues available than others (e.g., dark blue).

Yellow Book

Based on the Red Book (audio CD standards). This standard has two modes, which distinguish between error checking and maximum data transfer rate.

Mode 1: One sector contains only 2048 bytes of usable data, with 280 bytes reserved for additional error correction. This format requires 12 synchronization byes and four header bytes, above and beyond the number stated in the Red Book, for data handling.

Unlike audio CDs, every single sector must be accessible in a data CD. Therefore, the 12 synchronization bytes are used to access the number of each sector, as stored in the four header bytes. This permits fast access to each sector.

As this standard is based on the Red Book, 784 bytes are reserved for normal error checking, as well as 98 bytes for processing in a sector.

A statistical algorithm can resotre the 280 bytes used for additional error correction to the total usable data, when only a small part of the usable data can be properly read. This generates the odds of finding one read error within 1000 gigabytes.

Mode 2: This mode permits accelerated reading spped as well as additional error correction. In this case, only the 12 synchronization bytes and four header bytes are required from the 2352 bytes of usable data (this specified by Yellow Book specification), leaving 2336 bytes. The bottom line is a maximum data transfer rate of 171K per second (75*2336). The odds of errors occurring are slightly higher.

YUV

Abbreviation for a video signal based on brightness and color. YUV follows VHS conventions.

Appendix

We've compiled this comprehensive resource list of the hardware and software firms that were discussed in **The Photo CD Book**. We also included several companies that have advertised their Eastman Kodak Photo CD capabilities. If you're looking for further information on these products, you can contact the manufacturers directly.

It's important to note that the Photo CD world is changing rapidly. Therefore, the products and manufacturers are also changing. The names, addresses, products and information in this appendix is subject to change.

Thank you very much for purchasing The Photo CD Book!

Hardware

Adaptec, Inc.
691 S. Milpitas Blvd.
Milpitas, CA 95035
Tech support: 408-945-2550

CD Technology Inc.
766 San Aleso Ave
Sunnyvale, CA 94086

Chinon America Inc.
660 Maple Avenue
Torrance, CA. 90503

Corel Systems Corp
1600 Carling Ave.
Ottawa, ONT K1Z 8R7

Creative Labs Inc.
2050 Duane Avenue
Santa Clara, CA 95054

CTC Computers
1928 Old Middlefield Way
Mountain View, CA 94043-2503

Eastman-Kodak Company
343 State Street
Rochester, NY 14650-0519
(800) CD-KODAK

Genesis Integrated Systems Inc.
1000 Shelard Pkwy #270
Minneapolis, MN 55426

Hitachi America LTD
2000 Sierra Point Parkway
Brisbane, CA 94005-1819

IBM
Old Orchard Rd.
Armonk NY 10504

Media Vision Inc.
47221 Fremont Blvd.
Fremont, CA 94538

MicroSolutions Computer Products
132 W. Lincoln Highway
De Kalb, IL 60115

Mitsubishi Electronics America
991 Knox St. Systems Division
Torrance, CA 90502

Mitsumi Electronics Corp.
35 Pine Lawn Road
Melville, NY 11747

NEC Technologies Inc.
1255 Michael Dr.
Wood Dale, IL 60191-1094

Panasonic Electronics
2 Panasonic Way
Secaucus, NJ 07094

Philips Consumer Electronics
1 Philips Dr. POB 14810
Knoxville, TN 37914

Pioneer Comm. of America
600 E. Crescent Ave.
Upper Saddle River, NJ 07458

Sony Corp Computer Peripherals
655 River Oaks Parkway
San Jose, CA., 95134

Sun Moon Star
1941 Ringwood Avenue
San Jose, CA 95131

Tandy Corporation
700 One Tandy Center
Fort Worth, TX 76102

Texel America Inc.
1080 E. Duane Ave
Sunnyvale, CA 94086

Toshiba America
9740 Irvine Blvd
Irvine, CA 92718

Software

Adobe Systems Inc.
1585 Charleston Road
Mountain View, CA 94039

Alchemy Mindworks Inc.
POB 500
Beeton, ONT L0G 1A0

Aldus Corp.
411 First Ave. S. Ste 200
Seattle, WA 98104

Andover Advanced Technology
239 Littleton Road Ste 2A
Westford, MA 01886

Berkeley Systems Inc.
2095 Rose St.
Berkeley, CA 94709

Cerious Software
5424 Chedworth Dr.
Charlotte, NC 28210

Commix SP, Inc.
8201 Greensboro Dr. Ste 451
McLean, VA 22103

Digital Quick Color Inc.
30 Mauchly Ste B
Irvine, CA 92718

HSC Software
1661 Lincoln Blvd. Ste. 101
Santa Monica, CA 90404

Iterated Systems Inc.
5550-A Peachtree Pkwy Ste 650
Norcross, GA 30092

JASC
10901 Red Circle Drive Ste. 340
Minnetonka, MN 55343

MicroGraphx Inc.
1303 E. Arapaho Road
Richardson, TX 75081

MicroTek
680 Knox St.
Torrance, CA 90502

Microsoft Corp.
1 Microsoft Way
Redmond, WA 98052-6399

NorthCoast Software
POB 459
18A Shipley Rd.
Barrington, NH 03825

Procomm Technology
200 McCormick Ave.
Costa Mesa, CA 92626

Seattle FilmWorks
Elliott Bay at Pier 89
1260 16th Ave. W.
Seattle, WA 98119

Sir Speedy, Inc.
23131 Verdugo Dr
Laguna Hills, CA 92654

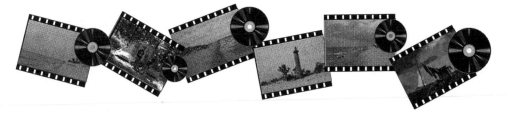

Index

Index

Index

Index

389

Index

Index

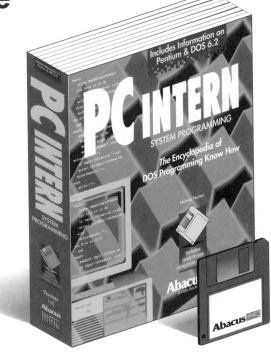

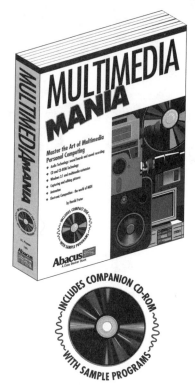

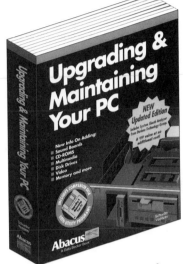

0-325kB in one second

Introducing the world's fastest CD ROM

The new Toshiba XM-3401B CD ROM is the fastest drive in the world.

While the standard Data Transfer Rate is currently at 153kB per second, our XM-3401B rockets ahead to read at over 300kB per second. With 600+ MB capacity, the XM-3401B stores massive amounts of data. And with a MTBF of 50,000 hours, compared with an industry average of 30,000 hours, we're taking CD ROM to new heights of reliability.

Ask about the new Toshiba XM-3401B drive. For the most dazzling performance ever.

TOSHIBA

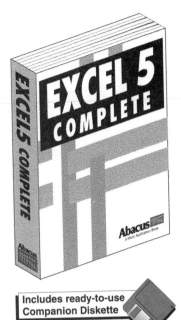

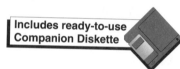

LET ME SEE!

With Film Processing Orders: Send any 35mm color print film. Select prints, slides or prints and slides. Add Pictures On Disk™ for only $3.95 ($5.95 for 36 exp.)

From Your Existing Photos: Send either 3½ x 5 or 4 x 6 prints, slides or 35mm color negatives. Your prints, slides or negatives will be returned with your disk.

NAME _____

ADDRESS _____

CITY _____ STATE _____ ZIP _____

100% Satisfaction Guaranteed!

PROCESSING SERVICES Prices include new film!	20 or 24 Exp.		36 Exp.		AMOUNT
	No. Rolls	Price	No. Rolls	Price	
PRINTS: Choose 3½ x 5 or 4 x 6					
☐ 3½ x 5, one each		$8.50		$12.25	
☐ 3½ x 5, two each		10.50		14.75	
☐ Deluxe 4 x 6, one each		9.50		13.75	
☐ Deluxe 4 x 6, two each		11.50		16.25	▼
PRINTS & SLIDES: From one roll					
☐ 3½ x 5 prints and slides		$11.95		$15.50	
☐ 4 x 6 prints and slides		12.95		16.95	▼
SLIDES: From any 35mm color film					
☐ One each		$5.25		$7.25	
☐ Two each (not available from chrome film)		7.75		10.75	▼
PICTURES ON DISK: See System Requirements below					
Specify disk size: ☐ 3½ ☐ 5¼					
☐ With film developing		$3.95		$5.95	
☐ From existing prints or slides		9.95	▷ ▷ ▷ ▷		
☐ From 35mm color negatives		11.95	▷ ▷ ▷ ▷		▼

SHIPPING: Choose Standard or FedEx* (check one)

*Priority Mail to P.O. Boxes, AK and HI. Chrome film orders and reprints shipped separately.

LIMIT OF LIABILITY: The photographic material you send us for handling will be treated with care. However, our responsibility for damage or loss, even though due to negligence or other fault, will be limited to the cost of unexposed film unless you have declared a higher value and paid a premium for that value in advance. SFW is wholly separate from any shipper and all other warranties, express or implied, and all incidental or consequential damages are specifically excluded.

☐ Standard 1-3 rolls ....add $1.35 per roll	
☐ FedEx 1 or 2 rolls ....add a total of $3.95	
☐ FedEx 3 or more rolls ...add a total of $4.95	
	▼
SUBTOTAL	
WA residents add 8.2% sales tax	
TOTAL PAYMENT	

PICTURES ON DISK!

ENCLOSE PAYMENT
☐ Check or money order   ☐ VISA   ☐ MasterCard

VISA/MasterCard Account Number (all 13 or 16 digits)

Signature _____   Exp. Date _____

26510

Thank You!

Seattle FilmWorks • 1260 16th Ave. W., Seattle, WA 98119   Call: 1-800-445-3348